The Put-in-Bay
Road Races,
1952–1963

ALSO BY CARL GOODWIN

*They Started in MGs: Profiles of
Sports Car Racers of the 1950s* (McFarland, 2011)

The Put-in-Bay Road Races, 1952–1963

CARL GOODWIN

McFarland & Company, Inc., Publishers
Jefferson, North Carolina

Library of Congress Cataloguing-in-Publication Data

Goodwin, Carl, author.
The Put-in-Bay road races, 1952–1963 / Carl Goodwin.
      p.   cm.
Includes bibliographical references and index.

ISBN 978-0-7864-7930-6 (softcover : acid free paper) ∞
ISBN 978-1-4766-1459-5 (ebook)

1. Sports car racing—Ohio—Put-in-Bay—History—20th century.
2. Automobile racing drivers—History—20th century.
3. Put-in-Bay (Ohio)—History—20th century.   I. Title.

GV1029.15.G66 2014   796.7209771'212—dc23   2014026203

British Library cataloguing data are available

© 2014 Carl Goodwin II. All rights reserved

*No part of this book may be reproduced or transmitted in any form
or by any means, electronic or mechanical, including photocopying
or recording, or by any information storage and retrieval system,
without permission in writing from the publisher.*

On the cover: A field of 18 cars approaches the green flag at the start/finish line
during Put-in-Bay's race weekend of 1959 (Rollin LaFrance)

Printed in the United States of America

*McFarland & Company, Inc., Publishers
Box 611, Jefferson, North Carolina 28640
www.mcfarlandpub.com*

To my father, C. Ray Goodwin, who drove us all up to Put-in-Bay the first year we saw the races; to my mother, Dr. Gladys Foulke Goodwin, who helped me buy my first car, a Siata Gran Sport that had raced at Put-in-Bay in 1956; to my wife Nancy, who was always there during adventures and misadventures with old sports cars and rope-towed me for probably about two thousand miles over the years (and then the Formula Ford ran over her foot in the paddock at Road America); to my brother David and sisters Penny and Suzy; to sons Brian and Douglas, who went with me to Mid-Ohio in rain or shine; and to grandsons Will and Ben, who actually like flying monkeys instead of cars, but who knows, they may come around some day.

Acknowledgments

An effort was made to compose this book of first-person stories from drivers, photographers, mechanics and race officials, so thanks to them all. With apologies to those missed, the book could also not have been written without Joe Brown, and Georgia Brown, who provided essential photographs for this and my early articles on the 'Bay races; Stu Kerr, supplier of many photographs for many years at Put-in-Bay; Tom Saal whose consistent encouragement kept me going on the project; Bob Satava, a constant source of information from someone who was on the scene; Christopher Kintner, information authority and grandson of the race organizers; Rollin LaFrance, photographer of a key year, 1959; Bob Karol, chronicler of the 1959 race; Len Griffing, writer of the 1958 record-setting year; and to Brenda Griffing; John Birchfield, planner of the original race details; Dick and Betty Henn, race chairman and race registrar; Bill Gorris, photographer in the year 1955; Dave and Sheila Bly, for pictures and information; Mickey Mishne, for help and encouragement; Sally and Jim Carroll, for racing stories; Lee McLaird and Stephen Charter at Bowling Green State University for their help on the early years; and to Jack Holth for his help on the last year. Then to my friends Charlie Hazle, Dick Lamport, Bill Brooks, Bill Sebelin, Mike Coyne, Tom Ireland, David Jones, Bob Eastman, Sam Kinney, Bill McLaren and Dan Holmes.

Plus, the Cleveland Sport Car Club, NE Ohio Region Sports Car Club of America, Beth Lunney of Classic MG, John Treible of Emerald Necklace MG Registry, Art and Dutch Brow, Ralph Cadwallader, David Gardner, Jim Sitz, Bill Green of the International Motor Racing Research Center at Watkins Glen, and, again, the Center for Archival Collections, William T. Jerome Library at Bowling Green University and Suzy Cooper of the Lake Erie Islands Historical Society.

Oh, let's not forget to mention Eric and Shelley at Our Photo Lab in Sandusky, Shipley Office Supply, Wolf Camera, Mike's Camera and Godec Photography, plus Bill Ellis, Griff Davies, Jim Raymond, Dwight Davies, John Ojala and Mike Hedge. The list goes on, with Jack Woehrle, Manley Ford, Bob and Linda Williams, and Roger Linton of the Put-in-Bay Road Race Heritage Society, Charlie Foss and the late Paul Henry, who was dedicated to keeping alive his father's memory and the memory of this great race.

Table of Contents

Acknowledgments — vi
Preface — 1

1. Put-in-Bay—A Summer Paradise in 1951 — 7
2. The Last American Road Race, 1952–1959, 1963 — 15
3. 1952: The First of the Last American Road Races — 36
4. 1953: What Is So Fair as a Day in June? — 57
5. 1954: The Technology of Sport — 75
6. 1955: Safety in Sports Car Racing — 92
7. 1956: A Likeable Little Race — 114
8. 1957: A Typical Day at Put-in-Bay — 136
9. 1958: The Year of the Lap Record — 158
10. 1959: The Last CSCC Race — 181
11. 1963: The Secret Road Race — 210
12. Farewell to Put-in-Bay—It Was a Wonderful Race — 229

Appendix: Special Contributors — 243
Bibliography — 256
Index — 259

"There was nothing like that race. It was like a dream of anybody who would just like to get in his car and go fast. It was just going to some little town and driving your heart out."

—Lorrain Holder

The Holder brothers, Lorrain and Manny, had a machine shop on the west side of Cleveland, the Diecast Finishing Co. They were interested in sports car racing and bought a Porsche Spyder, the 550RS model. They did an excellent job of preparing it for races, making it lighter and faster than the factory cars. Lorrain drove the national events, such as Watkins Glen, and Manny drove the regional races, such as Put-in-Bay. In 1958, Manny set the course record at 89.9 mph, the best drive of his life. It is a record that will stand forever at Put-in-Bay.

Preface

Every car enthusiast has a favorite racing course. Porsche champion Lake Underwood liked Bridgehampton the best. Historian Bill Green likes Watkins Glen. Fred Egloff, editor for SCCA's Chicago Region, likes Road America. Elva champion Chuck Dietrich liked Mid-Ohio. And I like Put-in-Bay. That's why I wrote this book.

If the Put-in-Bay races were so great, why weren't they as famous as Watkins Glen or Elkhart Lake? That's a fair question. The Put-in-Bay races were on a scenic island with a good race course and a good safety record. It was a well-organized event, so why did fame and fortune not follow it? Well, fortune did—it was a very successful event in every respect, including financially. But the reason it was so safe also kept it from being well-known. The 2-liter displacement limit kept the big-name cars and drivers out of the race. No Cunningham, no Kimberly, no Fitch, no Walters, no Shelby, no Phil Hill or Masten Gregory. No Ferrari Monza, Mondial or Testa Rossa; no C- or D-Type Jaguar; no Maserati 200S or 300S. With the right gearing, a D-Type Jaguar could reach a speed of 183 miles an hour. The presence of such cars with their high speeds and spirited and ambitious drivers would have likely caused the lesser entrants to crash, possibly into spectators. It's just as well that the 'Bay races were full of dozens of TRW engineers driving their own MGs. They wanted to get out on the track, come back safely and tell their co-workers around the water cooler at work, "I had the time of my life. I drove at the Put-in-Bay road races."

In the period immediately after World War II, there was a great national appetite to forget the past conflict. For many this meant pouring oneself into the job and into recreational activities. These included golf, bowling, gardening, fishing, hunting, boating ... and auto racing. There were many different kinds of racing—drag racing, midget racing, stock car racing—but they all had one thing in common. At the time most forms were amateur. You didn't need a sponsor, you didn't need a team; anyone could do it. Many people liked the road courses, which had many features—hilly terrains, turns to the right and left, or wet or dry tracks. And, might it be said, some liked this format better since the driving was cleaner and the drivers more sportsmanlike.

Since the sport was new, at least in America (setting aside the ARCA years), road racers had no place to race—that is, until Cameron Argetsinger closed off the roads in 1948 at Watkins Glen for the first postwar sports car race. Bruce Stevenson followed closely, with his 1949 Bridgehampton race. Then the 1950 race at Elkhart Lake, Wisconsin, and the West Coast races of 1950 and '51. The following year had the inaugural 1952 race at Put-in-Bay.

Many of these early races have been featured in books. They include Watkins Glen, Bridgehampton, Elkhart Lake, Palm Springs (1950), Pebble Beach (1950), and Torrey Pines (1951). I have to admit I've never been to the three California courses, though I've driven a

An exciting moment at the Put-in-Bay road races is immortalized in this George Ivanyi watercolor: Art Brow gets the #3 MG-TD out-of-sorts at Cemetery Curve on the 3.1-mile course, recovering shortly afterward. This was the incident when the heater shook loose and fell down on Art's feet so he couldn't brake for the corner. The car was borrowed from Bill Staufer (George Ivaniyi, collection of Art Brow).

racing car at the first three eastern courses. Each is a beautiful place and there's no denying their history. But what can match racing on a picturesque island in one of the Great Lakes, an island with a crescent harbor filled with boats and another island inside that bay? Imagine the scene: The cruising boats are at anchor; the motor yachts are tied up at the dock. The children's park at the waterfront is filled with little kids on the swings, the slides and the jungle gym. Then, outside of town, one finds vineyards by the score. There's a small-town atmosphere that is unmistakable. And, once a year, the racing cars come. Somebody should write a book about this place.

That's eventually what I did. This book on the old Put-in-Bay sports car races started with a proposed article to *Automobile* magazine. I asked the late David E. Davis, Jr., if he would like to see one. He had been to Put-in-Bay and he told me to send it in. I got some photographs from people in the Cleveland Sport Car Club—Dave and Sheila Bly, Bob Satava, Reed Andrews—the MG Car Club, Betty Henn and others. Betty and her husband organized the race. I had a little get-together with her at the home of Charlie and Ruth Ellmers, both participants in the event. Driver John Tame was there, too, as well as Fred Steger. I went down to the Rumrunners nightspot in the Cleveland flats and interviewed Lorrain and Nancy Holder. They had a Cigarette boat tied up at a dock on the Cuyahoga River. It would go close to 100 miles an hour. Their car—a Porsche Spyder—held the speed record at the 'Bay, with Lorrain's brother Manny at the wheel going 89 miles an hour! It was 1958. I saw the race myself. He was flying. It was the best drive of his life.

The piece that resulted was published in the October 1986 issue and was art-directed by the great Bob Forlenza, one of the many talented people that David E. had brought to the fledgling *Automobile* magazine.

Of course when it came out, I sent copies to the people who had helped with the article. A few months later, I got a call from the now-late Mickey Mishne, who was the motorsports editor of the *Cleveland Plain Dealer* and a longtime member of the Cleveland Sport Car Club. He asked if I would come to the club's annual banquet and put on a slide show about the Put-in-Bay races. I told him it was a little like hauling coals to Newcastle, since, of course, his club had put on the 'Bay races, but I happily agreed. I didn't have any slides and it cost me the price of an engine overhaul for my Formula Ford to have slides made from borrowed prints. I arranged to have surviving drivers from the event come and sit at a table during the show and comment as the slides came up. This worked very well. The event was held at the Manakiki Country Club in Metamora, Ohio, and had Mickey's racing posters plastered all over the walls. My wife Nancy and I drove down from Detroit in sub-zero temperatures. The heater in our Mercury Zephyr station wagon barely kept up with the cold.

Three more articles on the Put-in-Bay races followed, for *Vintage Motorsport, Classic MG* and *British Car,* and then a big 12-page article again for Randy Riggs at *Vintage Motorsport*. This was generously praised by Chris Economaki in *National Speed Sport News*. You may think of Chris as a circle track guy, but he liked sports car racing a lot more than you would imagine. What Chris said, in his May 21, 2003, column, was this: "The best magazine reading of the year is long-time NSSN reader Carl Goodwin's 'The Last American Road Race' in the March-April *Vintage Motorsport* magazine. It's a great piece on the sports car road racing of the 1950s held on Put-in-Bay island in Lake Erie in Ohio. Get there on a ferry or aboard a Ford Tri-Motor. No guard rails, no full-face helmets, no charge for admission, no prize money, nothing but pure enjoyment."

During production of this piece, I acquired the road racing photographs of Joe Brown, a Cleveland watchmaker and a fine local photographer who had covered the bay races extensively, and I also got the use of the photographs of Rollin LaFrance, a very talented Cleveland photographer who was an architect by profession. With the number of photographs I had, plus a few more that trickled in gradually, it looked like I had almost enough for a book.

I wanted to tell the story year-by-year, and I had been collecting stories and facts for 27 years. But I could find no photographs for the first year, 1952. Finally, due to the help of Manley Ford, Charlie Foss and Roger Linton, all connected with the Put-in-Bay Reunion, I learned of the Robert J. Dodge pictures in the Center for Archival Collections at Bowling Green State University. Curator Lee McLaird and Head Librarian Stephen Charter arranged for me to use the images, and the path to the book was then made clear. I was helped with story material by Sally Carroll, president of the Cleveland Sport Car Club, and by John Treible of the Emerald Necklace MG Club. Then I found that I was also short of material on the mysterious last race, in 1963. I got a leg up from Jack and Carol Holth and from Porsche guru Vic Skirmants. Further help came from Carol Clemens, the only woman to race at the 'Bay, and from ace photographer Stu Kerr.

☙ ❧

The era of road races, the late 1940s and early 1950s, is an interesting one for many reasons. America was changing economically, politically and culturally. Jazz was a popular music form, although a new sound called rock 'n' roll was emerging. We were changing over from Duke Ellington and the big band era to smaller groups such as Charlie Parker and then to

Artwork of MG-TCs racing at Put-in-Bay in the early fifties, complete with MGTCs, hay bales, snow fences, corner workers and spectators (Ralph Cadwallader, collection of Chuck Linick).

modern jazz, including players such as Dave Brubeck, Art Pepper, Max Roach and Clifford Brown. Harry Truman and Dwight Eisenhower were our presidents. The economy had a few ups and downs, but basically anyone who wanted to work could have a job. In a metalworking economy such as the Midwest, a man would go into a machine shop and ask if he could sweep the floors. A year later he would say to the boss, "Could someone teach me how to run that lathe?" In another year he would ask to operate the Bridgeport machine. Then he would become the shop foreman and then a vice president. That is, if he wanted to work. Of course, this was before the global economy really took hold.

In the sports car scene, clubs of all kinds were forming. One of them was the Cleveland Sport Car Club. Founded March 5, 1951, it was formed just before the NE Ohio Region of the Sports Car Club of America came to be (on October 29, 1952). The stalwarts of the CSCC got together to drink beer, rebuild carburetors and organize events. And organize events they did. Over an eight-year span, CSCC ran eight races at Put-in-Bay and four races at Akron Airport, as well as several rallies. But we're getting a little ahead of ourselves. In 1951 meetings were held at the Bratenahl, Ohio, home of Dick and Chuck Irish and even included a dog—a retriever named Cricket. They had a club picnic in August 1951. In the spring of 1952, they scouted out the location for that first race. John Birchfield and Norm Bradley went over to South Bass Island, a popular vacation place, and mapped out a course for the CSCC's first race. The start/finish line would face Put-in-Bay, historic home of the American navy that defeated the British in the War of 1812. The first race would be in 1952, 140 years after the start of that war.

CHAPTER 1

Put-in-Bay—
A Summer Paradise in 1951

Unless you live in Northern Ohio, you may not know that there's an archipelago of 28 islands offshore in Lake Erie. Three of the most prominent are North Bass, Middle Bass and South Bass islands.

The latter is the home of Put-in-Bay. This was where America beat the British in the War of 1812. Admiral Oliver Hazard Perry flew a battle flag inscribed "Don't Give Up the Ship." He declared with confidence, "If a victory is to be gained, I will gain it!" And his

A panoramic view of the crescent-shaped harbor at Put-in-Bay. The ferry boat docks are to the right of the picture, the town park is in the center and the front straightaway of the race course is at the left (Dick Henn, Jr.).

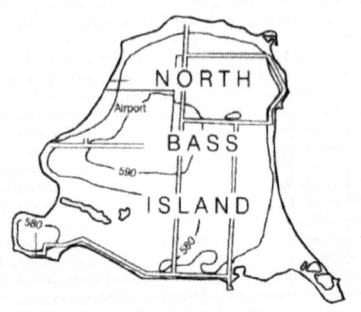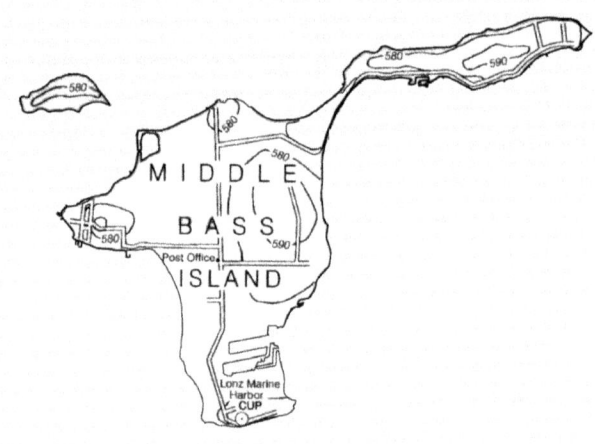

Activity around the gas dock includes a big Lyman cruising boat, a Thompson runabout and a large offshore sailing yacht. In the foreground is a chain hoist for stepping sailboat masts (Carl Goodwin).

report after the Battle of Lake Erie was, "We have met the enemy and he is ours." There's a big memorial—Perry's Monument—on South Bass Island.

The island had been built up with white Victorian cottages, their ornamentation harkening to an earlier day. You can almost hear the ragtime music playing on the piano in someone's parlor. In the early 1950s, the whole place had a pleasant, small town atmosphere, and the taxi cabs were Lincoln and Packard phaetons of the 1930s. Facing the ferry boat landing was a row of bars downtown, which are still there. The town hall and police station were at the right facing inland. Much further right was a state park with campsites. The cottages were inland, anywhere that there were not stores, bars or vineyards. The soil and climate of the island were ideal for growing grapes.

The bay itself has another island—Gibraltar—in the middle of it. That means you can anchor or dock your boat in calm water. Four- to six-foot waves are not uncommon on the lake, and the most I have seen is about ten. When you sail into Put-in-Bay, you can anchor your boat out in the bay towing a dinghy and row in to shore to get a pizza at Frosty's.

There was every type of boating activity available there, as there is today. If you like to fish, the waters are teeming with delicious perch, walleye and bass. A nearby waterfront town, Port Clinton, has a walleye festival once a year. Wonder what happened to the perch

Opposite: **Navigation chart of Lake Erie shows the three Bass Islands, just north of Sandusky, Ohio. Scenic Rattlesnake Island is to the west; Lonz Winery is on Middle Bass Island; and the sports car race was on South Bass.**

Top: With Gibraltar Island in the background, a Thistle Class sailboat completes a tack in front of a moored Alden 36. *Bottom*: Boat docks on the west side of South Bass, with Gibraltar Island behind them, and the author's Finn Class dinghy at the dock (Carl Goodwin).

Top: A popular boat around the 'Bay area and down the Lake Erie shoreline was *Merdeka*, owned by Herman Black and his sons Pat and Jim. Gathered about the mast are (left to right) race crew Charlie Ellmers and Fred Steger, with Jim Black. Both Ellmers and Steger were war heroes, but that's another story for another time. *Bottom*: Gerry Steger is at the helm of *Sinbad*. The 30-foot boat was owned by Gerry and husband Fred, also an MG racer. Over the span of about ten years, they managed to amass over seventy trophy flags in Put-in-Bay and other Lake Erie races (Collection of Jane Steger).

festival? Go out to one of the limestone reefs and reel them in all day. Take a friend and a cooler of beer. Many think that freshwater fish like these have much more flavor than fish from the ocean.

Other people like to go cruising in a motor yacht—something with living accommodations and a

This is the Cleveland Sport Car Club badge. It was designed largely by Dick Irish, with input from other club members. The design objective was to not look like either the SCCA or Metropolitan Sports Car Club (NYC) badges. The CSCC succeeded admirably, with one of the best-looking car badges ever (Joe Brown, collection of Dick Irish).

Among those at the March 5, 1951, founders' meeting of the Cleveland Sport Car Club, we see (left rear, in white shirt and sport jacket) Dick Bosley, creator of the Bosley Mk. I sports car; (center rear, white shirt and sport jacket) Dick Gent, owner of a Cisitalia and several other Italian cars; (center rear, in V-neck sweater) Earl Johnson, owner of a 2½-liter Riley roadster; (front center, white blouse) club secretary; (seated behind table) Dick Irish; (back row, white shirt) Frank White, owner of an MG-TD, an XK-120, then a DB-2 Aston Martin; (front row right, white open-collar shirt) Cornelius "Corny" Scheid, who had the first VW Beetle in town; (under table) Cricket, "our lovely Golden Retriever/lab mix dog"; (front, left of table) Andy Zimmerman—crippled by polio, he had an MG-TD with hand controls. At the meeting, Dick Irish was voted president. Not pictured is photographer and club member Joe Brown (Joe Brown, collection of Dick Irish).

1. Put-in-Bay—A Summer Paradise in 1951

galley. They usually pull up to the dock, pay a fee to the township, and sightsee on the island, or barhop or cruise to different islands in the group.

And sailing is very popular here. People sail from docks and moorings on the island or on the mainland. They sail from boat clubs all along the south shore of the mainland, such as Mentor Harbor Yachting Club and Cleveland Yacht Club, or from the Put-in-Bay Yacht Club. They sail the 17' Thistle class, the 19' Lightning, other centerboarders and plenty of keel boats. They day-sail, they cruise and they race. Every year the PIB YC sponsors a major regatta called Bay Week about the first weekend of August. It draws entries from up and down the Ohio shoreline as well as the Detroit area and the Canadian clubs. This has attracted as many as 400 boats.

One of the first things that happens with either boats or cars is that someone wants to

The registration table at the 1951 Cleveland Sport Car Club picnic, with club president Dick Irish (seated) and two helpers (Joe Brown).

The menfolk sit around the picnic table. CSCC, 1951. No doubt the topic is how to rebuild an S.U. carburetor (Joe Brown).

race with them, and this is what happened with the early sports cars, such as MG, Triumph, Porsche, and Alfa Romeo.

In the immediate postwar era, interest in cars flourished, including sports cars such as the MG TC, manufactured in England starting in late 1945. GIs started bringing them back as they finished their tours of duty. They were not just a utilitarian transport; they were made for pure pleasure and were a heck of a lot of fun to drive.

The problem was an absence of racing venues. Of course there were no purpose-built racing courses as there are now, such as Mid-Ohio, Nelson Ledges, Lime Rock and Road America. Beginning with Cameron Argetsinger's terrifically successful 1948 race at Watkins Glen, New York, the road races began on public roads that were closed for the weekend. Then they expanded to Bridgehampton, New York, Elkhart Lake, Wisconsin, a couple of West Coast locales and then Put-in-Bay.

There was a pretty good crowd at the CSCC picnic (1951) as a couple of MG-TDs headed for home. Bidding them farewell is Andy Zimmerman on crutches at the entrance to the Dick Irish farm. A little dachshund dog is approaching the cameraman (Joe Brown).

This happened through the initiatives of the Cleveland Sport Car Club. The club itself, as early member Betty Henn noted, was established in 1951. Most of the members were east-siders such as the Irish brothers, Dick and Chuck, the Henns, Dick Bosley, Dick Gent, Andy Zimmerman, Corny Scheid and others. Proposed for membership was Bob Lossman, known as "that plumber up on Lorain Avenue who has those cars for sale." Later, after founding Lossman Motors, he would be called "the millionaire plumber." One of the members was a retriever named Cricket. Meetings were often at the Irish home in Bratenahl on Lake Erie, and Dick Irish was elected the first club president.

The story of the race course has been told many times, so I'll make it short. Somebody—possibly Dick Gent—suggested Put-in-Bay as the venue for a race. Dick had a boat up there. So in April of 1952, John Birchfield and Norm Bradley went over to have a look.

John had organized rallies in Erie, Pennsylvania. Norm later owned a shop called Fine Cars, in partnership with driver Reed Andrews. Norm was a short, barrel-chested man, ex-navy. He wore a crew cut and smoked a cigar. They mapped out a 3.1-mile course on the island.

    The Race Committee talked to the city fathers. They would be happy to shut down a few roads for one day a year. The race would bring a lot of participants and spectators, who would spend a lot of money. And did they ever. The first race was planned in conjunction with a grape festival in September of 1952. We'll get to that year's story after a brief preview.

CHAPTER 2

The Last American Road Race, 1952–1959, 1963

For European-style races on public roads, Bridgehampton, Watkins Glen and Elkhart Lake are surely the best-known American venues. But there's one place where the racing went on longer and later than any of them: Put-in-Bay. Though it lacked the grand scale of the European distance races—Mille Miglia and Targa Florio—its charm was greater than that of the shorter round-the-houses events such as Aix-les-Bains in Belgium, and it was far safer.

Those who were not favored by a visit to this enchanting place on the 'Bay may be excused for their envy. It was a picture-book setting even more glorious than the Hamptons of the early fifties, the pastoral setting of rural Wisconsin and Elkhart Lake, or even the lovely race course in the rolling hills of central New York state.

Many race-goers were eager to make the lake crossing by Ford Tri-Motor. Was it faster than the ferry? Possibly. Unconcerned passengers wait while some routine maintenance is performed. No need to worry about the dripping oil (Rollin LaFrance).

Imagine an island in Lake Erie with a crescent bay and another island inside that bay. At the waterfront is a collection of Lyman runabouts with brightly varnished decks, a variety of offshore sailboats, the majestic R-Boats, Chris Craft Sedan Cruisers and Thistle class sloops. The Miller's Ferry docks are there too.

There's a little park with a bandstand and several cannons dating to the War of 1812 and Admiral Oliver Hazard Perry's defeat of the British fleet in Lake Erie there—Perry's Monument is just on the outskirts of town. Children's swings and benches ornament the square. Then there's a neat row of stores. There are bars, ice cream stores and places to buy picture postcards.

The front straight and the start-finish line are just ahead of those stores. As eager spectators leaned precipitously against the snow-fence there, Manny Holder's Porsche 550 RS was doing ninety miles an hour, two or three feet away.

For a week or two before—and after—the race, the winding country roads south and east of Cleveland would be busy with racers and would-be racers sharpening up their driving techniques—you would go after dark so you could see the headlights of approaching cars and get back into your own lane. The forest would ring with the sound of sports car exhausts. They would depart Linsay's Tavern, a sports car hangout in Shaker Heights, and head for Chagrin River Road, Eagle, Merkle or Rte. 615, all of which were, and are, terrific driving roads—no doubt the reason so many members of NE Ohio SCCA have done so well in national racing.

03 80

The Porsche Speedster of Roy Orr and Ernest Davis' TR-2 are loaded abroad Miller's Ferry at Catawba before the race. All are looking forward to a day of racing (Rollin LaFrance).

2. The Last American Road Race, 1952–1959, 1963

The Put-in-Bay Road Races ran from 1952 through 1959; in other words, the era of Chico Hamilton, Thelonius Monkπ15, penny loafers and dark blue LaCoste shirts. They were conducted by the Cleveland Sport Car Club, with an "outlaw" race run in 1963 by Detroit and Toledo enthusiasts. Roger Johnson of the Northwest Ohio Region (Toledo), SCCA, put on some autocrosses from 1981 to 1984, too. In comparison, the races on public streets at Bridgehampton ran 1949–1953, Watkins Glen 1948–1954, and Elkhart Lake 1950–1952. Brynfan Tyddyn ran from 1952 to 1956. Put-in-Bay was, in fact, the last American road race.

The site was found in much the same way as the others. Put-in-Bay, the bay on South Bass Island just offshore of Sandusky, Ohio, was a popular vacation spot for Clevelanders. CSCC member John Birchfield recalls, "Norman Bradley and I went to the island in April of 1951 and drove around in Norm's XK120. We laid out the course and decided, due to the rough narrow roads and sharp bends, that it should be limited to 2 liter unblown and 1500cc modified cars. That was quite altruistic of Norm because he really wanted to run his Jag." It was more or less rectangular and was spiritually akin to Bridgehampton, with curbs as hazards instead of Elkhart's deep ditches beside the racing surface. The Glen, dangerously, had both. Instrumental in making the arrangements was Bob Lossman, proprietor of MG Motor Sales

Inside the hold of the Miller's Ferry boat, shoehorned in are (clockwise from left) Bob Karol's Fiat/Nardi 600, Dick Henn's XK140, the no. 69 Arnolt-Bristol of Chuck Dietrich, a Fiat 600 Multipla, Charlie Ellmer's Lester MG, and an unidentified MG-TD (Rollin LaFrance).

To get a little extra practice time, a few competitors, and even non-competitors, ran the course in the middle of the night, such as Norm Bradley from Cleveland, seen here in his Fiat-Abarth Zagato with his nurse girlfriend in the car (Rollin LaFrance).

in Lakewood, Ohio, according to former employees Fred Troyan and Art Brow. "Bob knew everyone on the island," Brow recalls. "He really got them to support the race."

Luminaries of this wonderful event were Dick and Betty Henn of the CSCC. Two more energetic and personable characters could not be imagined. Dick was a retired army colonel who ran the event in a military fashion, but more affably—with the personality of your favorite uncle. He had the Ohio National Guard set up the communications system as a training exercise. Betty was warm, bouncy and bright. She ran the registration and enlisted Bill and Nancy Schmidt to organize the corner workers.

"And she got Bill Gorris to handle timing and scoring and Bob Kintner on race communications," John Comey adds. Gorris modestly ducks this recognition, noting that Bob Morrison did more than he did.

The first race, in 1952, almost did not come off. The night before the race, the mayor of the island insisted on seeing the insurance certificate for the event, which Dick Henn kept in a safe back in Cleveland Heights. When Bandini owner Dick Gent heard of the dilemma, he said, "We can still race. Get in my speedboat." Fortunately, Lake Erie was calm that night. It usually isn't. They tore off at record speed in a Marcel Riveau French racing boat, picked up the certificate, and returned to South Bass before the start of the race.

2. The Last American Road Race, 1952–1959, 1963

Except for the first year, the races were always on the first or second weekend of June. MG-TD owner John Comey went to every one of them—as a competitor in the first two and as course marshal in the rest. "In 1952," he says, "it was run in the fall—September I believe. I had the distinction of being the 1st car into the 1st corner in the 1st race. I was in the front row and got a good start. Then, on Airport Straight, I was passed by some cars that were going 7 or 8 miles an hour faster. We were all supposed to be stock, so the lesson here is that some cars were more stock than others. It started raining and I was getting wet so I stopped at a farm house and put up the top. I ran the car again the next year and, going into the gas station chicane, a number of cars came together. I had a tough time avoiding them but I did not avoid the telephone pole. That meant the end of my racing, since the MG was the car I drove to work. Then I became the course marshal. I would go up two days ahead of time, sweep the gravel off the corners and get farmers to bring in hay bales." Comey was also known for his Bugatti pace cars, a Type 55 that King Leopold had owned and a Type 57 convertible.

Competitors would arrive on the ferry boats Friday morning in order to perform technical inspections and practice. In fact, some, such as Chuck Stoddard, would come up very early Saturday morning. "The whole island was shut down and there was nothing to do," he recalls, "so I would just get up early and drive the Siata from Willoughby to get there at 9 o'clock. I would race my car, put it back on the ferry and be back home the same night."

Since there was no time for qualifying, the grid was formed by drawing numbers from a hat. Most of the cars were new, so inspection didn't reveal much. Brake tests and the rest of the tech inspections were held at Joe Parker's garage on Catawba Avenue. As race worker

Hank Becker in the #7 MG-TD gets his car teched by Joe Kovach at Parker's Garage. Seems to be race-ready! (collection of Hank Becker).

Mickey Mishne recalls, "Joe Kovatch was the technical inspector. One of his main concerns was that a car braked in a straight line. The driver would speed up slightly upon entering Parker's Garage, step on the brakes and raise both hands. The result was that many drivers learned how to keep their steering wheel straight, with their knees."

At the time, it was also common to test handbrakes. Only one car ever went through the back of the garage, as spectator and motorcycle road-racer Bob Karol relates: "Accelerating the length of the garage during the hand-brake test, Frazer-Nash driver Bo Miske disappeared, speed unchecked, out the back door. Returning from his trip around the building, he explained, 'I knew I forgot to connect something.'"

John Comey recalls, "There was a lot of racing the night before the race and a friend of mine went in the lake off the South Dock. It was Mike Caparon, in an MG. He claimed that mayflies made the dock slick!"

There were a certain number of inns and guest houses available for vacationers, and when these were used up, people made other plans. TD driver Art Brow recalls, "One time I couldn't find a room so I slept on the porch of Dr. Sam Sheppard's cottage." Sheppard was later accused of murdering his wife and was hounded by the newspapers thereafter. He also raced an MG-TD at the 'Bay in 1953 and '54. John Comey and his friends would rent an entire house and split the cost: for 50 people it was 50 cents each. "There were people sleeping everywhere," he comments.

Hardly anyone had a trailer. If you did, you left it at one of the ferry parking lots—Port Clinton, Catawba or Marblehead. Your car numbers were made of masking tape or maybe tempera paint, not die-cut vinyl. Safety equipment was simple and basic: a seat belt and a

Put-in-Bay's paddock was merely a corner lot, which served its purpose most efficiently. There seems to be a monopoly by MGs here! (Dave and Sheila Bly).

helmet. Roll-over bars and fire-retardant coveralls were not required until 1958. Of course you didn't need to go to drivers' school and you didn't need to get a competition license — you just showed up with your car and taped the headlights. Then the more technically astute would change their spark plugs and add some air pressure to their tires.

There weren't many rules, but "by 1957 there was one stipulation," Mickey Mishne recalls. "Drivers had to be members of the Cleveland Sport Car Club, which cost about $10. This rule ballooned club membership to 225 members!"

If you were a spectator, you would come over from the mainland on Saturday morning. If you didn't know any better, like the writer, you would take the Miller's Ferry from Port Clinton. It was an hour and 15 minutes versus the shorter 45-minute trip from Catawba. That's 30 minutes less pounding by the relentless waves of Lake Erie against the scow-like hull of the ferry boat.

Some preferred the adventure of flying on a Ford Tri-Motor. One year Chuck Stoddard arranged to have his car escorted over on the ferry, while he took the plane. "It was airborne at about 35 miles an hour," Stoddard recalls. "It trundled down the runway and suddenly you would realize, 'It's in the air!' Everything vibrated. It was like a flying tin can. I don't think it flew any higher than 200 feet over Lake Erie."

Normally, these boats would carry four regular cars like your Uncle Harold's Buick. If you were early enough, you would see, instead, eight or so little machines like Siatas, Abarths, Triumphs and, of course, MGs. If this was the first time you had seen them, it would intrigue the hell out of you. The impact of this would be intensified as you reached the shore and

To keep speeds down, cars larger than two liters were not permitted to race at Put-in-Bay, but cars such as the C-Type Jaguar of Douglas Maier (right) were allowed to pace the races (Dave and Sheila Bly).

the gangplank dropped down. When the din of the ferry boat subsided, you were left with the howl of racing engines, so you sprinted across the park to see them blasting by. What a magnificent sight!

On Saturday, the first event of the day was the all-MG race. It's unfortunate, now, that some vintage races don't even have a single T-series MG entered. Then, of course, that's about all there was. In fact, MGs could potentially run in four of the five races. Race worker and MG restorer Bob Satava recalls that 25 was the maximum starting grid for the 3.1-mile course. Each event was sent off with a rolling start, behind a pace car that was a Jaguar, Ferrari, Corvette, Bugatti or other car with enough power to outrun a field of up to 2-liter production or 1.5-liter modified cars.

"I drove the pace car several times," Betty Henn recalled. "It was one of our old Jags. I remember the first time. I was never so scared in all my life. All these louts were leaning against the snow fence in front of the hotel, with a bottle in each hand. They'd see us coming and they'd lean out further for a better view."

Not exactly mugs with tattoos and beer-bellies, most of the spectators were engineers from Thompson Products (which later became Thompson Ramo Woolridge and then TRW). Chuck Stoddard, among others, worked for them, on oil consumption in the nailhead Buick. On the other hand, they were not exactly Boy Scouts. Dick Heckman recalled an MG driver who stopped at one of the island's wineries and ducked in to buy a bottle during

The MG race comes into town past the Sohio station with Bob Shea's #12 TC leading. Behind him is Charlie Ellmers in the TC of the Funny Face Auto Racing Team and the rest of the 23-car field (Ruth and Charlie Ellmers).

the race, to make sure he had enough wine after the races. "I had someone try to pour beer on me, on Main Street in my racing car," complains Harry Constant, who drove there four times. "The only people worse were the yachtsmen. They never stopped drinking."

The 'Bay has a sailing tradition that begins before Admiral Perry and the War of 1812 and continues to this day with major Great Lakes regattas. Many of the people whose cars drove at the 'Bay later raced sailboats there, including Charlie Ellmers, Fred Steger, John Tame and this writer.

Contenders in the MG race, over the years, included Charlie Ellmers in a TD and then a borrowed TC, Ralph Cadwallader in a TC, Chuck Henry in a TC, Ralph Durbin in a TF, Jim Dever in a TD, Art Brow in a TD and John Tame in a TF. Ellmers, an overseas veteran of both World War II and Korea, recalls, "I was discharged from the navy after my stint aboard the *Essex*. I had some money saved up and thought I would buy a new car and drive it home. I was considering a Studebaker but thought I would check out the new MG-TD. The TD was $2,020, about the same as the Studebaker. The guy at the MG dealer wouldn't let me drive one of the MGs in the showroom but he did take me for a ride in his TC. That cinched it. After I got home, I stopped at our gang's favorite watering hole, the Monticello Bar in Cleveland Heights, and parked next to a TD identical to mine. Black and red. My close friend Johnny Reinhart had just bought it."

Ellmers later became the competition chairman of NE Ohio Region SCCA, the one who first gave a racing license to Roger Penske. As an MG driver, Charlie describes the course at Put-in-Bay. "We would follow the pace car until it went straight at Turn One. You could take that in first gear in a TD. Then there was a dog-leg a block later, past an old barn, and

Two charging Porsche Carrera Speedsters round the Colonial Ballroom, with Tom Payne leading Doc Curran. The Colonial claimed to have the world's longest bar (Rollin LaFrance).

The #80 Fiat-Abarth Zagato of Bob Stein charges down main street to the delight of spectators not used to seeing such diminutive automobiles ... and so fast! (Rollin LaFrance).

you went down a long straight to the Airport Turn. From there you went through the vineyards on a very bumpy road. Your speed was actually limited by the bumps you were hitting. Some of the cars were stiffly sprung and did not do well on this section."

Siata driver Al Beasley recalls, "I was following Mel Sachs in his Bandini, and every time it hit a bump it went two feet in the air so I could see the underside of his car." If your machine survived that, you would soon come to Cemetery Corner, not a very appealing name for a turn on a race course. This was always full of picnicking spectators, since it was well shaded and gave an excellent view of two straightaways. The last leg of the course was named Cooper Straight. At the end of this mile-long stretch was another dog-leg at the gas station and then the last corner into town and the start/finish line.

Cooper Straight was named for the restaurant where you could get the best perch dinner in the world. People offered other patrons 50-dollar bills for their dinner table at Cooper's. Just before the dog-leg was a bump where some of the cars became airborne. The Holder brothers' 4-cam Porsche Spyder was going 130 over this bump and went airborne for about 35 feet, alighting just in time to brake for the dog-leg. If you could not make the corner onto the front straight, the escape road led off the end of the dock, and then splash into Lake Erie.

An account of the MG Race is provided by "Haybale Harry" Constant, who went to the 'Bay twice with a TD and once, each, with an Alfa and a Siata. Constant, a longtime Detroit Region SCCA racing official, acquired his nickname by putting his car on top of the haybales during an event at the old Mt. Clemens Speedway. Anyway, Harry and his friend Ralph Durbin were put well back in the pack when the grid positions were drawn. But then there was an accident at the end of Airport Straight. "Cars were scattered everywhere," Harry recalls. "Ralph and I made it through the carnage and suddenly went from last to first. I led going into Cemetery Turn. Then there was a TC that seemed to come from nowhere. He and Durbin both passed me and raced down Cooper Straight. The TC nudged Ralph's car at the kink. He snapped around and went backwards from the gas station to Main Street, about 50 yards. He spun the car back around and we both took off after the TC but never caught it."

An incident photographed by the *Cleveland Plain Dealer* put Art Brow's borrowed MG into the hay bales. "I was driving Bill Staufer's TD and one of the fan blades broke off," Art says. "So I had to move my shift points up. Then the vibration backed out the screws on the heater assembly and it fell on my foot, pinning it and the accelerator to the floor just as I approached Cemetery Corner. There were a few anxious moments as I tried to regain control of the car and I went into the ditch on the exit of the turn." After putting the heater in the passenger foot-well he drove back onto the course and barely finished the race. "The imbalance bent the shaft three-eighths of an inch. It wouldn't have lasted too much longer."

Longtime MG racer Ralph Cadwallader ran his TC every year but the first one: "I missed 1952," he confesses, "and I never won at the 'Bay. I didn't have very good luck—one year I broke an axle, another year the brakes went out. The closest I came was in 1953. I was ahead of Chuck Dietrich for eight laps. But my exhaust pipe came loose. Every time we came by the marshal, Chuck would point to the pipe hanging from my car. Finally I was black-flagged and had to come in. I ripped the exhaust off my car and got back in the race. I had lost the lead but I still finished the race."

Cadwallader staged a meeting of former Put-in-Bay drivers at the Cleveland Sport Car Club's 40th annual banquet in 1992. All were there to recollect and to savor the unique character of the event—the beautiful setting, the great racing machines, the excitement of competition and the companionship of friends in the sport. In closing the event, Ralph paraphrased King Henry V before the battle of Agincourt, saying,

> We few, we happy few;
> We loyal band of brothers.
> He who race with me this day,
> Shall always be my brother.

Well after the MG race, stalwart drivers of the marque from Abingdon would sometimes brave the F-Production Porsche event—their option because of the displacement class. It was never an easy race to contest, since the German car was a newer design, lighter and more powerful. "An MG never beat a Porsche," recalls TF driver John Tame. "It just never did." In some events, they would allow a Siata Gran Sport to enter; Charles Allen's Siata took a 3rd in 1956.

Also racing in the under–1500-cc production event were the H- and G-Modified cars. This race was usually won by Chuck Stoddard in a black Siata with the cartoon figure "Tweety Bird" painted on the side. In that car, Stoddard, at 6'4", looked like Bill Spear in a Ferrari 166—like an adult in a kiddie car. "I found the Siata in Dayton, Ohio, where I was an aircraft maintenance officer at Wright Patterson. I had raced my TD at Thompson, Connecticut, when I was going to school and I was looking for more of a race car," he says. "I put a Crosley

The scene in the paddock says it all. Put-in-Bay was more than just a race (Rollin LaFrance).

engine in it and visited Lou Fageol to get some parts for it. The engine was 750 cc and had about 70 horsepower." A perennial competitor was Mel Sachs in the Dick Gent H-Modified Bandini.

In 1958, Stoddard switched to a 1300-cc G-Production Alfa Romeo twin-cam. "I had started my car business by then," he notes, "and Max Hoffman wouldn't sell you Porsches unless you bought Alfas. I liked the Alfa and decided to race it—there were no 1300-cc Porsches racing at the 'Bay then, but plenty of Alfas."

Stoddard later wrote a very good article on race-preparing an Alfa in *Sports Car,* the SCCA magazine. In 1958, he had a dramatic finish. While leading on the last turn of the last lap, he downshifted and blew up the engine. The crankshaft broke, in a cloud of white smoke. He had the presence of mind to stick in the clutch and coast over the finish line for the win. "At Put-in-Bay, if you won a race, you would stop after you crossed the finish line and Dick Henn would hand you the checkered flag for your victory lap. When I stopped I said, 'my car won't go any further.' Right away, Dick said, 'Just stay in your car and we'll wait for the rest to go past. Then we'll just push your car into the paddock.'" MG entrant Art Brow adds, "Stoddard was the only driver to get a first in class *and* the blow-up trophy that year."

On Monday morning, Stoddard called Karl Grassow at Hoffman Service to explain his (shall-we-say) warranty problem, and discovered that the 'Bay race was known nationally. Max himself came to the phone, speaking in accent: "Congratulations on vinning your race at Put-in-Bay," he began. "But as you should know vell, Mister Stoddard, vee dohn't guarantee zee cars for racink!"

Bob Kuhn's No. 6 Siata leads Chuck Dietrich's supercharged MG-TC, but just temporarily. Moments later, Chuck passed the exotic Siata with its 2-liter, V-8 engine (Betty Henn).

Ben Hall leads the pack through town in 1958 in his AC Ace (collection of Betty Henn).

The sedan classes were popular and fielded Volkswagens, Karmann Ghias, Renault Dauphines, 4CVs, Simcas, Goggomobils, DKWs and Morris Minors. John Comey remembers two young men who borrowed their mother's new VW beetle. "When they got to the 'Bay, they thought it would be even more fun to enter a race," he recalls. "They weren't able to decide who should drive, so each lap they stopped at the Finish Line, the doors flew open and they swapped places!"

In 1959, there was a 750-cc class "I" that pitted Saab GTs, Crosley Hotshots and Ben Shoemaker's Fiat 600 against Fiat-Abarth Zagato GTs and that meant a spirited contest, as race-goer and motorcycling author Bob Karol relates: "At the start of race two, Will Grant's Saab was fighting off the triple Fiat-Abarth threat of Bradley, Stone and Stein. As Al Beasley's smoke-screening Siata coasted into the pits, the Abarths, finally passing and outdistancing the remaining modified cars, set their sights on the leading Lotus VI of Robert Samm. Valve trouble eliminated Bradley's Abarth, permitting Stone's dark blue double-bubble to move up, but he spun in a last-minute effort to shake Stein, whose Abarth then grabbed a class win. Recovering in time, Stone secured a second in class, the not-too-far behind Saab managing a class third."

The H-Production class sprang to life in 1958, with introduction of the Austin-Healey Sprite and the Turner, a fiberglass-bodied English sports car. "Ralph Durbin had the first Sprite," says John Birchfield. "It was a red one." Art Brow, who had raced a TD in 1957, got

Tony Stica's red Sprite sails through the corner at the end of town, followed closely by the white Sprite of Meacham Hitchcock (Rollin LaFrance).

a new Turner. "It had a 948-cc Morris Minor engine," he says, "and a large-diameter tube frame, similar to the AC Ace. In 1958, I took a 2nd place with my Sprite. I started second to last and worked my way up to 3rd in 3 laps. I picked up one more position and finished the race that way."

"Well, 1959 was not such a good year for Art and his Turner," Ralph Cadwallader recounts. "He was leading the pack when his seat cushion slid out from under him, leaving Art sitting on the floor, seeing nothing but dashboard. When he hit a bump, he would come up for a quick snapshot of the race course and then down again on the floor. Finally he got the seat back under him and continued the race." A few laps later, a cam bearing froze, the cam gear sheared off and the entire assembly ceased to operate.

The stalwart in G-Modified was Chuck Dietrich. Dietrich raced until August of 2002, in a Martini SV in Formula Atlantic. At Mid-Ohio, that year, he placed sixth in a field of all newer Toyota-engined machines. This was at the age of 77. In 52 years of racing he has driven at 63 courses ("most of them closed now," he quips). "I ran my supercharged MG in '52 and '53," he says:

> Then I bought a Lester MG from Don Marsh in Columbus. It actually had a pre-war MG-TA frame, with a Lester aluminum body. Marsh had a new nose built in Columbus—the pointed tail was original. I ran that in '54 and '55, and sold it to Charlie Ellmers.

Then I read about a new car in an English car magazine. John Bolster wrote about the Elva Mark I. I contacted Frank Nichols and he said he had one that had been made for a Canadian who was overcome by fumes in his garage. It was supposed to have been prepped for Sebring, but it had no lights! I bought it and it was the first one in the country. I became the exclusive importer for a couple of years until it became too much work. I had a new one every year and won G-Modified at the 'Bay every year. One year I hit a tree and still won. In 1956 I had the Mk. I, in '57 a Mk. II, in '58 a Mk. III and a Mk. IV in '59. I could sell the Elva and make money on it. An Elva was about $2,000 from Frank Nichols, cheaper than a Lotus or Lola, but just as fast. At Elkhart in 1960, the winners in Race 5 were a Porsche RS60, a 550 then my Elva in 3rd, a Lotus and about three 2-liter Ferraris.

In 1957, there was a great battle between Dietrich in his Mk. III Elva and Tom Hallock of Grosse Pointe, Michigan, in a Cooper Climax. Race worker Mickey Mishne, best known as the motorsports feature writer of the *Cleveland Plain Dealer,* recalls a near miss at his station in about 1958: "Harvey Winograd and I were working the flags on Cooper Straight and we saw Doc Wylie headed straight for us in his Lotus. He didn't turn away, and at last minute we dove off to the side as he came sailing through our station and back onto the road."

Suzy Dietrich was also an outstanding pilot ("one of the most aggressive drivers I've

Race Chairman Dick Henn (left) awards a first place to Elva driver Doug Wearn at the trophy presentation in 1959 (Rollin LaFrance).

ever seen," observes Mishne), and it was frustrating to her that women were not allowed to race at the 'Bay. She did, however, drive the pace car once, a supercharged MG TC, and she didn't spare the horses. "Sure I remember when Suzy drove the pace car," Art Brow remarked. "It was the fastest lap I ever drove!"

"Some believe the fastest lap was set by Herb Swan in his Offenhauser-engined Siata," says Mickey Mishne. "I was at the flag station on the corner halfway to Airport Straight when Herb comes blasting up, brakes hard, and makes a right turn toward Cooper Straight. The only problem was, it was one corner too soon, cutting about a mile off the course. I wonder how that looked at the timing stand." Swan's Offenhauser engine later appeared in his Ferrari 166, for which, still later, the original engine was rebuilt by John Ferrante and this writer.

F and E-Modified classes consisted of modified MGs at first—Chuck Dietrich's supercharged TC and the Lester MG of Charlie Elmer's syndicate. Then, in 1955, the Porsche 550-As came along and, with its marvelous 4-cam engine, completely dominated the class. Spyder drivers included the record-setting Holder brothers, Manny and Lorrain, Jack Manting from Detroit, Carl Haas from Chicago and Bernie Keller from Mansfield. Another car is recalled by Art Brow: "Lou Fageol had a highly modified 1953 Porsche cabriolet. It had a Pepco supercharger. The car could accelerate with the Spyders but, as Lou soon found out, it couldn't corner with them." The course record was set in 1958 by Manny Holder's 550RS at 89.9 mph, and the record still stands. In fact, it always will.

The E-P cars included a ton of Triumphs—TR-2s, 3s and 3As—a few Morgans, AC Aces, AC Bristols, Arnolt Bristols, Bo Miske's Frazer Nash and the occasional Siata 208S. The ranks of E-Production drivers included Quay Barber, Ben Hall, Tom Payne and, of course, Reed Andrews. Reed got out of racing only recently. A Cleveland stockbroker and hail-fellow-well-met, he would slap the menfolk on the back and heartily kiss their wives. He was notorious for his lack of mechanical ability. At one of the races, Reed burned a couple valves in his TR-2 during practice. He was packing up his things in the car when his friends the Holder brothers came by. They had a machine shop in Cleveland and had completely redone the gears in their 550RS. "What's the matter?" Lorrain asked. Reed only knew his car was running on three cylinders. "Let's take a look," Manny said. In no time at all the head was off, and the burnt valves were confirmed. They called a dealer on the mainland and located the parts, then flew over to get them. By late afternoon the car was back together and ready to race the next day. "I took a 3rd place in E-Production," Reed recalls, "thanks to Manny and Lorrain." The Holder brothers took a 1st, of course, with Manny driving the fast silver Spyder. He drove the victory lap with Barbara in the seat beside him, holding the checkered flag as it snapped in the wind. It is a scene that will live forever in the memory of anyone who saw it.

"Put-in-Bay was like utopia," Chuck Stoddard recalls. "It was always nice. No one ever got hurt. Oh, sure, a few cars got bent and then people would joke about 'How's he going to get home?' but it was very idyllic. Even though the safety record was very good, insurance was becoming more difficult to get. In 1959, a guy in a Sprite went off course at Airport Turn and hit a spectator. You know the sloping hood that a Sprite has? Well, this spectator went up the hood, over the cockpit and down the back deck. Which spectator was it? The insurance man—he promptly increased the insurance premium!"

John Comey elaborates: "Because of the layout at Put-in-Bay, you couldn't charge admission. So Bob Lossman would go around to the local businesses after the race and pass the hat. They made an awful lot of money. They made so much money that when the state of

At the 1990 Put-in-Bay MG Revival, race organizer Betty Henn rides in the MG-TD of former race worker Bob Satava (Carl Goodwin).

Ohio passed a law against racing on public streets, the Put-in-Bay merchants got a specific exemption passed for their race. The ferry boat company built a new dock at the south end of the island to make more trips and bring in more money. But insurance costs were going up too. At the end, insurance costs just outstripped the ability to pay for it. Then too, crowd control was getting more difficult."

But 1959 wasn't exactly the last race there. It was revived in 1963, on a shortened course that did not go out of town. "The last 'Bay race was said to be a Detroit event," turn marshal Jack Holth recalls, "but that's not quite true." Jack and his bride Carol were newlyweds, and both worked corners at the last race. "The organizers were Dick Reder in Toledo, Al Blumberg in Toledo and Ed Houlehan, who was the starter at Waterford Hills for years and years. It's probably correct that most of the entrants were from Detroit, though."

Longtime Porsche driver Vic Skirmants drove down to the race from Detroit, in his '58 coupe, with a neighbor from Pontiac, Larry Boice. "I remember the course was pretty simple," Vic recalls; "four ninety-degree turns. I knew a couple of people from Waterford—Ralph Durbin in his Arnolt-Bristol and Frank Cipelle in his 1300 Porsche coupe. It was interesting to watch the cars going through town, and of course I remember the accident. It was a front-engined Elva, which hit the telephone pole a little off center. Instead of pushing the engine back into the driver, it sheared off the intake manifold, which probably saved him."

The driver? Where was he? Race-worker Jack Holth recalls: "The Elva went out of control trying to avoid a spectator who had run across the course. It was a terrible wreck and the car was completely demolished. They couldn't even find the driver. He was sitting at the base of a tree having a cigarette. That was the end of wheel-to-wheel racing at Put-in-Bay."

In 1981, '82, '83 and '84, the Northwestern Ohio Region of the Sports Car Club of America put on its autocross events. A pylon course had been set up around the town square. It was nice to hear racing engines again at the 'Bay, and some good performances were turned in by Gary Lownsdale in his rapid Lotus Elan.

Then, on June 2, 1990, on the 31st anniversary of the races, Bob Satava, the "MG King of Cleveland" and a former course worker in the early days, organized a very nice MG T-series reunion at the island. About 35 cars were ferried over to partake in the festivities. One event was the staging of MGs at the start-finish line as if gridded for a race, which occasioned lump-in-the-throat nostalgia for old-timers who saw it. In the lead car, Bob Satava's vintage racing TD, with the hood side-panels off and carburetor air horns tilting jauntily upward, was race organizer Betty Henn, a spry 89 years old at the time. A member of the new breed of MG owners—yes, I'm afraid he was the one who wore a ship captain's hat and shifted his car at 1500 rpm—said patronizingly, "Here, let me help you get in." As Betty clambered under the roll bar she said, "Don't worry, sonny, I've done this before."

Like everyone, Manny and Lorrain Holder, and their wives Nancy and Barbara, loved Put-in-Bay. It was more than the competition, and Lorrain was able to put it into words: "There was nothing like that race," he said. "It was just like a dream of anybody who would like to get in his car and go fast. It was just going to some little town and driving your heart out."

Description of the 3.1-Mile Cleveland Sport Car Club Course Used at Put-in-Bay from 1952 through 1959

STARTING LINE (Start-Finish): The start was taken as a rolling start, rather than the standing start common in Europe and in some U.S. races. Dick and Betty Henn believed that a rolling start would be safer—which it is. The rolling start was behind a pace car that was as fast or faster than the class being started. It could be a Ferrari 250 LWB, John Comey's Type 55 Bugatti, Doug Maier's C-Type Jaguar, Betty Henn's Jag 140, Suzy Dietrich in her supercharged MG-TC or Dave Weisenberger in his Triumph TR-3. They would take the field around once, the starter would give them the green flag and the pace car would go straight as the field went through Turn One.

TURN ONE: A 90-degree right flat turn. There was a ditch on the inside, so drivers were advised not to cut it short or they would drop a wheel off the road. It was the site of congestion and anxiety as the 25 cars from the starting line funneled past the pits into a turn that, as Chuck Stoddard recalls, was "three cars wide at the entrance and two cars wide at the exit" as it went toward the airport straight. The Bayshore Hotel, where many of the drivers stayed, was off to the left.

TURN TWO: This was another right turn, but half right, and it was an extension of the airport road. It was a deceptively hard turn that caused a number of spins of first-lap cars whose tires had not warmed up.

AIRPORT STRAIGHT: 5,825 feet long. This was a fairly smooth road, and the highest speeds were posted on this straight. This is where Chuck Dietrich ran out of gas one year; he borrowed some from a farmer and got back in the race.

TURN THREE, AIRPORT CORNER: Another site of spins, particularly Morgans, as the macadam pavement turned to mush in the hot summer sun. This was a 90-degree corner that was not entirely flat. It had an off-camber falloff on the outside of the turn that caused trouble for some. It had an escape road; namely, the airport road went straight for about half a mile, ending on a dock in Lake Erie. One car was rumored to have gone off this dock. It was probably Mike Capron from Detroit in his MG-TD. Mike claimed that mayflies on the dock made it slippery, and that's why he went into the lake.

Road from Airport Corner to Cemetery Corner: Very bumpy, supposed to be an axle breaker, but there were no known incidents of breakage. We did have a few cars up in the air, including the Mel Sachs/Dick Gent Bandini: Al Beasley, following in his Siata, said he had seen the rear axle of the car on one bounce. Other cars, heavier cars, were not as affected by the bumps. This road was 1,375 feet long. It was on this road, too, that Reed Andrews had his famous crash.

"It was about 1957," says Reed. "I was driving my E-Production Triumph TR3. I was passing an Ace Bristol, which was on my right side. We were just about even when all of a sudden the bumps got to me! The car spun and got airborne. I went backwards, between a fence and a tree, and there was quite a bump when I landed, in among some small trees and bushes. It was a miracle that I didn't hit the other car. I thought I might go upside down. Out of the corner of my eye I saw people scrambling to get out of the way. I was going backwards pretty fast, with my foot on the brake. Finally I stopped. Racing spectator John Clark was the first to get to me. "Reed, are you all right?" he asked. "Yes. Is everyone else all right?" I said. He told me no one had been hurt. "Then let's get this foliage out of the car," I told him, "so I can get back to the race." Of course by that time I had lost a lot of positions and didn't finish all that well. The next year, the race chairman, Dick Henn, said there would be no passing on the airport-to-cemetery road. That was 1957, and the rule also applied to 1958 and '59.

Turn Four, Cemetery Corner: Right turn—site of the famous or infamous Art Brow incident in which the heater in the borrowed Bill Staufer TD fell on his foot so he couldn't lift off the accelerator, causing a near spin and a few anxious moments. Just before the corner there was a dip and then a short uphill section; you started the turn going uphill, and the exit was reverse camber. There was no escape road, only haybales and then a graveyard on the right.

Cooper Straight: going back into town; 5,025 feet in length. Most people thought the straight was longer than the one from the airport, but of course it wasn't. In the middle of the straight was Cooper's Restaurant, home of the world's best perch dinner. Most of this road was fairly smooth and downhill into town.

Whoop-te-do at the end of Cooper Straight: Just before the corner at the gas station was a little rise that would launch the cars off the ground for a few feet. That's what the MGs would do. But the Porsche Spyders, going 125–130 mph down Cooper Straight, would be in the air about 30 to 40 feet, landing just in time to put on the brakes, downshift and make the corner at the gas station. If you were watching the cars come in to town, the most dramatic—and longest flight—would be Manny Holder in his Porsche Spyder.

Turn Five: The left turn at the gas station (see above). On the right side was the gas station and on the left side was the church. One time, the day after the race, Jim Carroll was doing some spirited driving in the Crosley-engined Siata. He came through that corner just as the parson came out of the church. The parson jumped a foot in the air and perhaps thought uncharitable thoughts. Another incident, in 1955, involved the MGs of Detroiters Ralph Durbin and Harry Constant. Harry notes, "Going down the straight Ralph passed me, but I kept on his tail. A TC passed me, got behind Ralph and gave him a nudge as we approached the gas station. He spun Ralph, and Ralph drove backwards down the sidewalk, hit the front straight, went forward and continued. A very interesting bit of driving. I'll never forget Ralph looking over his shoulder, driving backward."

TURN SIX: The turn into town and down Main Street to the start-finish line. It was a 90-degree right turn after the short downhill straight from the gas station. There was an escape road that went straight to the lake, but it was about a half a block away. If you had any ego at all, you wanted to make this a good turn so your friends would see what a good driver you were and hold speed onto the main street straight through town. One of the best old photographs is the one of Chuck Henry taking this turn in his MG-TC, picture perfect. On another occasion, Chuck Stoddard blew up the engine of his Alfa Giulietta just before the turn, while in the lead. He had the presence of mind to stick in the clutch and coast through the turn and across the finish line. He got not only the win but also the blowup trophy. Event organizer Dick Henn would usually hold the race winner at the start-finish until the other cars had passed, and then send the winning car with a checkered flag in hand for a victory lap. In Stoddard's case, this tradition was dispensed with.

FINISH LINE (Start-Finish): Located approximately at the site of the trophy presentations. As mentioned above, the practice was to hold the winning car in each race until the track was clear and then send them around with the checkered flag. To every winning driver, this was a great occasion. But no finish was so triumphant as the record-setting race of Manny Holder in 1958, his silver Porsche Spyder winning decisively over Sidney Baughman's Spyder. Manny drove the victory lap with his wife Barbara in the seat beside him, holding the checkered flag as it snapped in the wind, with the wonderful sound of that 4-cam engine. It is a scene that will live forever in the memory of anyone who saw it.

TOWN PARK: the site of trophy presentations. After the races, trophies were awarded by Dick Henn to the winning drivers at a site in the park just across from the start-finish line. The lap record was set by Manny Holder of Cleveland, in his Porsche 550RS Spyder, at 89.90 mph. It is a record that will never be broken.

Thanks to help from Put-in-Bay racing drivers Harry Constant, Hank Becker, Reed Andrews and Chuck Stoddard for compiling these descriptions.

CHAPTER 3

1952: The First of the Last American Road Races

September 14, 1952

Little information remains on the 1952 version of the classic Put-in-Bay road races. Sally Caroll of the Cleveland Sport Car Club has provided some. Suzy Dietrich has shared some of her remembrances, and John Treible of the Emerald Necklace MG Register and Chris Kintner, grandson of race organizers Richard L. and Betty Henn, have provided even more material. In addition to stories saved from conversations with drivers who are now deceased, this is material saved from the 40th anniversary meeting of PiB drivers, as organized by longtime MG TC racing driver Ralph Cadwallader. It includes Cadwallader's memories of the part John Birchfield played in organizing the event. "John Birchfield is a name that has become little known in the history of Put-in-Bay," Ralph says, "so before too much fades from memory and John's contribution becomes vague and unappreciated, I think it is important to recount his part in getting the races started."

Ralph Cadwallader continues on Birchfield's role: "When I talked to John he was unassuming and very low key about what he did. However, I confirmed that he was asked to handle this embryonic race because he had put on a very successful rally for the club and, if he could do that, then a mere road race would be a walk in the park.

"Dick Henn and Andy Zimmerman handled the politics while John took over the actual mechanics of the race. He and Norm Bradley went to the island in April of 1952, drove around in Norm's XK-120, laid out the course and decided that due to the rough narrow roads and sharp bends that the course should be limited to 2-liter unblown and 1500-cc blown or modified. That was quite altruistic of Norm since he really wanted to run his Jag. The Cleveland Sport Car Club started and ran the Put-in-Bay Road Race, assisted later with the help of the SCCA and the MG Car club." This applies only to the first race, as subsequent events involved Dick Henn as the race chairman.

John Birchfield describes in more detail how the race course at Put-in-Bay came to be chosen. "Richard Gent had a boat and he took it up to the 'Bay every year. It seemed to offer a place that was good for racing. It was inexpensive then, and easy to get to. Another reason was that you could control who got there and make sure everyone was interested in the sport." According to Sally Carroll, Birchfield was elected by the Cleveland Sport Car Club to find a course on the island and decide on the running of the race. He asked Norm Bradley to drive his Jaguar up there to find one. Norm had taken John's wife Helen on a spirited tour of Shaker Heights; this was his chance to demonstrate that he could drive more conservatively. They went over in April of 1952. It was the first survey for the course. "I found a good course," Birchfield recalls, "and then we went around it several laps trying to decide where to put the flagmen. We also found a good place for tech inspection and a place to park the cars—the pits. The people who rented cabins were very enthused about the race and the extra business it would bring them."

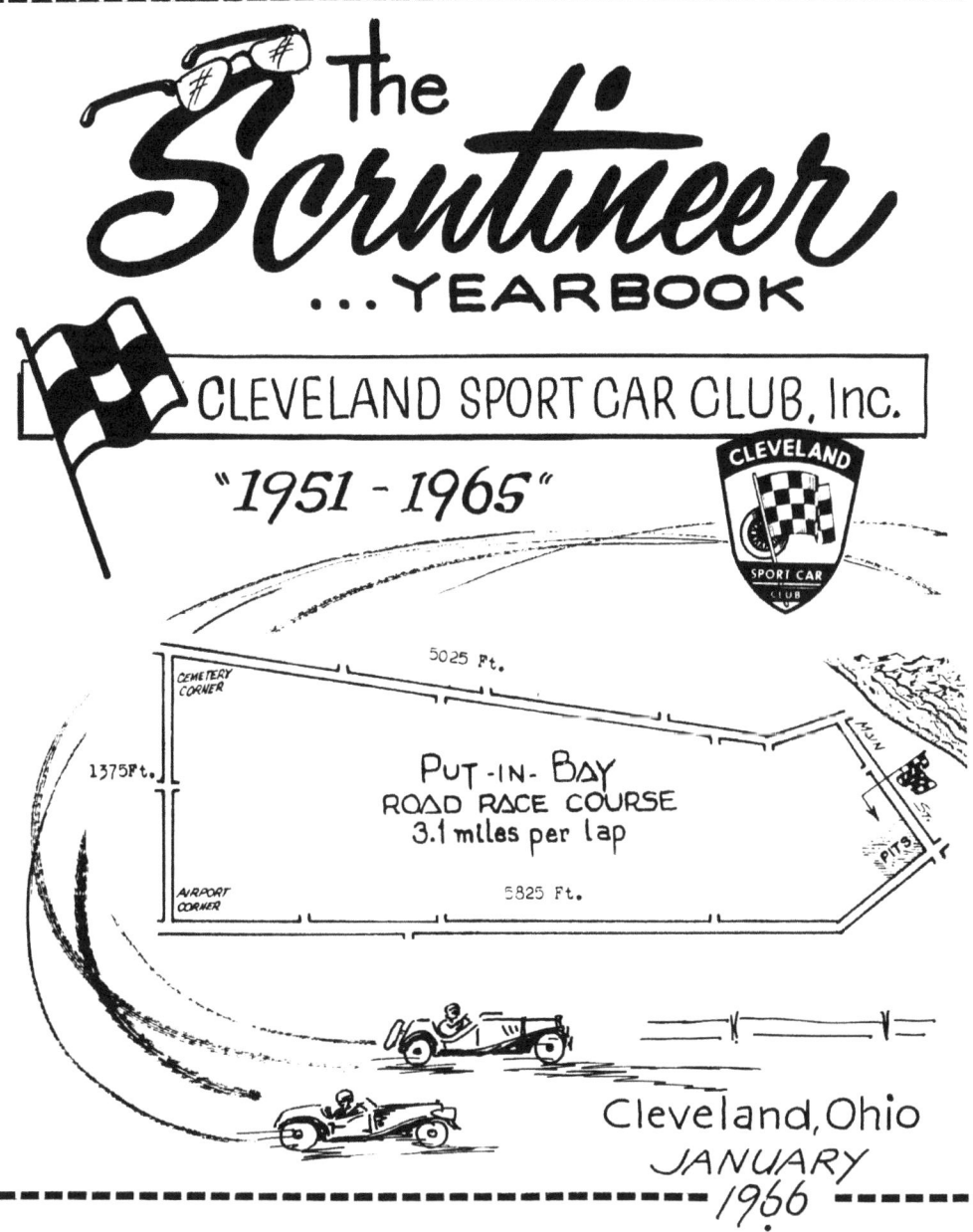

Sketch of the 3.1-mile Put-in-Bay race course as shown on the cover of *The Scrutineer*, a publication of the Cleveland Sport Car Club. The original course was sketched out on a restaurant place mat by race chairman Dick Henn (collection of Bill Gorris).

The length of the course was 3.1 miles. If you have a map of Put-in-Bay, you will see that the start-finish line is on Delaware Street, right on front of the bars and souvenir stores. (Officially, Main Street is the closest one to the lake. However, everyone who went to the races called Delaware St. "Main Street.") Then the course goes right for a short stretch along Toledo Avenue, which takes an oblique right onto Langham Road out to the airport. Here again, perception being reality, these were called "Airport Straight" by the racers. The course takes a right onto Thompson Road, the bumpy road past the vineyards. As far as I know, this never had a name unless it was "the back road." At the cemetery was a peculiar corner, part of which was off-camber. The cemetery was named Crown Hill. Then you were on your way to the popular Cooper's Restaurant and into town, where the road took a slight left-hand turn, known as the dog-leg turn, at about the Sohio gasoline station. Locally, this was called Catawba Avenue, but was always referred to as "Cooper Straight" by the racers. At the corner was, again, Delaware, aka Main Street. This had snow fences from end to end, not to keep the cars from the spectators but the other way around. When they had the extra race in 1963, the course was 2.4 miles in length and cut across one street behind Delaware.

Back to Ralph Cadwallader: "They decided the old grape field was the ideal spot for the pits and that Parker's Garage was the place for technical inspection. From there John pretty much managed what became, in September of 1952, the first of eight very successful Put-in-Bay road races. I think it was the first race that was rain-delayed, and when the rain stopped John got everyone out on the track to drive round and round to dry it off so the race could start."

An MG-TD drives down the ramp from the ferry boat to the dock at Put-in-Bay—the dock downtown, across from the children's park (Center for Archival Collections, University Libraries, Bowling Green State University).

As the race went on year by year, John Birchfield's role became smaller, and the involvement of Dick and Betty Henn became greater. Each contributed in their own way. Birchfield notes: "I had been running events in eastern sports car clubs. The Henns were politically connected. They were society people. They were known by the rich crowd on the east side and it was a mark of prestige to have them running the race." As Chuck Stoddard says, "Without Dick Henn, the Put-in-Bay road races never would have happened." Dick Henn was the race chairman for each of the Put-in-Bay events except the first one.

Dick (Richard L.) Henn and Betty Henn were race managers *par excellence*. They

Giant tents set up for the 1952 Put-in-Bay Wine Festival provide plenty of room for the connoisseurs of the grape (Center for Archival Collections, University Libraries, Bowling Green State University).

got the race announcements out on time, they got the entries logged and confirmed, they established a cadre of race workers for every need, they made sure the town was taken care of, they got the races running on time, and they kept them that way with the kind of leadership and management that made a successful event.

Stepping back a couple of years, and to others in the cast of characters, it was 1950 and Jim Carroll was dating Sally Vaughan. In the spring of 1951, Jim bought an MG TD and they started on a life in the sports car scene. A year later, Jim traded the TD even for a TC. Later yet, they would run it at the Akron Airport sports car races. As the sports car movement was under way, Jim and Sally were involved, with others, in the formation of two notable car clubs, the Cleveland Sport Car Club and the MG Car Club. The CSCC would be the founder of the Put-in-Bay and Akron Airport road races, before the Sports Car Club of America became involved with either event.

Originally, the meeting place of the CSCC, on March 5, 1951, was in the basement of the house of Dick Irish in Bratenahl. It was a very relaxed place, where even the dog named Cricket, a golden retriever and lab mix, could attend meetings. Later on, meetings were shifted to Sports Cars Limited at 45th and Euclid, which was less convenient to the members and not too accommodating for dogs. Early members included Dick Bosley, Dick Gent, Dick Henn, Earl Johnson, Frank White, Corny Scheid and Andy Zimmerman. Andy had had polio and walked with crutches; his MG TD was fitted with hand controls to compensate for his condition. Nothing kept Andy from being active in the sports car club. Dick Irish was elected president in 1951 and Dick Henn became president in 1952. The subsequent presidents were Andy Zimmerman, 1953; Dick Henn, 1954; Joe Brown, 1955; Charlie Ellmers, 1956 and 1957; Dick Henn, 1958 and 1959. In addition, Henn was a charter member of the famous Race Communications Association, founded in 1951 by Fred German at Watkins Glen. It was the first organization in the country for planning safety and communications at speed events. Training includes flagging, communications and the handling of emergencies. Other CSCC members in RCA included Bill Cowan and Bob Kintner.

Going back to 1951, the Lake Erie Centre of the MG Car Club was formed by Jim and Sally, as a branch of the Chicago MG club. The MG club originally met at a tavern on Lee Road just south of Mayfield in Cleveland Heights. Later, it would have a long-time address at Linsay's Tavern in Shaker Heights.

"Bob Lossman was very much involved with it," Suzy Dietrich remembers of Put-in-Bay. "He had a boat up there and knew all the townspeople. He made the arrangements with them. An older couple from Cleveland [Dick and Betty Henn] put the race on. As I recall, it was in mid to late September. I was very anxious to drive because it was held where I lived. But they wouldn't let me drive. There was trouble in Congress—if a guy got hit, well that's too bad. If I got hit, it could cancel all the races. That's the way they thought."

Lossman, of course, was the owner of MG

In front of the Round House Bar we see the fabulous Cisitalia 202. This example, car #62, is owned by Richard Gent, Sr. (Center for Archival Collections, University Libraries, Bowling Green State University).

Dick Irish sits in the #65 Siata Gran Sport at the start-finish line of the 1952 Put-in-Bay road race. The man in the white shirt is his brother, Chuck. Dick did not drive the car in the race but it is the same car that he and Bob Fergus drove to a class win in the March 15, 1952, Sebring 12-hour race (collection of Dick Irish).

Motors and three other sports car dealerships on Cleveland's west side. Bob knew all the local people on South Bass Island. He ensured the cooperation of the locals. As soon as the races started, the local merchants made so much money they couldn't count it.

As the word got out, entries began to come in. The first of them, for the fall race, arrived August 14, 1952, from Ralph Durbin of Detroit. All in all, there were 30 entries. Durbin called it "the biggest bash of the year."

While there were from three to five races in the day's event during later years of the Put-in-Bay sports car races, there appears to have been only one in 1952, because the race was scheduled on Sunday, in the afternoon. The MG race absorbed other cars, including a Siata Spyder and a Fiat Balilla. One of the entrants was John Comey with his MG. That was the car he drove to work. His hobby car was a Bugatti Type 55. As Ralph Cadwallader noted,

John Comey was active in course preparation from the earliest years, and it was people such as John and Bill Gorris, plus Bob Morrison on timing and scoring, and, later on, Bob Kintner on race communications, who worked long and hard to make the race a success—these guys made the race happen.

Comey entered his stock TD in the first race in 1952 and was lucky enough to draw pole position at the drivers' meeting, so the rest of the stock T-type MGs were lined up two abreast behind him on the starting grid. He had managed to get through the first turn in the lead when Charlie Ellmers shot past. Then the parade past him started. By the time he made the first lap everybody had passed him—Comey's comment: "Some MGs are more stock than others." During that race it started to rain (again), so John pulled off the track, put up his top and side curtains, and comfortably finished—dead last. The complete finishing order of the first race has been lost to the sands of time. All we know is that Charlie Ellmers was first and John Comey was last.

The story of the rain and its effect on the race is the subject of some controversy. The account above—about stopping to put up the top and finishing the race in the rain—was told to me in person by John Comey while he was still alive. And, of course, it is common for sports cars to race in the rain—road racing is the only form of motorsports in which this is the practice. I, personally, have raced several times in the rain. It's the same as racing on a dry track, only slower. Ralph Cadwallader recalled, "I think it was the first race that was rain delayed, and when the rain stopped John Birchfield got everyone out on the track to drive round and round to dry it off so the race could start."

In his very fine book titled *Isolated Splendor: Put-in-Bay and South Bass Island,* island resident and photographer Robert J. Dodge states that the race was canceled due to rain after only four laps of a ten-lap event. However, the account of John Comey, in which it rained during the race, contradicts this. The account of John Birchfield, who said that the cars drove around to dry out the track, also contradicts this and would suggest a postponement rather than a cancellation, and at the beginning of the race. Also in contradiction is the account of Betty Henn, who noted that seven laps were completed. Betty was the registrar of the race, closely involved in all its aspects. Between the comments of these three people, it appears that there was one race, the start of it was delayed, and it ran seven laps. Also, it appears to have been held on Sunday afternoon, instead of Saturday as were all races from 1954 afterward.

The rain affected more than the number of laps. Betty Henn told this story: "Some of our more dashing drivers had read of the glamorous colored jumpers worn in Europe and, not to be outdone, showed up with their coveralls dipped in the brightest reds and yellows made by the Tintex Company. And then—the rains came." The colors were not fast, so at the feet of each driver was a puddle of red or yellow rainwater.

As Suzy Dietrich recalls, "The course was easy to learn. They had the pits at the corner going out of town and a fast bend after that. I saw a car go into a sideways slide onto somebody's lawn there. Then a guy came out with a pitchfork and the car drove away."

Overall, according to Suzy Dietrich, there were about 50 entrants (actually fewer). And attendance was fairly good for the first year—"There were a few hundred people watching," said Suzy.

Other than the air shuttles, ferry boats were the only way to get spectators or race cars onto the island. In 1952, the first year of the race, the captain of the Miller's Ferry boat to the island was Bob Schmidt. He remembers the big tents for the wine festival that that was held along with the sports car races. He remembers the MGs and other cars he took over for

The drivers' meeting in 1952. The speaker (white shirt, back to camera) is Cleveland Sport Car Club official John Birchfield, who originated the design of the 3.1-mile course and its racing features (Center for Archival Collections, University Libraries, Bowling Green State University).

the races. Many people were under the impression that the ferry boats were just converted fishing boats. Not so, says Schmidt: "The Miller boats were originally built to take cars and passengers. They were specifically built for that. We eventually had four boats. These were all under 65 feet—they were probably 64 feet, eleven inches—to meet the Coast Guard crew regulations! There was a crew of three—the captain, the deck hand and the purser, who also served as a deck hand. At first he collected tickets on the boat and later they set up a ticket booth on the dock. The first of the four boats was named the *South Shore* and built by the Stadium Boat Works in Cleveland. The next one was called the *West Shore* and built at the John Rowan Boat Works in Sturgeon Bay, Wisconsin. After that it was the *William Miller*, also built in Wisconsin, and the *Put-in-Bay*, again built in Wisconsin. The capacity for cars was nine or ten, or more if they were small like an MG—we really crammed them in there!"

Jim Etzkorn, from Chagrin Falls, a college student at Baldwin Wallace in Fairview Park just south of Rocky River, was a member of the Black River Sports Car Club. His interest in sports cars had been growing. He had begun high school in Indianapolis. "I got hooked on *Motor Trend* magazine," he admits:

> We moved to Cleveland in 1949. I had a summer class at West High School and while on the bus I passed a speed shop that had copies of *Road and Track* in the window. This was when they

A fine photograph of the paddock on the corner at Put-in-Bay. What a wonderful-looking paddock, all full of MGs and drivers who are just regular guys. No sponsors, no logos, no cash prizes. It's right in town, near the old water tower (Center for Archival Collections, University Libraries, Bowling Green State University).

Here we see the starting grid lined up, ready to make the first lap around the course. Most of the cars are MG-TDs (Joe Brown).

were only an annual magazine. I drove back there and bought one. Then I was reading the *Cleveland Plain Dealer,* I think it was the sports section, and I saw a tiny notice about the race. That morning I drove up to the airfield in Gypsum, near Port Clinton, I got on the Ford Tri-Motor to the island. It took us 15 minutes to get there, going 75 miles an hour. There was a perpetual oil leak in the right side engine. The window was covered with oil. I overheard a passenger mentioning this to the pilot and he said, "don't worry about it." As we banked to come into the airport, I could see the huge wing that was holding us up. As we taxied in, I caught a view of the Bugatti Type 35. I think it belonged to Bob Fergus. Before the races, the organizers were trying to get volunteers for crowd control. There was a real strange collection of cars, with Chuck and Suzy Dietrich and their supercharged MG, Dick Gent and his Fiat Balilla and a few others. After the race, we went back to the airport. Somebody shouted, "Run for it—if the wind changes you'll have to go on the next flight!" I remember I ran and ended up in a big puddle.

At Put-in-Bay in 1952—the year of the first race—Hank Becker was up there with Chuck Irish and Bob Fergus. Bob had just bought a Type 35 Bugatti. They were downtown when they all decided to go back to the hotel, the Bayshore Hotel, which was beyond turn one on the other side of town. "How will we get there?" someone asked. "We'll drive," Fergus announced. He piled in the driver's seat, Chuck Irish got in the passenger's, and Becker had to sit on the rear deck with his feet dangling dangerously close to the spoked wheels. "With the engine turning over, Fergus got on the gas, upshifted, accelerated, braked for the corner, downshifted and managed to make the corner. I'm still hanging on," says Becker; "We made it out to the hotel without mangling my feet in the spokes but I don't know how."

Charlie Ellmers was a navy combat veteran of both World War II and the Korean War, actually a war hero, before he got into sports cars in 1950. "I was discharged from the navy

Another photograph of the starting grid, with the camera pulled back to show the #87 MGTD and the #83 MGTC, as well as a spectator's wood-sided Chevrolet station wagon (Joe Brown).

after my stint aboard the *Essex*," Charlie said. "I had some money saved up and thought I would buy a new car and drive it home. I was considering a Studebaker but thought I would check out the new MG-TD. The TD was $2,020, about the same as the Studebaker. The guy at the MG dealer's wouldn't let me drive one of the MGs in the showroom, but he did take me for a ride in his TC. That cinched it." He joined the Cleveland Sport Car Club in 1951. He was an excellent driver and won the first race, the first year at Put-in-Bay in 1952, in his black MG-TD. He also drove the TD at Put-in-Bay in '53 and '54, and drove at Elkhart Lake and Lockbourne Air Force Base. "He raced it at Watkins Glen," notes Ruth Ellmers, "and blew up the engine. He was so disgusted he sold it on the spot. Besides, he didn't have a tow bar."

☙ ❧

Jim Carroll and his wife Sally were among the early organizers of the Cleveland Sport Car Club, which sanctioned the race. Their account centers around Jim's driving an aluminum-bodied 1,000-pound H-Modified Siata Spyder.

"1952 at Put-in-Bay? I was there," says Sally Carroll:

> Jim had the Siata 750, I was pregnant with our first child, the car had to be push-started and the mechanic only weighed 110 pounds. It was a September race and the baby was born the first week of December. We drove down the day before the race. We drove the Siata from Cleveland to the island and we blew out the steel wool that we put in the exhaust pipe, so it was a pretty noisy trip. This was the same year that Dick Irish went to Sebring with his Siata, only it was a 1400. When we got over to Put-in-Bay, we did have a hotel room but it was upstairs right above the bar, so we didn't get any sleep.

3. 1952

An early spat-fendered Jaguar 120 is the pace car, leading a field of MGs past the bars on the main street and the old water tower. The driver of the Jag is Norm Bradley, who later raced at the 'Bay in a Fiat-Abarth Zagato (Center for Archival Collections, University Libraries, Bowling Green State University).

There was a Crosley engine in the Siata and we could not keep it running. Just before the race, we tuned it at a garage just across the street from the church downtown. Then they flagged the cars off and I was in the pits waiting. Jim went by a few times and then we didn't see him for about four laps. With every lap of not seeing him, I became more worried. Finally, he appeared again. It turned out that the carburetor linkage had come off at cemetery turn and it took a little time to figure out what had happened and fix it.

After that incident, Jim swore off racing and so did Lou Barber, who was on our pit crew. He was planning to get into racing but suddenly lost his interest.

At Ralph Cadwallader's request, Jim Carroll wrote a somewhat more detailed account in 1999 and, if you'll pardon a small amount of repetition, here it is: "Since Ralph Cadwallader is doing a retrospective of the Put-in-Bay Races and talking to those who participated," Jim began, "he asked me to write something that I remember about my one and only race at the 'Bay. It was 1952. I was working as a salesman at Sports Cars Limited at 45th and Euclid Avenue. Sports Cars Ltd. was owned by David Blauschild. David also owned Blauschild Chrysler Plymouth and probably a lot of other things I didn't know about. Mr. Blauschild was a super gentleman and would give you the shirt off his back. Dick Irish was the other salesman and he and I persuaded (conned, would probably be more accurate) David to

MG #21 sprints down to the dog-leg past the film store. Hay bales are there to protect both cars and spectators (Center for Archival Collections, University Libraries, Bowling Green State University).

field a couple of race cars so that we would win races and get the name of Sports Cars Ltd. known throughout the sports car world. Actually, what we really wanted was to race the cars and have someone else pay the bills.

"Dick was very persuasive and I was very eager. So David agreed to supply a Siata 1400 and a Siata 750 to the program and Dick and I were off and running. Dick Irish was a successful race driver, driving his own Jaguar XK-120 and a Formula III Kieft, while I managed to get beaten on a regular basis in my TC. Dick Irish took the Siata 1400, a white car with blue between the wheel wells, to the twelve-hour race at Sebring."

Dick got a pit crew and co-driver in Columbus and drove both the Vero Beach 12-hour race, and Sebring the following weekend. They had a lot of trouble with head gaskets—they

A nice overhead shot of the black TD by Robert Dodge as the car heads out of town. The crowd shows that this is a good place for spectators (Center for Archival Collections, University Libraries, Bowling Green State University).

blew four of them—and finally got one to last at Sebring. The Siata had outstanding handling qualities and beat four Ferraris and three Jaguars car-for-car for a third overall, second on index and first in class. When the car came back, Blauschild inexplicably re-painted it gold and blue.

Dick Irish, by the way, was at the '52 race, just as a spectator. He no longer worked for Blauschild, but his old Sebring class-winning Siata Gran Sport was there, ostensibly for another driver, even though there was nothing on the entry list and no sign of the driver. The car was spiffed up in Blauschild livery. "We had nicked the right front fender on the way down to Sebring," says Dick, "and so the car was repainted as soon as it got back. For some strange reason, it was repainted gold and blue instead of the white and blue it wore during the race. Then, it had thrown a rod after the race and Blauschild had a shop in the basement, Sports Cars Limited in Cleveland, where they rebuilt the engine. It was race-ready but I don't remember that it ran. I was enthralled with the Tri-Motor and wanted to go on that, but I was with some friends and they were going to take the ferry to Port Clinton, so I went along with them."

Jim Carroll continues the story:

I was assigned the Siata 750 to race at Put-in-Bay. The Siata 750 came from the distributor [the irascible Tony Pompeo] without an engine but was designed to take a Crosley engine. We managed to find one in a junk yard. One of my pals from my days as a mechanics helper at the New York Central Railroad, George ("Clarky") Clark, agreed to be my mechanic. A long time friend, Lou Barber, became (with my wife Sally) my pit crew. We managed to get the engine in and running, after a fashion. The engine came with a Holley carburetor which we knew very little about and with lots of tinkering by Clarky, we managed to get it running quite respectably. "We may not be fast but we sure as hell are loud" was our watch-word. We had no muffler at all. We ran the exhaust out the right side through four pipes and because we had no trailer, or tow car for that matter, we had to drive from Seventieth and Euclid to the ferry dock at Port Clinton. To muffle the car so we didn't get arrested at the first stop light, we stuffed steel wool up the tail pipes and put a nail through to keep it from being blown right out. This worked quite well as long as I was very gentle with the throttle, but when I tried to accelerate so that I could keep up with Clarky and the support car I blew the steel wool out in fiery balls (really an impressive pyrotechnic display). The ensuing noise was ear-shattering.

We left rather late, because we were attending to last minute details, like putting safety belts in so we could pass inspection. While driving through one small hamlet we saw four little dogs playing, fighting, tumbling and having a great time. When we turned onto their street they all stopped and lined up at the side of the road to watch us go by. Apparently they had never seen a car that small or that loud ever before. It was approaching midnight when we stopped at a gas station which was still fortunately open, a bit west of Lorain. After refilling the tank I asked my expectant wife to push the car to get it started. Clarky weighed about 114 pounds, not heavy enough to push start the car, and Sally didn't know how to drive. The guys in the station heard this and, feeling sorry for her, offered to carry the car to Port Clinton for us. They successfully lifted the car, as part of the joke, but when they went to put it back down they realized that although it was tiny, it still weighed MUCH more than they expected.

It was apparent that we were not going to make the last ferry that day, so we looked for a place to stay, but found none. At about two o'clock in the morning, I said, "I can't drive any further." We found a nice soft field in front of a billboard which gave us adequate space to park our cars safely and laid out a couple of tarps to sleep on and promptly went to sleep. I had just dropped off, or so it seemed, when the whole world came to an end with a thunderous roar, the earth shook, a brilliant white light was shining in my eyes and then came the shriek of a thousand banshees. Believe me, I was awake and running in six directions at once. My infanticipating wife was sleeping next to me, but I didn't think of her. It was every man for himself. I was halfway across

As the Siata Spyder speeds down the front straight, a spectator in the fashionable bobby socks, saddle shoes and Shaker High School skirt looks down the track toward the corner. Note: this year there was no snow fencing along this stretch (Center for Archival Collections, University Libraries, Bowling Green State University).

the road before I realized that the billboard that we were sleeping under was directly in front of the railroad tracks and to all intents and purposes the train was about to get in my sleeping bag with me. So that was all the sleep we got that night.

We got to Port Clinton in time for the first ferry and made it to the island in time for tech. inspection, but we must have looked a pretty sight, dirty, unshaven, disheveled, irritated, tired and surly. We managed to pass tech. inspection and take a couple of laps around the course, but we were not happy with the carburetion and kept fiddling with it.

Suzie Dietrich came around and asked if she could drive the car. We acceded with alacrity as Suzie was a gorgeous gal and one of the best drivers in the SCCA, male or female. She came back after a short while and gave her opinion that it was a very nice car, handled well and went

Trying to keep the Fiat Balilla in sight is Jim Carroll in the Siata Spyder entered by Blauschild Motors of Shaker Heights. Jim had a problem with his throttle linkage and had to drop out for a while (Joe Brown).

well but there was something wrong with the carb. This after Clarky had done everything he knew to get it to run properly. There was a definite flat spot that we couldn't get rid of. I went to bed early, knowing that I shouldn't go out drinking and carousing the night before a race. (What did I know?) I was not aware, however, that the room we were assigned was almost directly above the carousers. It took some time to get to sleep that night.

Early the next morning we decided to see if we could improve our performance a little. We spent more than a little time exchanging spark plugs in an attempt to match the heat range to the expected heat of the day. If we actually helped any, we were never sure. This work was conducted under the semi-shade of the tree next to the only garage in town. Someone once wrote, "There was a certain Crosley powered Siata at Put-in Bay being operated by some rude person who tested its maximum RPM range, through four straight pipes directly outside the church door as the congregation was exiting from Sunday morning services."

On race day, before our race we are all sitting in our cars on the starting grid. I was a little nervous but feeling proud, too. The car looked terrific painted a two tone blue and gold with a big white #1 on both doors the hood and the back. I was sitting there idly wondering when we were going to get the word to start our engines and go racing. I looked to my right and I saw a pair of hands on the top of the passenger's door. I couldn't see anything else. Now this car was tiny and the top of the passenger's door could not have been much more than thirty inches from the pavement. A small boy pulled himself up to his full tippy toe height and looked me square in the eye and said, "What kind of breakfast cereal do you eat, mister?" Well we had a little discussion and allowed as how Wheaties were OK, but I really preferred Cheerios. That was the right answer because his face was wreathed in smiles and he gave up his little impromptu cereal survey, not bothering any of the other drivers, whether that was because my car said I was number one or whether he couldn't muster the height to look over any of the other doors. Maybe it was simply because he had the answer he wanted.

3. 1952

Charlie Ellmers in the #3 MG-TD—the first winner of the first Put-in-Bay race. Charlie was a member of the Cleveland Sport Car Club and NE Ohio SCCA, of which he was the head of the competition board. The man with the hat and the flag is John Birchfield, and leaning in to talk with Charlie is Ted Jayne (collection of Charlie and Ruth Ellmers).

After a while the race started and I was doing very well. I don't remember what lap I was on but I was happily in first place, a spot that I had never been in before, driving like crazy, when all of a sudden a fella in a prewar Fiat Balilla went screaming past me. I caught him at the corner, but on the long straightaway he started lengthening his lead on me, so I started to flutter the accelerator pedal, hoping that by moving the throttle in and out I could activate the accelerator pump in the carb and thereby dump more gas into the engine. It turned out to be a pretty dumb move because, not only does that not work, it also caused the throttle linkage to fall off. This seriously slows one down and it takes a little while before you realize what you have done. The engine is still running, the clutch and gearbox are still working, but you aren't going anywhere.

Pull over, jump out, lift the hood and see what has happened. Pop the linkage back on and go tearing after everybody else. Of course the whole field has passed me by this time and I am all alone, but I am still having a good time driving as fast as I can, without worrying about a policeman arresting me. It doesn't get any better than that. Back in the pits Sally is waiting to get my lap time and knows I should be the first car past, but there is this blue Fiat and then another car, then another car, then everybody else but no Jim Carroll. She is standing there thinking the worst, with visions of raising a fatherless child. That's when Lou Barber said, "I looked at your wife's face and swore I would never put my wife through that." He never did go racing, which was something he really had wanted to do. I managed to catch up quite a bit and finally got back to fourth place. But that wasn't good enough, so my racing days for "Sports Cars Ltd. Racing Team" were over.

Thus began one of the greatest races in America. Thanks to Dick and Betty Henn and the other race workers, it was the safest road race run in those days. As nice as the races were elsewhere—Cam Argetsinger's Watkins Glen, Bruce Stevenson's Bridgehampton, Elkhart Lake, Brynfan Tyddyn and the others—it was hard to compare with the start-finish line right there at the waterfront, the charming Victorian cottages lining the race course and the allure of being on an island in the middle of Lake Erie, which none of the other courses could claim. In closing his comments about the first year of the 'Bay races, Ralph Cadwallader

This nice TC is Ben Hitchcock's car, with his wife "Spook" in the driver's seat. No one knew her real name. She was a wealthy heiress who was some of the money behind the Rand Corporation, where Ben was a vice president. Ben's team, the Funny Face Auto Racing Team, was an interesting cast of characters that included war heroes, builders of submarine torpedoes, sailing champions, businessmen and engineers (Center for Archival Collections, University Libraries, Bowling Green State University).

notes: "It was a wonderful era for a lot of us—the beginning of a time in our lives we shall never forget—and for this we thank you, John Birchfield." Likewise Cadwallader praises the Henns, saying, "Much has been said of Dick and Betty Henn, but never will all the things be known that make them so special to all of us. And each of us has his own special reason to love them."

☙ ❧

The pictures that accompany this chapter are the best pictures that have been found, so far, of the 1952 race. They were made available to the Put-in-Bay Road Race Reunion by

Pausing for a little post-race refreshment at the Coke sign is an assortment of cars of the era: an MG-TD, a Morris Minor convertible, a nice Cadillac and another MG. In the MG is Betty Henn, registrar of the event, and in the Morris Minor is Bettsy Kintner, mother of Chris Kintner, descendent of the race organizers (Center for Archival Collections, University Libraries, Bowling Green State University).

Stephen Charter and Lee McLaird at the Center for Archival Collections at Bowling Green State University, through the Robert J. Dodge collection. They were located by Roger Linton, Manley Ford and Charlie Foss of the Put-in-Bay Reunion organizers. Later, some photographs from the great Joe Brown were also located.

1952 was the beginning of one of the greatest races in America, a real road race in the era before the airport courses and purpose-built racing circuits. It went from '52 through '59, with an extra race in '63. It included hundreds of drivers and thousands of spectators and dozens of race workers.

Driver Ralph Cadwallader said it best: "It was a wonderful era for a lot of us—the beginning of a time in our lives we shall never forget."

CHAPTER 4

1953: What Is So Fair as a Day in June?

Sunday, June 14, 1953

In 1953, the second year of the races, it was decided to move the date from September 14 to June 14, also a Sunday, in hopes of avoiding rain. Advance notice of the race was reasonably good. It appeared in the *Cleveland Plain Dealer*. So early on Sunday morning, spectators would get on the ferry, either from Port Clinton, Marblehead, Catawba or Sandusky. If you were lucky you'd share it with late-arriving race cars. If you were not lucky, there would be a nasty chop on Lake Erie. Those unaccustomed to the lake could get queasy—or worse. If you actually liked these boat rides, the one from Port Clinton was your best bet since it was about twice the distance of the others but didn't cost any more. Though it's not true, many of the ferry boats were believed to be converted fishing boats. Why the bows were so bluff and the ride so rough, I don't know. All of the boats I ever had had pointed bows.

Finally arriving, race-goers could enjoy a dramatic introduction to the event. As the ferry approached the harbor, the noise of racing engines could be heard over the racket the boat made, and nearing the dock you could see the cars. As soon as the gangplank was down, you'd run across the town square as if hurrying would keep you from missing something important. In town you had to stay behind the snow fence to watch the cars. They would come by, at speed, a yard away.

Forty drivers entered the 1953 event. Most of the drivers were from Ohio, with the exception of eight from Michigan and four from Pennsylvania. The race was co-sponsored by the Cleveland Sport Car Club and the recently formed NE Ohio Region of the Sports Car Club of America.

One of these eager race-goers was Art Seyler from Cleveland Heights. Art had an MG-TD but his wife was leery of letting him race, so he went up just to work a corner. He promised her he would not race. But a long and honored tradition at the 'Bay was night practice, in which everyone who was not racing, and some who were, would blast around the island on the race course at all hours of the night. The more prudent ones would putter past the very fat police chief and, when they got to the edge of town, stand on it, through the airport and cemetery corners and halfway down the back straight. This is exactly what Art did on the first weekend in June 1953. At midnight Friday, he and a friend, seeing that the chief was not in sight, blasted off towards Cemetery Corner at high speed. Flashing red lights from three cruisers suddenly lit up, and the racers came to a screeching halt. The chief said, "That will be enough of that," and it was, at least until 1954.

Sports cars roll out of the Miller's Ferry boat to compete at Put-in-Bay. An MG-TC with cycle fenders leads the way, with a TD following and a pickup truck already on the landing. The boat is the all-steel diesel ferry that photographer Robert Dodge refers to in his book (Center for Archival Collections, University Libraries, Bowling Green State University).

But in 1953, Art worked the race at a flag station right at the kink into town. "The cars were coming right at me," Art recalls. "Chuck Dietrich sped by in his supercharged MG, about three feet away. I was completely absorbed in watching the races, but I began to experience the symptoms of Rose Fever, which I am susceptible to. It took me several minutes to realize I was standing next to a bed of roses." Later that summer Art bought himself a Jaguar XK-120.

Of the 40 entries, 33 were MGs, showing the importance of this marque in the beginnings of the sport. Others were—one each—an old Simca sedan, one of those great-handling Siata Spyders, the beautiful Cisitalia, an exotic Fiat Balilla, the aluminum-bodied Singer,

Here we see the Aston Martin DB2 pace car down at the boat docks, ready to lead the racers around the 3.1-mile course. It's in front of a 1953 Studebaker Starliner. The Aston was owned by Frank White, of the family that owned the White Truck Company (Center for Archival Collections, University Libraries, Bowling Green State University).

the glamorous Arnolt MG and a Porsche 1500. None of the cars came on trailers, and formal safety requirements were relatively few. Helmets and seatbelts were the only real requirements. Roll bars were not used at the 'Bay until 1957. But everyone had his own plan for what he would do if the car rolled—one enterprising fellow had a grab handle installed on the passenger side floor.

The entrants would usually arrive a day before the races, Saturday, and stay over at one of the island's many hotels and rooming houses. There were several on the road running alongside the harbor. One of them was the Friendly Inn. (That was where the Funny Face Auto Racing Team stayed—but more about them later.) This place was run by Mary and

Local dogs were kept inside during the races, but this one is no doubt standing here before the races, looking down the street and thinking of how much fun it would be to go for a ride in one of those nice little sports cars (Center for Archival Collections, University Libraries, Bowling Green State University).

Walter Liscowski. It had five sparsely furnished rooms, each amply lit by a single bare bulb hanging by its cord from the ceiling. Walter could entertain with rope tricks and usually sported a Wallace-Beery-style undershirt against which he would lean a generous stack of breakfast toast that he handed out to the guests on the morning of tech inspection, for those who had not had their cars looked over the day before.

An important influence on the races was the mandatory drivers' meeting the day of the race. Chairman Dick Henn got the drivers together in the Town Hall and stood at the podium before them. Event worker Bob Satava describes the tone of the meeting: "Colonel Henn made it clear that the organizers would not put up with anything that compromised

Three MGs are lined up for tech inspection at Parker's Garage, a white TD, black TD and black TC. Car #65 is Don Janik from Cleveland (Center for Archival Collections, University Libraries, Bowling Green State University).

safety. He told them they were going to race like gentlemen or not race at all. In the way he spoke they knew he meant business."

Drivers—the cast of characters—included the always-smiling Charlie Ellmers, a heck of a driver too; Hank Becker, recently graduated from Cornell; Ralph Cadwallader, driving the MG-TC he had disassembled on a carpet in his garage; Ron McConnell, a frequent sight at the Linsay's Tavern MG meetings; John Comey in his waterproof TD (he stopped to put the top up); and Ed Hugus from Pittsburgh, trying out his hand at racing an MG. Then there was the dapper Dick Gent, connoisseur of Italian machines; Bob Shea, MG tuning expert; Bob Lossman, proprietor of Lossman MG; George Webber, Bob's business partner; John Moncur, Jaguar Cleveland mechanic; ace Ford engineer Tony Stica; Sam Shep-

It's tech inspection for the #21 MG-TD of Earl Kornfeld from Twinsburg, Ohio, at Parker's Garage. Note the windshield covered with safety tape (Center for Archival Collections, University Libraries, Bowling Green State University).

pard, before he got in trouble with the Cleveland newspapers who believed (mistakenly) that he had murdered his wife; celebrity Cleveland disc jockey Bill Randle in an MG-TD specially race-prepared by John Moncur; and finally Alan Patterson in the white #12 MG-TC.

As Fred Troyan notes, Bob Shea was involved in the Put-in-Bay races as both a tech inspector (along with Joe Kovach, Ron McConnell and Walter Jarmain), and a driver. The tech team's approach was to help the drivers pass tech rather than keep them out for some trivial thing. Bob was also a very good racing driver. He had an MG-TC that he drove for a number of years. He was car #51 in the Put-in-Bay MG race in 1953. He was car #36 in the Put-in-Bay MG race in 1954. He was #5 in a TC in 1955 and #15 in 1956. He was entered

Top: John Comey's red TD #16 leads the pack through town in the first race of 1953. Trailing are Eugene Smith in the black #20, Earl Kornfeld in #21, Thomas Richardson in #8, Philip Thomas in #2, and a host of other TDs. *Bottom*: The pace car of John Comey takes the second race field around to the start. Comey, a longtime race official at Put-in-Bay, owned both this Type 37 Bugatti and a Type 55 that had been owned by King Leopold. Note the puddles and wet pavement: the schedule switch to June did not entirely eliminate rain showers (Joe Brown).

in '57 as #12 but did not drive. "He had bursitis in his shoulder that year," says Dutch Brow. "He was sick during the race and went back to the place where he was staying. He let Chuck Dietrich drive the #12 TC, and Chuck won the race with it. Art ran the same car in the G-Production race. Shea also raced at the Akron Airport sports car races in #28, the familiar TC. He was a good driver," says Dutch, "but he had to quit. He had shrapnel in his back. His doctor thought it was moving, and the racing could shift it closer to his spinal cord and paralyze him." As Art Brow relates, Shea had been an army infantry lieutenant in World War II, serving in combat during the Battle of the Bulge. He once gave a bag full of pistols and swords to co-worker Fred Troyan. He had no love for Germans, and during a less-than-pleasant exchange with one at the dealership, said, "I think you're one that we missed."

The #30 Dick Gates Simca leads the pack in the second race, at least for now. Coming up for the pass is Dick Yares in his Siata. Three MGs are just making the turn at Cemetery Corner (Center for Archival Collections, University Libraries, Bowling Green State University).

Ralph Cadwallader is not exactly a household word in racing, but he was a Cleveland club racer who loved his MG and loved the Put-in-Bay races. As racer Art Brow recalls, Ralph was the general manager of MG Motor Sales on Madison Avenue in Lakewood, Ohio, during the 1950s and '60s. The MG store was first owned by George Webber in partnership with Bob Lossman, who later bought him out. One day, a customer who owned a Jeepster came in looking for a sports car. He was Bob Shea, who was operating a dairy. He was immediately hired to be the service manager for MGs. Lossman Motors also sold Volkswagens from Midvo, the VW distributor in Columbus owned by Don Marsh and Bob Fergus, and it also sold MGs. As VW began to grow, it suddenly decided it didn't want its dealers handling any other brand, so the MG operation had to move. When it did, Bob Shea went with it, and Cadwallader became the manager. Art Brow stayed at the VW store as a mechanic, and his wife Dutch was employed in the office on warranty work and other details. Incidentally, Art says, both Bob Shea and Ralph Cadwallader were combat infantry veterans of the Battle of the Bulge in World War II.

Meanwhile, in about 1950, Ralph bought an MG-TC. He put a carpet in the garage and disassembled the entire car on it. He drove it on weekends and then, when the Put-in-Bay races came up, entered them. "I ran my TC every year but the first one," Ralph said. "I missed 1952, and I never won at the 'Bay. I didn't have very good luck—one year I broke an axle, another year the brakes went out. The closest I came was in 1953. I was ahead of Chuck Dietrich for eight laps. But my exhaust pipe came loose. Every time we came by the marshal, Chuck would point to the pipe hanging from my car. Finally I was black-flagged and had to come in. I ripped the exhaust off my car and I got back in the race. I had lost the lead but I still finished the race."

The great-looking #40 Cisitalia roadster of Richard Gent takes the turn out of town and heads for the airport (Joe Brown).

With that peculiar pavement and the off-camber line, it was easy to go astray at Cemetery Corner, as these three MGs have, in the second race (Center for Archival Collections, University Libraries, Bowling Green State University).

Alan Patterson, mentioned among the MG drivers, bought his car in 1951, from importer J.S. Inskip. A resident of Boston, Pennsylvania, he raced it at Pennsylvania hill climbs from Pittsburgh to Hershey in 1951, then in 1952 at Brynfan Tyddyn. In March of 1953 he went to Sebring with Hubert Brundage, finishing 7th in class F and 28th overall. In June of '53, he decided to race at Put-in-Bay and drove up there from the University of Miami. That's not Miami of Ohio, that's the one in Coral Gables. He pulled up to the dock just as the ferryboat was leaving. Luckily his brother Charles was already on it and he was able to persuade the captain to back the boat up.

Patterson ran in two events, the second and third races, and doesn't remember where he finished in either. Heck, it was 58 years ago! Also in the second race was an interesting

car entered by Dick Gent of Cleveland. It was a Cisitalia with a Motto roadster body. Gent's son Richard remembers the car: "It was a light car to begin, with but he kept trying to lighten it up some more. We had a separate garage with two stalls for hobby cars and another stall for a pony we had. He kept it in there and worked on it. The car was powered by a modified Fiat 1100 engine, but the casting was poor so he got a Simca block, which was similar but better. In the race, I was standing near the start/finish line looking down the straight when I saw him drive off the side on the grass to pass several cars."

Top: Corner workers and spectators alike are helping to sort out this mess in the hay bales at—you guessed it—Cemetery Corner. *Bottom*: As the grid forms up for the third race of 1953, we see a smiling Bob Lossman in car #52, his supercharged MG (Center for Archival Collections, University Libraries, Bowling Green State University).

As the star of the third race, the name Chuck Dietrich is legendary in the Midwest among sports car racing enthusiasts. Like many of the leading drivers of his era, he started in an MG. He won his first race in 1951, in an MG-TC at the old Detroit Fairgrounds. Chuck modified his car by drilling the tappets full of lightening holes, grinding the weight off the rocker arms and carefully balancing his engine while adding a Marshall-Nordec supercharger. He first won fame at the Put-in-Bay road races, with his fast MG in the 1953 event.

Backing up to describe the Bill Randle entry, as Hank Becker notes, "Bill was a Cleveland disc jockey. He did a lot to make rock and roll famous. Then he decided he wanted to go racing. John Moncur was a Brit who worked for Jaguar-Cleveland. Bill had John set up an MG-TD for him. This was going to be a state-of-the-art, stand-back! racing car. God knows what it cost. It had bike fenders, headlights mounted low and lots of engine modifications. The most notable result of this car was the classic photograph from Put-in-Bay, of Randle's car up on two wheels—it was a miracle it did not roll that day. Later Bill got a Kieft MG with an aluminum body and an MG engine, made by the same English company that produced the highly successful Kieft Formula III car driven to many race wins by Clevelander Dick Irish."

ॐ ॐ

With the third race underway, we see the #101 supercharged MG of popular disc jockey Bill Randall leading a Porsche and a Singer roadster (Center for Archival Collections, University Libraries, Bowling Green State University).

4. 1953

A decision was made to race on Sunday in 1953, just as in 1952. There was no conflict with the morning church services because the three races were run in the afternoon.

Attendance at the race was OK but certainly not at the levels we would see in later events at the 'Bay. Most of the publicity was word-of-mouth, of course including members of the sanctioning organization, the Cleveland Sport Car Club, and related groups including NE Ohio SCCA, the Detroit Region SCCA and the people at Waterford Hills. So only people in the know went. One of those was a 15-year-old student at Shaker Heights high school named Dick Lamport, Jr., who had just moved to the Cleveland area from Chicago. His father, also Dick Lamport, had been the steward of the meet at Elkhart Lake the previous year. At the end of the school year, Dick Jr. asked a few of his friends, "How'd you like to go to the sports car races at Put-in-Bay?" We all said, "What are those?" One of the group, Charlie Hazle, recalls, "We were all 15 years old, so nobody could drive. We had to get your father [the author's] to drive. He took the Lincoln up to Port Clinton, smoking a cigar all the way. We put the car in the parking lot and got on the ferry boat. We arrived on the island just after the first race had started. Ray [my father] went into a bar to hear the baseball game." I remember that we walked up to the Cemetery Corner, past Cooper's Restaurant and the winery. Brooks stood outside the winery asking people if they would buy a bottle of wine

The #83 Porsche of mechanic John Moncur pursues the #95 supercharged MG of Avery Morris from Detroit (Center for Archival Collections, University Libraries, Bowling Green State University).

The classic shot of Bill Randle nearly rolling his MG-TD near Airport Corner. His recovery seemed to defy the laws of physics (Joe Brown).

for them. We didn't walk around the whole course, just up to the cemetery and back through town to the pits.

Dick Lamport remembered the relative safety of Put-in-Bay. "At the old course at Elkhart Lake, they had no curbs out of town but they did have them in town. The smaller-displacement engines made it safer at Put-in-Bay—no Jaguars, Allards or Ferraris. I liked the Bay race," says Lamport, "I liked the boat ride over and back, I liked the Ford Tri-Motor even though we didn't go on it, and I had a great time. I'm not sure your dad wanted to go, but he was a good sport—he took us there and we went more than once."

On the way back home we got a flat tire. Charlie fixed the flat and we motored on to the east side of Cleveland in the Lincoln, which was the same kind that had won the Mexican Road Race. The race had been a great experience. The sound of the racing engines had been audible over the noise of the ferry boat as we first pulled into the dock. We all got interested in sports cars and all owned them after that. In particular, we all had Porsche Speedsters at one time or another: Charlie Hazle had a red '56 with beehive tail lights, Dick Lamport had a black one, Mike Coyne had a red one and I had a white '57 with teardrop tail lights. I had that car for 25 years. It's now in Eugene Binder's museum in Marfa, Texas.

In the pattern of subsequent races—since the one-race event in 1952, those of 1953 and 1954 were three-race programs, held in June—this would have been the race for 1.5-liter and 2-liter production cars, namely pre–356A Porsches and flat-radiator Morgan 4/4s. Other entrants in the feature race included class H- and G-Modified cars as well as the ever-present Modified MGs.

☙ ❧

Moments after the Morgan rolled at the airport, people are rushing to help. The flat-radiator Morgan was a late entry in 1953 (Center for Archival Collections, University Libraries, Bowling Green State University).

Other road races run in 1953 included Watkins Glen, having moved up the hill to Dix Township; Brynfan Tyddyn, which was held in concert with the Giant's Despair Hill Climb at Wilkes Barre, Pennsylvania; and the quirky 8-mile race at Callicoon, New York, held only one year, 1953. Elkhart Lake had had its last road race in 1952; they were planning their permanent road course already, and the era of racing on public streets was already coming to a close. But they didn't know that at Put-in-Bay.

The airport courses were somewhere between road courses and closed circuits. Although they were flat, they were interesting in their own way, particularly the SAC base series in 1952, 1953 and 1954. These were the exact opposite of Put-in-Bay; with mile-long runways and open spaces, they ran the big cars at speeds up to 174 mph. The series on the

Corner workers and spectators have reached the rolled Morgan and are starting to roll the car back on its wheels (1953). Fortunately, accidents were never serious on Put-in-Bay (Center for Archival Collections, University Libraries, Bowling Green State University).

Strategic Air Command bases was the result of an agreement between General Curtis LeMay and the Sports Car Club of America. Since each base was fenced, unlike the road-racing towns, spectators could be charged an admission. The bulk of the money went to the air force's Living Improvement Fund. This paid for recreational facilities including gyms, bowling alleys, nurseries and garages for working on hobby cars. The idea was to provide these things to increase re-enlistment and improve morale, which it did. There were enormous spectator crowds at these events—60,000 people on October 26 at Turner AFB in Albany, Georgia, for example (at $2 a ticket!). Other airfields were McDill in Tampa, Florida; March Field at Riverside, California; Hunter AFB in Savannah, Georgia; Chanute AFB in Rantoul, Illinois; Offut AFB in Nebraska; Atterbury AFB in Columbus, Indiana; Westover AFB in

4. 1953

Winning drivers pose with a table full of trophies at the 1953 Put-in-Bay road races. These drivers are from all walks of life, such as mechanics, bus drivers, stockbrokers, doctors, advertising men, machinists, engineers and the military (Art and Dutch Brow).

Massachusetts; and Moffett Field in California. There were also races not far from Put-in-Bay, at Lockbourne AFB near Columbus, Ohio, run in 1953 and '54

June 14, 1953, Entry List

First Race

10 laps (31 miles), for stock MG

Car	Driver	Address	Make	Displ. CC
1	John Whitlock	Pontiac, Mich.	MG	1250
2	Philip Thomas	Cleveland, Ohio	MG	1250
3	Charles Ellmers	Chagrin Falls, Ohio	MG	1250
4	Richard Quinn	Cleveland, Ohio	MG	1250
5	Lawrence Murtaugh	Lorain, Ohio	MG	1250
6	Malcolm Boardman	Detroit, Mich.	MG	1250
7	Henry Becker	Cleve. Hghts., Ohio	MG	1250
8	Thomas Richardson	Alliance, Ohio	MG	1250
9	Ralph Cadwallader	Cleveland, Ohio	MG	1250
10	Ralph Durbin	Grand River, Mich.	MG	1250
11	Ronald McConnell	Cleveland, Ohio	MG	1250

Car	Driver	Address	Make	Displ. CC
12	Alan Patterson	Boston, Penn.	MG	1250
15	Peter Reece	Willowick, Ohio	MG	1250
16	John Comey	Chagrin Falls, Ohio	MG	1250
18	Elmer Riedel	Cleveland, Ohio	MG	1250
20	Eugene Smith	Akron, Ohio	MG	1250
21	Earl Kornfeld	Twinsburgh, Ohio	MG	1250
22	Bob Hugus	Pittsburgh, Penn.	MG	1250

Second Race

12 laps (36 miles), up to 1350 cc

Car	Driver	Address	Make	Displ. CC
12	Alan Patterson	Boston, Penn.	MG	1250
25	Stiles Twitchell	Cleveland, Ohio	MG	1250
26	Wesley Staples	Birmingham, Mich.	MG	1250
30	Dick Gates	Cleveland, Ohio	Simca	1090
31	Dick Yares	Cleveland, Ohio	Siata	736
32	Edward Tierney	Cleveland, Ohio	MG	1250
33	John Antos	Pontiac, Mich.	MG	1250
40	Dick Gent	Cleveland, Ohio	Cisitalia	1090
44	Elmo Howell	Cleveland, Ohio	MG	1250
45	Philip Forsyth	Elyria, Ohio	Fiat	990
66	George Phillips	Pontiac, Mich.	MG	1250

Third Race

15 laps (47 miles), up to 1950 cc

Car	Drive	Address	Make	Displ. CC
12	Alan Patterson	Boston, Penn.	MG	1250
51	Robert Shea	Cleveland, Ohio	MG	1250(s)
52	Robert Lossman	Cleveland, Ohio	MG	1250(s)
60	Philip Cole	Maumee, Ohio	Singer	1497
65	Don Janik	Cleveland, Ohio	MG	1250(s)
72	George Webber, Jr.	Cleveland, Ohio	Arnolt MG	1250(s)
83	John Moncur	Akron, Ohio	Porsche	1488
88	Anthony Stica	Detroit, Mich.	MG	1399
95	Avery Morris	Detroit, Mich.	MG	1288(s)
99	Sam Sheppard	Cleveland, Ohio	MG	1250(s)
101	Bill Randle	Cleveland, Ohio	MG	1250(s)

(s) indicates that car is supercharged

As you will note the size of European-type engines is listed in cc (cubic centimeters). In the U.S. we use cubic inches. To give you a basis of comparison, here are three popular American cars in cubic inches and cubic centimeters:

Ford V-8	239.4 cu. in.	3923 cc
Chevrolet	235.5 cu. in.	3859 cc
Plymouth	217.8 cu. in.	3583 cc

The popular MG has a displacement of 1250 cc and the Ford has 3923 cc, making it slightly over three times as large, but it has only twice the power.

Chapter 5

1954: The Technology of Sport

June 12, 1954

The year 1954 at Put-in-Bay brought in a number of new machines as the technology of sports cars advanced. The most sophisticated of these was the Siata 208S, from the small constructor in Turin, Italy, which based its models on Fiat components. It was said that Siata was to Fiat as Shelby was to Ford. Central to the car's engineering was a small but powerful 2-liter V-8. Fearing a conflict with Ford copyrights, Siata named its engine the 8-V, or Otto Vu. This was mounted well back in the chassis for balance, as was the Siata practice. The

Ready to race and sitting in the starting grid is the MG-TD of Joe Weber, from Cleveland Heights. Apropos the informal conduct of the 'Bay races, Joe told his parents that he was going to the race but forgot to mention that he would be in it (collection of Joe Weber).

chassis, in turn, was a large-diameter tubular frame with an advanced independent suspension in the rear and tried-and-true, unequal A-arm independent suspension in the front. In other words, it was more up-to-date than many other current cars, although it was designed in 1952. The body was aluminum, designed and built by Motto.

These wonderful cars were sold by "Mister Etceterini," Tony Pompeo, whose distributorship in New York City brought in cars not only from Siata but also from Bandini, Moretti, Stanguellini, Nardi and Abarth. Tony was a colorful fellow. He was a ladies' man and was rumored to have some connection with the Mafia. For all his love of cars, he was not a very good driver and once rolled a Siata, an almost impossible feat. He rolled it right in front of photographer Dan Rubin at Thompson Raceway, as Dan relates: "A bunch of us photographers are sitting around and a state trooper drives up. 'I want to see everyone's press pass,' he says. Just then there's a yellow Siata flipping and the flagman is running for his life. Inside the car was Tony Pompeo."

With all these car lines, it was difficult to maintain parts support. Alfa driver Chuck Stoddard once helped to maintain and race-prepare the Siata 208 of Lt. Col. Bob Kuhn, the very same one who ran at the 'Bay in '54. Both of them were air force officers at Wright-Patterson AFB in Dayton. On one occasion, they went to New York for some spares. Dropping in on Pompeo, Stoddard said, "Col. Kuhn here has a 208. Will you show us to your parts department?" "Certainly," replied Pompeo. "Follow me." Arriving at a small room in the warehouse, Pompeo announced, "Here it is. Just let me know what you want." Stoddard reports that the room held only ten boxes of miscellaneous parts for the variety of cars that

The back half of the grid for the first race in 1954 includes the #32 car of Malcolm Boardman and the #4 car of Sam Lewis (Dave and Sheila Bly).

5. 1954

The MG field comes through the left-hand jog into town at the 1954 Put-in-Bay race, with #7, N.P. deCourville of Akron, Ohio, in the lead (Joe Brown).

the business handled. Pompeo was a likeable, popular man, but not all customers were happy about the parts situation. I was, though. One time I got the last set of Siata 1400 pistons in the world from him.

Another new car of interest was something called a Lotus—Lotus Mk. VI, to be exact. This was originally configured as a solid-axle car with a flathead, four-cylinder Ford engine and used for field trials in England. By the time it got to Put-in-Bay, Colin Chapman had given the car several refinements. These turned the lightweight little car into a potent racing machine, as driven by Toledo, Ohio, importer Gunnard Rubini.

This race was the first appearance, at Put-in-Bay, of the Siata Gran Sport. With a solid rear axle and 1400-cc overhead valve engine, it lacked the refinement of its bigger brother, the 208S. However, it was an extremely well balanced car, with handling second to none. It had excellent brakes as well. According to Dick Irish, who drove one of these cars to a class first in the 1952 Sebring, it was a better handling car than any Ferrari on the road. At PiB, it was driven by Henry Dahl, who owned the Keystone Garage in Warren, Pennsylvania.

In the 1953 race, there had been one Porsche; now, in 1954, there were three. These great little cars got faster every day. First they were 1100 cc, then 1300 cc, then 1500 cc, then 1500 Super. The evolution never stopped. VW brakes were changed to aluminum Porsche brakes, and improvements were made in the suspension systems among other refinements.

Also entered in the feature race was one of the exotic Kieft center-seat sports racers. Powered by an MG engine bored out to 1467 cc, it was thought to be a real contender, just as the Kieft Formula III was. Elmo Howell of Bay Village, Ohio, entered and drove the car.

Paul Flickinger, a scientist from the atomic labs in Oak Ridge, Tennessee, brought an unusual car this year, an HRG. These cars, most of them prewar, featured a tubular steel frame, an aluminum body and the power of a Singer engine. With a 1497 cc displacement and lighter weight, it could out-accelerate an MG.

Then there was the Singer itself. It looked like an MG, and it had about the same engine size, but it was a single overhead cam design. It did not have the balance or handling ability of the MG. A nearby driver named Phillip Cole, of Maumee, Ohio, a Toledo suburb, was slated to drive the car.

That's in addition to the vast number of MGs of every type and color: The new TF, TD, TC, modified, supercharged, you name it. The so-called experts, the reviewers, didn't like the TF. But it was consistent with the other T-series cars, and it was actually faster on the straightaway than either the TD or TC. A lot of people liked the faired-in headlights. I know I did.

Among the many MG drivers who were interesting as race entrants and car enthusiasts was Herb Whiting. As a sometime racer, Herb ran his modified MG-TD in the second race at Put-in-Bay, 1954, finishing sixth. He ran the same Mark II TD at Akron. Then in 1957, he drove a Siata Spyder in the second race at Put-in-Bay, and at Akron. The following year at Akron he drove a Sprite, which he also drove at Watkins Glen, Dunkirk and Thompson, Connecticut. He was the founder of the Northern Ohio Region of the Porsche Club of America and owned a number of interesting cars, including a 1958 Porsche 356A coupe, a Porsche 550 Spyder, complete with 4-cam engine, a Jaguar XK-120, and a genuine World War II Jeep.

One of these MG TDs, the #35 car, was owned and raced by the soon-to-be-notorious

MG #32, Malcolm Boardman of Detroit, rounds the corner at the Colonial Ballroom. There's a pretty good crowd here, and the hay bales keep the cars from hitting the trees in the park (Joe Brown).

Dr. Sam Sheppard. Those who did not live in Cleveland in the mid-fifties can be excused for not instantly recognizing this name, but in Cleveland you could not pick up a newspaper without seeing his name.

On June 12, while Dr. Sam Sheppard was waiting to race his MG, he made a phone call, part of which was overheard by the son of the mayor of Cleveland. That part was, "I'll kill the bitch," punctuated by the slamming of a phone in the receiver. And 21 days later, his wife was dead. That began a long sequence of questions and answers that eventually materialized as a television series titled *The Fugitive*, with the main character modeled after Sam Sheppard.

Cornering briskly in his Lotus VI is Gunnard Rubini of Toledo. The lightweight Colin Chapman creation was the object of curiosity everywhere it went. Later, at the Lockbourne AFB race in Columbus, Luigi Chinetti and Alfred Momo addressed Rubini in Italian, alas he is Swedish (Center for Archival Collections, University Libraries, Bowling Green State University).

A race three weeks after the Put-in-Bay event is featured briefly in the transcript of an interview of the Cuyahoga County Sheriff's Office. Describing events of the days that led up to the murder of his wife, Sheppard said, "I told him [Officer Schottke] as I recall that I had attended stock car races two or three days previously with my wife, [football player] Otto Graham and his wife." Actually, if the murder occurred two days after the "stock car races," that's what they must have been—stock car—because the Put-in-Bay sports car races were held on June 12, 21 days before the July 3 death of Marilyn Sheppard.

Sam Sheppard owned a cottage on the island. He was popular on the sports car scene and so, when Art Brow mentioned that he could not find a rooming house, he said, "Well,

The #18 Siata Gran Sport of Henry Dahl from Warren, Pennsylvania, has just arrived in the ferry boat. It's a contender in the third race (Center for Archival Collections, University Libraries, Bowling Green State University).

5. 1954

The Aston Martin DB2 pace car leads the F-Modified field to the starter's flag at the 1954 Put-in-Bay feature. On the front row is the #31 Kieft MG of Elmo W. Howell (right), and the Siata Gran Sport of Henry Dahl (left) and behind them the HRG of Paul Flickinger (left) and several MGs (Joe Brown).

if you don't mind sleeping on the porch, you're welcome to do that." Art was a central part of the crew for the Jack Uhl #23 Porsche coupe. He and Jack had modified it extensively. They supercharged the engine with a Pepco blower. These commonly put out 15 pounds of pressure boost. If the engine didn't blow up, it was going to be very powerful. Plus, they put the 356 coupe on a crash diet by replacing doors, hood and engine hatches with fabricated aluminum. They got the weight down to about 1600 lbs by the time they were done. Between corners, the car was very fast. But the handling of the pre-A 356 models left something to be desired.

Not long after the races were over, the Sheppard case turned into a circus. The doctor claimed he had seen the murderer escaping, and the newspapers claimed the murderer had not; it was Sheppard. Accusations included the allegation that he may have had an affair with the wife of the owner of MG Motors, where he bought a Jaguar and an MG. His wife was going to get a divorce and drag his name though the mud. In the transcript Sheppard discusses seeing both Mr. and Mrs. Lossman at gatherings of the Sports Car Club but does not say which one. SCCA? Cleveland Sport Car Club? It referred to "functions ... here in the city," suggesting the Sports Car Club of America was meant, because it met at the Statler Hilton downtown whereas CSCC met in the suburbs. The transcript ends with Sheppard's seeing the unknown murderer running away on the beach as he falls down in the surf at the retaining wall on the lake.

Sheppard was convicted on circumstantial evidence and spent ten years in prison. But

The E-Production field rounds Cemetery Corner, with a white Triumph TR-2 in the lead, followed by the red #40 TR-2 and Col. Kuhn's Siata 208, going around on the outside (Center for Archival Collections, University Libraries, Bowling Green State University).

the real murderer, as noted by Fred Troyan, who worked at MG Motor Sales, may have been Dick Eberling, a groundskeeper and house cleaner for many west-side Cleveland families. He was in jail for another offense and allegedly boasted of the killing to another prisoner. Other evidence, brought forward by attorney F. Lee Bailey of Boston, freed Sheppard when he was found not guilty in a 1966 retrial. In the aftermath, Sam's son Chip filed a lawsuit against the State of Ohio and Fred Troyan delivered a new Jaguar XKE that his brother Richard had bought for Sam Sheppard.

In all the excitement about Sam Sheppard, one other car I forgot to mention is the newly-introduced Triumph TR-2, put on the track with the unpopular number 13. Successor to the Triumph 2000 touring car, this was more of a sports car, with its cut-down doors and

5. 1954

This Siata Gran Sport came from Tony Pompeo's distributorship in New York. See how flat it corners here at the Put-in-Bay road races in 1954, as driven by Henry Dahl of Warren, Pennsylvania (Betty Henn).

torquey two-liter engine. It was a car that many people would come to like in all its iterations, including the TR-3 and 3A. It was entered by an ex-WWII paratrooper, a veteran of many missions in the Pacific Theatre. On one of them, he was the 13th man out of the plane and all of the others were killed. The driver of the lucky-13 numbered TR-2 was Pittsburgh car dealer Ed Hugus.

The course, starting the previous year, incorporated no-passing zones. One would think that odd, but here's the way those worked, according to Art Brow: "There were four 90-degree turns on the course. The road was only 18 feet wide so they had to have something that made passing safer. These No Passing zones were marked with signs that said 'NP' and placed about 100 yards before the corner. If you were halfway past a car at that point, you could continue your pass through the corner. If you were not past the car beside you, you had to drop back. I was able to pass several cars by braking late and passing on the inside, off what you would consider a normal cornering line. The pit turn was exciting—the road got really rough there, especially on the inside of the turn. One time I hit a hay bale, turned to see what happened, and my visor blew off."

The no-passing zones were carried over from the old road-racing rules promulgated by the Sports Car Club of America. They were used at the early Watkins Glen course, where they also had "RP"—Resume Passing—signs.

And here we pick up the continuing saga of Art Seyler, from 1953. The following year—it was June 12, 1954—he again went to Put-in-Bay, this time with his brother Al, and again ran a few laps of night practice, this time in the Jag. Art relates,

Someone said to me, "If you really want to see the race, go to Cemetery Corner. You can see the back straight, the corner and the straight into town all from the same spot. But you've got to get there early because it fills up fast." We were hung over and sunburned so we turned in and got some sleep. Then we got up early to look for a good vantage point.

At 6 a.m. I dragged my brother out to the cemetery. He was bitching all the way—he didn't want to be there anyway. Sure enough, there were only a few places left, and we took a spot under an overhanging tombstone and lay down to get some sleep before the races.

I was lying on my back and almost asleep when a drunk who was wandering around there stepped on my leg. I got up, cursed him and told him to get out of there. When I lay down, I lay on my side, resting my head on my arm, at the base of this tombstone. Suddenly I heard a woman's scream. I sat up with a start, just as the top stone came crashing down. The same drunk had bumped it off. It raked the side of my head, putting a deep gash above my ear, and fell on my arm, pinning it to the ground.

My brother Al and another man lifted the 200-pound stone off my arm. We looked for the drunk, but he had fled in a fit of self-preservation. The lady who alerted me with her scream was nearby, wearing a cocktail dress and high heels that were sinking into the grass of the cemetery. Her husband was the sales manager of Jaguar-Cleveland.

I had abrasions on my arm but nothing serious. If I had not shifted positions to lie on my side, the stone would have crushed my skull and killed me, without any doubt.

It was a pretty good day of racing at Put-in-Bay. Afterwards we took the ferry boat back to Port Clinton, drove back to Cleveland, and I dropped my brother off. When I went in my house with bandages on my ear and on my arm the first thing my wife Lucile said is, "You've been racing!" And I said, "No, I haven't." Then I told her the whole story, ending it by saying, "If I can get killed sleeping in a cemetery at 6 a.m. on a Saturday, by a drunk pushing a tombstone on me, just waiting for a race, then racing must be safer, so that's what I've decided to do."

Chuck Dietrich in his supercharged #24 TC is setting up for a pass on the Siata 208 of Bob Kuhn. Moments later he was by (collection of Betty Henn).

A little later that year I was entered at the Akron Airport sports car race, in a borrowed and very tired, modified MG-TD, which my good friend Henry Becker wisely passed up to race a 1500cc Kieft.

Another spectator was a 14-year-old kid from Lakewood High School on the west side of Cleveland. He was Michael Lynch, now widely known as a racing historian who authored *American Sports Car Racing in the 1950s* with William Edgar and Ron Parravano. He had already been to a sports car race, the SAC base race at Lockbourne in 1953. General LeMay

A Kieft center-seat takes Cemetery Corner in the third race. Driver is Elmo Howell from Bay Village, Ohio. This car was originally purchased by disc jockey Bill Randle. The cars did reasonably well at the 'Bay and even better in the Mother Country. There was a curious little racing team known as the Monkey Stable in England, which ran modified MGs with some success, then switched to the Kieft (Center for Archival Collections, University Libraries, Bowling Green State University).

was a customer of his father, who did the graphics for the SAC planes as an executive of Dupont. Michael remembers that they got all kinds of credentials and enjoyed listening to the howl of the 4.1 engines as Kimberly and Spear flew down the straight in their 340 Ferraris. Michael says,

> I was a sophomore in high school, and I knew three seniors who were going to the race: the Munz brothers and Jerry Steigerwald. Jerry was a swimmer who went to Yale on an athletic scholarship. He had a date and was driving his MG up there with her. So I went with the Munz brothers. We took the ferry over from Port Clinton and walked up the back straight to watch most of the race from the graveyard. That year the TR2 had come out and a lot of drivers had moved up to it, not realizing how much more power it had. So there were a tremendous number of incidents of Triumphs not making that corner.
>
> I remember the festive atmosphere and the novelty of seeing two Bugattis, a Type 35B and a 57 with a swoopy body. We were influenced by the *pur sang* culture of the Ken Purdy books. I kissed the Bugatti badge on one of those cars! There was a Lotus Mk. VI with cycle fenders. It was very impressive. Visibly faster than the others in the corner. Dick Gent had an interesting car, a Cisitalia roadster, up there.
>
> One of the Munz brothers wanted to go back on the Ford Tri-Motor. I don't know how we got on it but we did. The other one took the ferry back and picked us up at the airport on the mainland. Later in the summer of '54 my family moved to Kansas City. I wasn't looking forward to it but as soon as I got there they had an SCCA regional race at the airport.

Another interesting car in the 1954 Put-in-Bay race is the #21 HRG of Paul Flickinger from Oak Ridge, Tennssee. These cars, easily mistaken for MGs, were imported to the States by enthusiast Jack Wherry, who lived in Iowa. Most of them had Singer 1500 engines on a C-section frame with semi-elliptical rear and quarter-elliptical front suspensions. The engine was set well back, the car was well-balanced, and it had an aluminum body mounted on a wood frame made of ash (Joe Brown).

5. 1954

The First Race

The first race was always the MG race. One of the highlights of this year was the win by Ralph Durbin. The Detroit driver was known as "the world's fastest bus driver" in his home town. Ralph made his living driving for the Greyhound line. His car—one of the new MG-TFs—was always well prepared, and he was an outstanding driver. Another Detroiter, Malcolm Boardman, took second. Clevelanders Ted Jayne and Charlie Ellmers, in fourth and fifth, did not do as well as expected. Jack Oettinger from Shaker Heights finished sixth.

Joe Weber in MG-TD #5 finished seventh but had as good a time as any. Here's how Joe describes it:

> I used to have a Rocket 88 Olds, and then I found out about sports cars and I joined the MG car club that met down on Lee Road at Linsay's Tavern. I went to a few gymkhanas and rallies and then I heard that the Put-in-Bay race was coming up. I was living in Cleveland Heights at the time, and several people I knew were going to the St. John's Cathedral Printers Mass, for those who worked at the newspapers, et cetera. It ended at midnight and we drove all night to get to Port Clinton. We made the 8 a.m. ferry and got over to the island. I had told my parents I was going to the race but didn't tell them I would be in it. They put the number 5 on my car, I got on the grid in the third position, and the race started. After a couple of laps, I got vapor lock and went into a field. I think it was out near the airport. A corner worker shouted to me, "You going to go back on the track?" I said, "sure." I was able

Top: TR-2 #40 goes wide at Cemetery Corner, pursued by a silver Porsche coupe. *Bottom*: On the outside of the turn at Cemetery Corner is this assortment of race officials, spectators and the driver of the #40 TR-2, formerly in racing condition (Center for Archival Collections, University Libraries, Bowling Green State University).

to re-start my car and found that everyone else had gone by and I was at the end. As I was trying to catch up, people were cheering me, as if I had won. I passed a few cars and finished in 7th place. I liked the race and I would have run more, but I moved to Florida after that year. I did drive Akron Airport in '54, where my folks came down to watch, unknown to me, and Cumberland, Maryland, plus an old horse racing track near Maumee, where a guy flipped.

"I remember passing Dr. Sam Sheppard's home in Bay Village on the way back to Cleveland from the 1954 Put-in-Bay races," Joe recalled, "and waving to him and a bunch of other sports car people in his driveway."

The Second Race

In the second race of the day, a modified MG-TC won. This car had the usual engine preparation that included boring the cylinders to 1320 cc, an MG competition camshaft, higher-than-stock compression, and balancing, which the British usually did not do. The winning car was driven by Leo McPherson, Jr., of Columbus—the #11 car. Ralph Durbin in his stock MG-TF took second place, with Bill Malion finishing third, also in a TF. The fourth-place car was the MG-TF of Bob Lossman, who figured heavily in the organizing of the event itself. In fifth place was Jim Dever. Jim was the brother of Neil Dever, and he was initially a mechanic at Lossman Motors. He was later a crewman on a lakes freighter that sailed beautiful Lake Erie until the gales of November. Then, in sixth place, was Herb Whiting, who was a judge and also a sailor at Mentor Harbor Yacht Club. Somewhere along the line, the nimble Lotus dropped out, with its promise unrealized.

A sedan race accompanied this one, and the winner was William Pickrel, Jr., who drove a 750-cc Renault CV4. Bob Fergus, a Volkswagen distributor from Columbus, was second in a VW, followed by a Morris Minor in third and Fergus' business partner in the Midvo Corporation, Don Marsh, driving a VW.

The Third Race

The third race was won by Lt. Col. Robert Kuhn in the aforementioned two-liter Siata 208S. Kuhn was a longtime racer who liked Italian cars and later drove an OSCA. Second place in the feature event was Ed Hugus in his Triumph. Hugus later drove both Sebring and Le Mans several times. Elmo Howell drove his Kieft MG to a third place and William Pickrel, Jr., drove his Porsche Super to fourth place. The #11 MG that had done so well in the second race had a mechanical problem and was sidelined out near the airport.

Chuck Dietrich in his #24 modified MG-TC had a promising start and actually passed Col. Kuhn's Siata at one point, but then he had a problem. Somewhere between the airport turn and Cemetery Corner, he ran out of gas in the supercharged TC. Sputtering to a stop in front of a farm house, he borrowed a can of tractor gas, dumped it into the tank and rejoined the fray. "I don't think I placed very well that year," Dietrich recalled, "but I did finish the race."

The Gunnard Rubini Lotus Mk. VI did not appear in the finishing results. At 1057 cc with a de-stroked MG engine, it had the smallest engine in the third race. "It handled well," says Gunnard, "and had good acceleration. It had a Laystall aluminum head, and we shaved it as much as we dared. Later in the season I raced it at Lockbourne SAC base, where I had an interesting talk with General Le May about the car and Briggs Cunningham looked it over closely."

In other news related to the Cleveland Sport Car Club, Dick Henn was elected president and several marriages occurred between members: Ruth and Charlie Ellmers, Penny and Ted Jayne, Joy and John Comey, and Bettsey and Bob Kintner. Later in the season, October 10 to be exact, the club put on its second race, the Akron Airport Sports Car Race. This was cooked up in a meeting at Linsay's Tavern and involved closing a part of the airport to make a 2.0-mile course. Like the 'Bay race, it was terrifically successful. It drew big-name drivers and cars such as the Jim Kimberly and Sherwood Johnston Ferraris; Ebby Lunken, the Ferrari driver from Cincinnati; and Jim Jeffords, from Milwaukee. Kimberly won in his 4.5 Ferrari. This was a car that could do 174 mph on the straightaway—exactly why it was not racing at Put-in-Bay. Sherwood Johnston was second after spinning out of the lead, and Chuck Hassan, one of the "Cincinnati Gang," was third in his Ferrari.

At this point, we pick up the trail of the Funny Face Auto Racing Team, commonly known as FFART. Team member Meach Hitchcock explains: "The origin of the FFART is somewhat obscure. The best available records show that it was formed at the Akron race in 1954 [that was on October 11, so it would have been after the 1954 Put-in-Bay race]. Ben Hitchcock's TC had made a total of half a lap under the hands of Charlie Ellmers in its debut and Ted Jayne's TD had not exactly burned up the course at the Glen earlier in the year. At Akron, while we had our problems, both cars finished their race. All concerned were so pleased that broad smiles were stuck on the cars' radiators with yellow masking tape. Since the smiles made it easier to spot the cars on the track, it was decided to use them as a sort of trademark."

So closed another wonderful year in the Midwestern sports car scene. There had been a new and improved race up at Put-in-Bay, plus Akron, a brand new airport race close to Cleveland, rallies organized by John Birchfield and Charlie Ellmers, and an annual banquet held at the Cleveland Skating Club.

June 12, 1954, Entry List

First Race

10:45 a.m., 10 laps (31 miles), for stock MG

Car	Driver	Address	Make	Displ. CC
3	F. Eugene Smith	Akron, Ohio	MG	1250
4	Samuel S. Lewis	Akron, Ohio	MG	1250
5	R. Joe Weber	Cleve. Hts., Ohio	MG	1250
7	N.P. deCourville	Akron, Ohio	MG	1250
10	R.M. Gubbins	Birmingham, Mich.	MG	1250
12	Tony J. Hogg	Columbus, Ohio	MG	1250
15	Charles R. Ellmers	Chagrin Falls, Ohio	MG	1250
16	Ted Jayne	Cleveland, Ohio	MG	1250
17	Jack Oettinger	Shaker Hts., Ohio	MG	1250
19	Ralph Durbin	Detroit, Mich.	MG	1250
20	Ronald McConnell	Lakewood, Ohio	MG	1250
22	Edward Shea, Sr.	Jamestown, N.Y.	MG	1250
32	Malcolm Boardman	Detroit, Mich.	MG	1250

Car	Driver	Address	Make	Displ. CC
33	Orlie C. Ward	Lincoln Park, Mich.	MG	1250
35	Dr. Sam Sheppard	Bay Village, Ohio	MG	1250
39	Don Janik	Lakewood, Ohio	MG	1250

Second Race

11:30 a.m., 12 laps (37.2 miles), up to 1350 cc

Car	Driver	Address	Make	Displ. CC
1	Robert Lossman	Rocky River, Ohio	MG-TF	1250
8	Gunnard Rubini	Toledo, Ohio	Lotus MKVI	1057
9	Herbert Whiting	Cleveland, Ohio	MG (mod.)	1250
11	Leo McPherson, Jr.	Columbus, Ohio	MG-TC (mod.)	1320
14	James S. Ryan	Cleveland, Ohio	MG (mod.)	1250
26	William Pickrel, Jr.	Dayton, Ohio	Renault CV4	748
27	John G. Whitlock	Pontiac, Mich.	MG (mod.)	1250
29	William Malion	Columbus, Ohio	MG-TF	1250
30	Jim Dever	Cleveland, Ohio	MG (mod.)	1340
34	Wallace Stickler	Dayton, Ohio	Renault	750
38	Louis Miralia	Cleveland, Ohio	Crosley H.S.	750

Third Race

2:15 p.m. 15 laps (46.5 miles), up to 1950 cc

Car	Driver	Address	Make	Displ. CC
2	Robert Lossman	Rocky River, Ohio	MG	1250(s)
4	Theodore Kessel	Massillon, Ohio	MG	1250
6	Lt. Col. Robt. Kuhn	Fairborn, Ohio	Siata V8	1996
8	Gunnard Rubini	Toledo, Ohio	Lotus MKVI	1057
13	J. Edward Hugus	Pittsburgh, Pa.	Triumph	1991
18	Henry J. Dahl	Warren, Pa.	Siata (mod.)	1400
21	Paul Flickinger	Oak Ridge, Tenn.	H.R.G.	1497
23	Earl H. Uhr	Lakewood, Ohio	Porsche	1488
24	Charles Dietrich	Sandusky, Ohio	MG-TC	1300(s)
25	William Pickrel, Jr.	Dayton, Ohio	Porsche (Super)	1495
28	George Phillips	Pontiac, Mich.	Porsche (Super)	1500
31	E.W. Howell	Bay Village, Ohio	Kieft MG	1467
36	Robert Shea	Cleveland, Ohio	MG-TC	1466
37	Phillip Cole	Maumee, Ohio	Singer SM	1497

Cars placing first, second, or third in the first two races were eligible to run in the third race. The size of European-type engines is listed in cc (cubic centimeters). In the U.S. we use cubic inches. For comparison, the stock MG displacement is 1250 cc, or 76 cu. in.

Put-in-Bay Race Results, 1954

First Race: Stock MG

1. Ralph Durbin, Detroit, MG 1250 #19
2. Malcolm Boardman, Detroit, #32
3. Samuel S. Lewis, Akron, #4
4. Ted Jayne, Cleveland, #16
5. Charlie Ellmers, Chagrin Falls, #15
6. Jack Oettinger, Shaker Heights, #17
7. R. Joe Weber, Cleveland Hts., #5
8. Orlie C. Ward, Lincoln Park, Mich., #33

Second Race: Class F and H

Class F

1. Leo McPherson, Jr., Columbus, MG-TC (mod), 1320 cc, #11
2. Ralph Durbin, Detroit, MG-TF, #19
3. Bill Malion, Columbus, TF, #29
4. Bob Lossman, Rocky River, TF, 1250 cc, #1
5. Jim Dever, Cleveland, MG (mod.), 1340 cc, #30
6. Herb Whiting, Cleveland, MG (mod.), 1250 cc, #9

Class H

1. Wm. Pickrel Jr., Renault CV4, 750 cc, #26
2. Fergus, VW
3. Kampe, Morris
4. March, VW

Third Race: Classes E and F-Mod, 15 laps

1. Lt. Col. Robt. Kuhn, Fairborn, Ohio, Siata V8, 1996 cc, #6
2. J. Edward Hugus, Pittsburgh, Triumph, 1991 cc, #13
3. E.W. Howell, Bay Village, Kieft MG, 1467 cc, #31
4. Wm. Pickrel Jr., Dayton, Porsche Super, 1495 cc, #25
5. Ralph Durbin, TF
6. Mahoney, TD

Source: *NE Ohio SCCA Blower* (newsletter), July 1, 1954

Chapter 6

1955: Safety in Sports Car Racing

June 18, 1955

This year's Put-in-Bay race happened only one week after the terrible accident at Le Mans, France, that killed 84 people, the worst racing accident in history. Many races were cancelled after the June 12 wreck, but not Put-in-Bay. It underscored the attention to safety that went into the planning at the island race. Of course, a true road race, as PiB was, always has its hazards, but, insofar as possible, this race had features that the others did not. Put-in-Bay, the history books will show, was the safest of all the races run on public roads.

Before the races, Chuck Dietrich drives the #24 MG-TC down the ferryboat ramps with a carload of spares, including three extra tires and wheels (Joe Brown).

Engine displacements and car speeds were reduced. Production cars were limited to 2 liters and the modified or sports racing cars were limited to 1½ liters. That ultimately included cars from the 750 cc Fiat Abarths to the 2-liter AC Bristols, with speeds of 90 mph to 125, and the 750 cc Crosley-engined Siatas to the 1500 cc Porsche Spyders, with speeds of 100 mph to 130+ mph. The Porsches were getting progressively faster as the factory in Germany found new ways to boost the horsepower. They were on the borderline of "too fast." By contrast, Watkins Glen and Bridgehampton had unlimited engine sizes in both the production and modified classes. They had Jaguars, Allards, Ferraris, Maseratis and more. Their cars would go 150 mph and over. Each of these races had a fatality, whereas Put-in-Bay never had a serious accident other than a few spinouts and roll-overs.

While some races used the standing start that was popular in Europe, the organizers of PiB—John Birchfield, Dick Henn and Betty Henn—used a rolling start with a pace car. This is inherently safer and it smooths out the natural confusion after the green flag is dropped. Rolling starts are used in Sports Car Club of America events to this day, while you see standing starts in the Formula One events.

Although most of the cars were new at the time, each received a thorough tech inspection just to make sure it was mechanically race-ready. Each entry had a 21-point inspection tag accompanying it at Parker's Garage. A copy of one of these was sent to me by Bob Satava, a race worker at Put-in-Bay and longtime MG enthusiast. At the very top was the entrant's club, whether Cleveland Sport Car Club or Sports Car Club of America. Then there were spaces for the car number, driver name and car. Then there were two columns: one headed

Two of Chuck Dietrich's cars are in view on the boat docks at Put-in-Bay: the supercharged TC (left) and the G-Modified Lester MG (#31). In back of the Lester is Joe Bojalad's AC Ace, which won the feature event (Joe Brown).

"OK" and the other "re-check," the second-chance column. The check list began with inspection record and then went to "insurance"—did the driver have it? Next was "waiver signed," then "entry paid." According to Bob Satava, the fee in 1955 was $12.50 per car per race (that is, if a car was in the first and second races, its total entry fee would have been $25). Next was "lights taped"—we wouldn't want glass scattered all over the course in the event of a collision, would we? "Horn" was next—does it operate? Then "stop lights" to alert following drivers of slowing for a corner. "Body measurement" was next. It was superfluous to the inspection and never done. Next on the list was "crash helmet," although many of the helmets appeared to be made of cardboard. All the drivers were grateful when we got to the stage of the Snell Foundation and really good quality helmets.

"Goggles" were next; these were pretty good, since they were either war surplus (U.S. Army Air Corps) or the fancy split-lens goggles from Europe. Then the side mirror or mirrors were examined—were they on tight? Were they aligned? The emergency brake was one of the trickiest inspections—some were too tight, some were too loose, some didn't work at all. After that was the safety belt check, for the condition of the webbing and the latch and

Everyone is settled in at the paddock, including this unusual Doretti sports car. Based on a Triumph TR-2 and created by Triumph distributor Dorothy Deen, it was brought to the 1955 event by Pittsburgh racer Ralph Ziegler (Dick Henn, Jr.).

then for a large-diameter, thick washer under the car that the mounting eye went through. Then the door locks—were the doors going to swing open in the middle of a corner? Steering. Was the steering loose? In most cases it was not, since many of the cars racing were new or nearly so. Tires were almost always road tires, but even then discerning drivers were beginning to pick out the better European brands such as Dunlop, Michelin and Pirelli. Condition was important, of course—excessive cord wear was unacceptable.

The "loose parts" line on the form was the predecessor to "nutting" on the later formula cars, in which "to nut" is used as a verb, meaning to go over the entire car and make sure each and every nut is tightened properly—a rather tedious process, but useful. The check for "leakage" was a perfect test of British cars, from which anything could leak: coolant, gasoline, engine oil or brake fluid. The "fuel test" meant testing for alcohol or AvGas, but it was never done. The test of the car's racing number was basically whether the number was on, whether it was the correct one and whether it could be seen by the timing and scoring people. Finally and most importantly, the brakes—did they grab right or left, did they work at all; that kind of thing. The tech inspectors at Put-in-Bay were understanding folks who made every effort to let an entrant race. When the "OK" column on the inspection card was successfully completed, the driver was given an "approved" sticker for his dash or, later, for the roll bar.

Local people from the island were also involved. "They put me in charge of safety," says Louis Heineman, president of the well-known Heineman's Wineries. "I went around getting hay bales and putting them in front of telephone poles, trees and fire-plugs. I remember Dick Henn was in charge of the race. They had to have the cars checked. They were going

Rear view of the Bugatti Type 55 of John Comey. It was used as a pace car at Put-in-Bay (Bill Gorris).

The grid at the start of the MG race at Put-in-Bay in 1955. Ted Jayne is at the wheel of the #1 MG-TD; Thomas Kramer of Huron, Ohio, is at the wheel of the #33 MG-TD. The truck in the background has some bleachers where the ladies of the timing and scoring crew sat (Bill Gorris).

into Parker's Garage. I think on the airport road they were supposedly going 90 miles an hour. I was 26 years old then and I'm 86 now."

Corner workers were selected from the memberships of the Cleveland Sport Car Club and the NE Ohio Region of the SCCA, with its crack safety crews from Bill Benham's Lake Erie Communications. A complete land line was set up completely around the course by the Ohio National Guard. There were also radio link-ups.

Everything that the club did to increase safety was helpful. Having worked in the field of racing safety with the late John Fitch for over 18 years, I know many of the things that can be done. My own view is that the beautiful little race on the island was watched over by God, and so no one was ever hurt. It was too nice an event to be marred by an injury accident.

Experienced race officials at Put-in-Bay included Dick and Betty Henn, Bill Gorris, Bob Kintner, John Comey, Bob Morrison, and Bill and Nancy Schmidt.

Dick Henn and John Birchfield conducted a mandatory and comprehensive drivers' meeting just before the event. In it, Colonel Henn cautioned everyone, "You will race like gentlemen or not race at all." And really, when you think about it, there's no reason to drive in an unsportsmanlike manner. If you can't get ahead without hitting another car, you don't belong on the track. As Chuck Stoddard reminds us, the good drivers are safe drivers—people such as Jim Clark and Graham Hill did not need to touch another car to do well in a race.

The grid at the start of the MG race at Put-in-Bay in 1955. There are 19 cars on the line in the MG race. Beyond Ted Jayne's MG-TD #1 is Malcolm Boardman of Detroit, driving the white #45 TD, and Allan Hess of Westlake, Ohio, driving the #19 TD. Ted Jayne in #1 is putting on his helmet and getting ready for the green flag. Behind him, Mike Ward of Lansing, Michigan, is driving the #161 TD (Bill Gorris).

Of course, danger is a relative thing, as this story about MG driver and Funny Face Auto Racing Team member Fred Steger reveals. The time came when he switched over to sailing, and his wife Gerry said, "When Fred got out of sports cars and into sailing, it made my mother very happy. She was always worried about the racing. I told her, 'Mom, they're all going the same direction.' Besides Fred had done a few more dangerous things than racing. He was a Marine combat rifleman in the Pacific during World War II. Assigned as a scout to his platoon, he participated in five invasions in the Philippines." In addition, driver Hank Becker adds, "He was also at Iwo Jima. If you had a bigger print of the famous flag-raising there, you would see Fred Steger about fifteen feet down and to the right, holding his rifle at the ready."

The popular Charlie Ellmers was in combat in World War II and then was called up again by the navy for Korea. Pat Black, a friend of his, tells us that Ellmers flew 33 night recon missions as a radar operator in a Douglas Skyraider, flying off the carrier *Essex* after dark. His plane was loaded with state-of-the-art electronic gear, unarmed and unprotected from enemy aircraft.

Race One

Charlie Ellmers had to borrow an MG-TC to be in the 1955 race, as wife Ruth explains. "After the TD was raced in 1952, '53 and '54, Charlie bought a Jaguar XK-120. It was red and he painted it black," Ruth recalls. "He drove it in rallies for a couple of years before we were married and won several of them. To continue racing at Put-in-Bay, since the Jag could not race there, Charlie borrowed an MG-TC from Ben Hitchcock, which he drove in 1955, '56 and '57." As Ruth recalls, that was the year that he missed the corner into town, went straight down the escape road, backed up, and still won the race. "I was impressed when he won that race," she adds. "Charlie had the TC in the MG race with Constant, Durbin and the other drivers from the Motor City."

As Meach Hitchcock reports, "The bright spot of the year [for FFART] was Charlie's hard-fought third place at the Bay despite a locked-up steering system on the TC. In 1955, the yellow smiling faces were seen at more races."

Another MG driver was Harry Constant from Detroit. "About two years out of college, in 1953," says Harry, "I was having lunch at a friend's house and he had a TD in the back yard. I asked him what he was going to do with it and he said, 'Race it.' At that time you had to own a sports car and be sponsored to join the SCCA, so I bought a used TD and my friend sponsored me.

Here's a close-up of the time and scoring crew on the stake-bed truck. Note that the ladies have their choice of either the fashionable coolee hat or the exotic pith helmet as a means to keep the sun off (Dick Henn, Jr.).

The grid forms for the second race at Put-in-Bay in 1955. At the front is Jack Manting in the #39 Porsche Speedster. It must have been one of the first in the country. Behind him in the #44 MG-TF is Jack Wilson. Over in the #5 MG-TC is Bob Shea, with the end of a cigar in his mouth. Behind Shea is Ed Hugus in his lucky number 13 Porsche Speedster. Beside him is Ron Kehl in the #4 MG-TF (Bill Gorris).

"My first race was Lockbourne AFB in 1954. It was a blast. They even assigned a GI to each car. I raced a stock MG for three years. But Put-in-Bay was fun. You could practice and race on Saturday and then party all night. We also raced Harewood and Greenacres in Canada. Even on two dirt tracks in Maumee, Ohio, and Mt. Clemens, Michigan. They put hay bales on the course to make you shift gears. That's how I learned about four-wheel drifts, not intentionally."

In '55, Detroit driver Harry Constant and his friend Ralph Durbin both started at the back of the field. There were a couple of cars spinning and a lot of confusion and soon they went from last to first. They were going side by side on the bumpy road from Airport Corner to Cemetery Corner, then down the straight. "Going down the straight, Ralph passed me," Harry recalls, "but I kept on his tail. A TC passed me, then got behind Ralph and gave him a nudge as we approached the gas station. He spun Ralph 180 degrees, and Ralph drove backwards down the sidewalk. He finally crossed the road into town, put on the brakes and accelerated down toward the start/finish line. A very interesting bit of driving. I'll never forget Ralph looking over his shoulder, driving backwards in the race. We never did find out who tapped Ralph."

Ken Askew notes, "Ralph and I became friends when I moved back to the Detroit area in 1954. I worked on his pit crew in 1955 and enjoyed his company. A fierce competitor on the track, he was a gentle and humorous friend. When I got a chance to drive an Alfa Romeo

As the second race gets going, we see that the #13 Ed Hugus Speedster has cut into the inside lane and already passed Bob Shea's #5 TC. Jack Manting's Porsche has gotten, shall we say, a favorable start (Bill Gorris).

owned by Jack Downey, I knew Ralph had to change cars to win in the under–1300 class. The night before the Put-in-Bay race of 1956, I took Ralph for a ride around the course in the Alfa. The Alfa was entered in the G-Production class, until after the morning practice, then it was moved to G-Modified. I finished second to Chuck Dietrich, who drove a Lester MG, and ahead of the class F MG-As. Ralph won the 1300 MG race that day but was convinced about the Alfa's future."

Yet another MG driver was Bob Barsantee, Jr., of Ann Arbor, Michigan, now living in Saline. Bob raced the #46 MG-TD at the 'Bay in '55 and never went back, but did do plenty of racing in the United States and Canada. He described the race course as basically a rectangle. He didn't remember where he started or even where he finished but he did remember the big water tower in town and the turn at the cemetery, and at least one car being in it. Bob says, "I had a good job; I was a tool and die maker and I had lots of vacation time. I raced at Harewood Acres, Canada, Grayling, Cumberland, Akron, Elkhart Lake and Mid-Ohio. I drove MGs, an Alfa, Sprite, Austin Healey, Jag 120 M and a front-engined Elva Formula Junior. I knew many drivers from Put-in-Bay including Harry Constant, Ralph Durbin, Chuck Dietrich and Chuck Stoddard. I raced against Stoddard in an Alfa one time but didn't win. His car was very fast. I had a car dealership for 25 years and my insurance wouldn't let me race, so I sponsored a few cars for other drivers."

The TDs were popular in 1955, with 13 of them entered, including the #34 car of Bob Beverly from Sandusky. "Chuck Dietrich taught me all I knew," he says, "but there were four TCs in that race and no way I could pass a TC with a TD. Their big 19-inch wheels gave them an advantage in top speed." Bob raced at Put-in-Bay, Cumberland, Akron and Milwaukee. Even his wife and sons raced. But his main interest was boating. A member of the Sandusky Yacht Club, he owned 13 boats over the years, including a fast Class E Scow, a 42-foot Chris Craft and a 45-foot Matthews, the latter two for cruising. "I've been on every lake except Superior," he notes.

At the finish of the MG race, Ron McConnell, the lawyer from Lakewood, was first; Ralph Durbin, of Birmingham, Michigan, was second; and Charlie Ellmers of Chagrin Falls was third. Harry Constant was sixth.

Race Two

The next race was for sedans, for those who did not own a sports car. The popular sedans of the day included Morris Minors, Volkswagens, Renault Dauphines and Simcas. John Comey told this story about one of the entries in the sedan race and the two guys who borrowed their mother's VW Beetle to go to the races: Once there they became caught up in the spirit of things and entered the Bug in the VW race. Both wanted to drive, so after each lap they would pull into the pits and change drivers. If you ever discover who they were, don't tell their mother.

As Joe Brown reported, "This was the fun race of the day, though maybe not particularly interesting from the spectator's standpoint. It was Hancock's race all the way. Hank Becker and Ralph Durbin in their VWs had a neat duel in the first few laps, but Hank's '55 passed the '54 and Ralph had to be contented with third place, though he nibbled on Becker's tailpipe all the way."

Leading another TF in the second race at Put-in-Bay in 1955 is Jack Wilson of Louisville, Ohio, in the #44 MG-TF (Bill Gorris).

At the end of the race, Jack Manting has won in his new Porsche Speedster. He even finished ahead of Chuck Dietrich in the Lester MG and Ed Hugus in the other Speedster (Bill Gorris).

Becker had been working for Jaguar Cleveland, and his employer wanted to get some exposure for VW. "We want you to drive it," they said. "Sure," replied Becker. So they took a new car, and mechanic John Moncur began the process of loosening it up. He told the parts gofer to drive it and never use fourth gear. He drove it home to Akron. But it was still way too tight. "You really want to make it run?" asked mechanic George Clark. "Then ask the owner if I can make it run."

"George put the car on the chassis dyno," says Becker, "and he took off the air cleaner. He poured most of a can of Boraxo drain cleaner into the engine. That really loosened it."

The Boraxo technique of engine preparation almost did the trick, since the finishing order, again, was Ed Hancock of Ypsilanti, Michigan, first; Hank Becker of Shaker Heights, Ohio, second; and Ralph Durbin third, all in VWs.

Race Three

Several interesting entries in this race were Ted Jayne in his MG-TF Special, Charlie Ellmers in the MG-TC borrowed from the Funny Face Auto Racing Team, Bob Shea—a great mechanic and a great driver, Michael Caparon—notorious for running his MG off the dock and into Lake Erie, former Siata driver Henry Dahl from Warren, Pennsylvania (in a TF), Dick Gent in his Siata Spyder, Chuck Dietrich in his new Lester MG and Ed Hugus in his Porsche Speedster. There were also two of the Crosley Hot Shot racing specials. One was entered by Norm Bradley, co-owner with Reed Andrews of the Fine Cars sports car

The third race on the 1955 schedule was the Volkswagen race. Here, ace MG driver Ralph Durbin, in the #20 VW, gets ready on the starting grid. Behind him in the #41 VW is Bill Pickrel from Dayton, Ohio. Over in the #47 VW is Herman Emmert of Cleveland. Bill Gorris knew Durbin and described him as "a nice guy, a good driver, but not as aggressive as some of the other drivers" (Bill Gorris).

garage on Carnegie Avenue. He previously owned a Jag 120 roadster and later owned a Fiat-Abarth Zagato coupe. The other Crosley was owned by Bert Lisicki of Cleveland. Bert had a store named Bert's Auto Parts, later Bert's and Son. His car was #50, not the usual #81 he had driven as a stock car at Sportsman's Park and Cloverleaf Speedway. He had driven stock cars in the 1940s and outboard-powered midget racers in the early fifties. His son Jim describes the way he got into sports car racing: "He had ten or fifteen Crosleys at the auto parts store and he decided to fix one up to race at Put-in-Bay. He took it up there in 1955. His friend, MG driver Ernie Dickens, went up there with him. But he rolled the car at Cemetery Turn. It's a wonder he wasn't hurt. When he brought the wrecked car back home and my mother saw it, that was the end of his racing! He went to several of the Indy races, and we went to Can Am races at Mid Ohio, too."

After racing the MG-TC, Chuck Dietrich bought a Lester MG from Don Marsh in Columbus. But he kept the MG. People sometimes confuse the MG-based cars of Harry Lester—and the famous Monkey Stable—with the cars of Brian Lister that came later (Lister Jaguar, Lister Corvette, etc.). This Lester had a prewar MG-TA frame with a Lester aluminum body and a new nose that Marsh had made of fiberglass. Ported and polished, with high compression pistons, the car ran with success in the F-Modified class. Chuck drove it in 1955 before selling it to Charlie Ellmers and the Funny Face Auto Racing Team, but that's another story.

Another interesting entrant was Jack Hannig from Wheeling, West Virginia. Listed on the entry sheet as Franz Hannig, he had a red Siata Spyder that he towed up through the hills of southern Ohio. This Siata was not the usual H-Modified variety but the faster G-Modified with an 1100-cc Fiat and two Weber carburetors. His nephew Bill Hannig, Jr., recalls his uncle's car hobby: "He had the first MG in Wheeling. It was made in the 1940s and had belts to hold the hood down. It was red with silver wire wheels and it had some car badges, which my brother still has. Then he had several Jags. He had a Porsche Carrera, which was his favorite car, and he had the Siata Spyder. All of these cars were red, his favorite color. He had a red car, a red trailer and a red tow car. He had a little symbol on the car of a green turtle on its back. It was holding a staff in its hand and drinking a mint julep. Jack used to go around to the races with a friend of his, Bunt Polack, also from Wheeling. He was the president of Marsh Wheeling Stogie Company—they made cigars. Another friend of his was Bill Cruise, who was the first VW dealer in Wheeling."

In the mid-fifties, Ed Hugus drove at the Put-in-Bay road races for four years: 1954 in a Triumph TR-2, 1955 in a Porsche Speedster, 1956 in a Porsche Spyder with his lucky number 13, and 1957 in an Alfa Giulietta Spider. In the 1956 race at Akron Airport, he drove a Porsche Spyder to a second place after Bob Fergus and ahead of Doc Wyllie in the Lotus. He also raced at Cumberland, Maryland, and was one of the founders of the Steel Cities Region of the Sports Car Club of America.

"In the third race," racing photographer Joe Brown related, "the Porsche Speedster of Jack Manting jumped to the fore and maintained that position, consistently lapping about

There's an advantage in your mother having a Volkswagen: when the Put-in-Bay races come up, you can borrow it for the day and nobody will be the wiser. That's what Don Black did in the 1955 'Bay races, and he had a great time (Don Black).

The feature race at Put-in-Bay in 1955 forms up in front of the Crescent bar, offering good food and beer. The #51 TR2 is Jim Brooks of Lansing, Michigan. The #28 TR2 is James Campbell of East Cleveland. TR2 #3 is race promoter Bob Lossman of Lossman Motors; beside him in the #24 MG-TC is Chuck Dietrich of Sandusky. The #43 Arnolt Bristol is Tom Payne (Bill Gorris).

Speeding by the hardware store is Ralph Ziegler in the handsome Doretti. What a great day for a race (Stu Kerr).

At speed down the front straight at Put-in-Bay in 1955 is Ben Hall of Willoughby, in his Morgan (Bill Gorris).

six seconds faster than his nearest competitor. Chuck Dietrich aboard his new Lester MG (1289 cc) finished first in class and directly behind Manting's Porsche." Ed Hugus from Pittsburgh was third, in another Porsche Speedster. The fourth-place car was Hank Dahl from Warren, Pennsylvania, in an MG-TF 1500. And Jack Hannig won his class in the GM Siata.

Fourth Race

"The big event of the day," said Joe Brown, "started with a field that included an AC Ace, a Doretti, an Arnolt Bristol, two Morgans driven by Ed Hebb and Ben Hall, three Triumphs, two blown MGs, a blown Porsche and an assortment of modified MGs, and the cars were paced by Peggy Wyllie in Phil Miller's ex–Fergus C Jag."

A Doretti was a Swallow Coachbuilder car with TR2 mechanicals. The Italianesque name was cooked up by Dorothy Deen, who was vice president of Cal Sales, Inc., the West Coast Triumph distributor, who collaborated with Swallow Coachbuilding to get the cars designed and produced. The name, combining the first part of her name and "etti," had been used as a signature on a line of sports car accessories in the late forties to early fifties. It was a nice-looking car that was reliable and reasonably fast, besting early Healeys on several occasions. According to Tom Householder of the Doretti Register, owner Ralph Ziegler, comptroller of a division of Blaw-Knox Corp., entered the car and drove it up from Pittsburgh.

And how did he get into racing the Doretti? Hap Ziegler, Ralph's son, remembers, "We first got a 1953 flat radiator, single-carburetor Morgan. The car was great fun and we, the family, enjoyed getting into the SCCA groove. My dad was bitten by the racing bug and entered the Morgan in several races. Frustrated by the performance (could not have been his driving, of course) and since he felt the Morgan was not competitive, he purchased the Doretti in late 1954 from European Motors of Pittsburgh, then located on Saw Mill Run Boulevard, later relocated to a Liberty Avenue site." From the racing records of Tom Householder, the Doretti ran at Put-in-Bay, Cumberland, Watkins Glen, and Sewickley (an SCCA-sponsored hill climb). Householder's son Herb notes, "I recall my dad saying he was retiring from racing because new rules required a roll bar and he didn't want to mess up the car. He had installed seat belts and had the engine balanced at a machine shop in Dayton, as I recall."

Ralph Ziegler's wife, Phyliss, won second place in the women's division at the 1955 Sewickley Hill Climb, driving the Doretti. As time went by, the two boys became the principal drivers of the Doretti. A few years after Ralph Sr.'s death in 1963, the car was sold.

The rapid AC Bristol of Joe Bojalad from Pittsburgh surprises the Porsche, and he drives off onto the side of the road. Bojalad went on to win the race overall (Lorrain Holder).

The blown Porsche was an interesting piece of work. It was the collaboration between owner Jack Uhr (listed in the entry forms as Earl A. Uhr) and crewman Art Brow. Art says, "Jack had a Porsche coupe and we wanted to make it faster. It had a 1500 engine and we decided to supercharge it. We used a Pepco supercharger. They were a Rootes-type blower, built in Akron. Then we decided to lighten up the car so we took off the doors, the hood and the engine hatch. We replaced those all with aluminum. The car was fast but it would have been nice if it handled better and had bigger brakes."

Another interesting entrant was Ben Hall in a Morgan. It was his first race; three years later he would win his class at Put-in-Bay driving an AC Ace. Siata and Alfa driver Chuck Stoddard has this one little recollection of Ben: "When I knew him, he had his own trucking company and ran nightly semi-loads from Cleveland to Chicago. One time I free-loaded a 10 p.m. ride in a semi with one of his drivers to Chicago, so I could pick up a car from Wacky Arnolt. They dropped me off in the bowels of Chicago at about 4:30 a.m. and I found my way. Sure wouldn't want to do that these days. Ben was racing a pre–Shelby AC with a Bristol engine—he asked me to co-drive his car with him in the Elkhart 500—about ½ way, the engine blew. I have not seen or heard from Ben in probably 40 years."

The Triumph TR2 of Jim Brooks led a couple of laps but spun on the slippery track, as his son Bob explains: "I was twelve years old at the time," he says:

> My dad led in the Triumph and then spun out. I was standing at cemetery corner and said to some bystanders, "That's my dad." But then he was back in 15th place, throwing hay out of the car while he was driving. In all, he spun three times.

The red AC Bristol of Joe Bojalad drives onto the ferry boat for the trip back home after winning the feature event at the 1955 Put-in-Bay road races (Joe Brown).

He raced sprint cars after the war—a Miller and an Offenhauser. Then he got an MG-TD and a TR2 and later a TR3. In the five or six years that he raced I followed him around. He went to Lockbourne, Watkins Glen and Akron Airport—I remember the Green Monster at the drag strip there. I remember Kimberly and Bill Spear in their big, fast Ferraris. We went to the Johnson Park hill climb in Grand Rapids—we were there with Jack Manting, Mike Ward, Dick Hall and some of the others. We had a sports car dealership, Brooks Imported Cars, and we took a

Bay race organizers Betty and Dick Henn on the ferryboat back to Marblehead after another successful event (collection of Betty Henn).

production MG-A off the floor for a race at Elkhart Lake. Dad's co-driver Pete Burgess was in gravel pit corner, forced off the road by a bigger, faster car and he rolled it. It was sad to see it all wadded up on the trailer; we were heartbroken. But back to Put-in-Bay, I remember the May flies there. At night at the gas station you could see them around the lights—millions of them.

The island roads were made of treacherous stuff. The surface was macadam, not asphalt. It was just tar and gravel. The more it warmed up, the more slippery it became. Many people spun on those roads.

Hebb's Morgan got out in front for two laps, only to be passed by Jack Uhr's blown Porsche. Then on the next lap, Chuck Dietrich in his famous number-24 supercharged TC took over for laps four and five. Joe Bojolad, riding the Ace for all it was worth, passed Dietrich and took over the lead for the balance of the race.

One of the more interesting cars in race four was the AC Ace driven by Joe Bojalad from Pittsburgh. It was the second one in the country. Joe says,

> When I was young I was enthusiastic about cars. I went to Watkins Glen and in 1952 I saw a car that was like a little Ferrari. I couldn't afford a Ferrari but I could afford this. In 1954 it cost 900 pounds, or about three thousand dollars. I ordered the car over the phone. They finished it in February, and it was the second one in the States. Some colonel had the first one. I raced it at Cumberland and met Carroll Shelby there. He was impressed by the car's handing. At this time, Ford was thinking of buying Ferrari. Ford sent its auditors to Ferrari, but Enzo kicked them out. As you know, most Italian companies have two sets of books. They didn't think it was any of Ford's business. After Shelby won Le Mans he got friendly with Iacocca. He conned the AC factory into stopping production, modifying the chassis and installing Ford 289 engines.
>
> At the 1955 race at Put-in-Bay, I almost left before the race. I didn't like the no-passing zones—they had two of them: one at Airport Corner and one at Cemetery Corner. I also didn't like my starting position, which was 13th. But I decided to stay. Soon I was behind Chuck Dietrich, about 40 feet behind. I was coming after him right near the airport. I had the lap record for several laps. I touched the hay bales going in and out of every turn. Near the corner, he hit the brakes and spun so I passed him. I went from last to first in five laps. I lapped the whole field.
>
> Then three laps from the end [of a 12-lap race], I started losing oil pressure. I had lapped everyone so I started to take it easy. At the end of the Cooper Straight, I looked in my mirror and saw a car. I assumed it was somebody I had lapped but little by little he was catching me. It was a red Porsche. After the last turn I put the car in neutral and shut off the engine. I had to save the engine and drive home to Pittsburgh. The Porsche didn't have enough to catch me.

He was right. At the finish, it was Joe Bojalad, AC Ace, first; Jack Manting, Porsche Speedster, second; and Bob Lossman, Triumph, third.

When the races were over, it was always nice to go back to the pits for a last look at the cars. You could feel the heat from their engines. You could smell their mechanical smells. This is the kind of thing that wouldn't matter to a lot of people now, but it mattered then.

Postscript: Joe Bojalad appeared as a special guest at the 2012 Put-in-Bay sports car race reunion. He talked a little about his experiences at the Put-in-Bay race, and then the organizers brought his son Joey out; he presented Joe with his old AC Ace. His son had located the car and managed to purchase it as a gift to his father. It had been through several owners and was even stolen once. But now it was back with Joe at Put-in-Bay.

June 18, 1955, Entry List

First Race

10:30 a.m., 10 laps (31 miles),
all MG class G, to 1300 cc and modified to TF 54 specs

Car	Driver	Address	Make	Displ. CC
1	Ted Jayne	Cleveland, Ohio	MG-TD	1250
2	Charlie Ellmers	Chagrin Falls, Ohio	MG-TC	1250
6	Ronald McConnell	Lakewood, Ohio	MG-TD	1250
7	Robert Rippel	Avon Lake, Ohio	MG-TD	1250
8	Michael Caparon	Cleveland, Ohio	MG-TD	1250
9	Ralph Cadwallader	Cleveland, Ohio	MG-TC	1250
12	E.H. Polack, II	Wheeling, W. Va.	MG-TC	1250
15	John P. Curran, M.D.E.	Cleveland, Ohio	MG-TD	1250
18	Jim Dever	Cleveland, Ohio	MG-TC	1250
19	Alan W. Hess	Westlake, Ohio	MG-TD	1250
21	Ralph Durbin	Birmingham, Mich.	MG-TF	1250
29	Dale Smith	Canal Fulton, Ohio	MG-Mk. II	1250
33	Thomas Kramer	Huron, Ohio	MG-TD	1250
34	Robert Beverly	Sandusky, Ohio	MG-TD	1250
36	Orlie Ward	Lincoln Park, Mich.	MG-TF	1250
40	Harry Constant	Grosse Pointe, Mich.	MG-TD	1250
45	Malcolm Boardman	Detroit, Mich.	MG-TD	1250
46	Bob Barsantee, Jr.	Ann Arbor, Mich.	MG-TD	1250
161	Mike Ward, Jr.	Lansing, Mich.	MG-TD	1250

Second Race

11:15 a.m., 10 laps (31 miles), Stock Volkswagens only, Class G

Car	Driver	Address	Make	Displ. CC
17	Charlie Ellmers	Chagrin Falls, Ohio	VW	1192
20	Ralph Durbin	Birmingham, Mich.	VW	1160
27	Ralph Wilson, Jr.	Princeton, N.J.	VW	1182
41	William G. Pickrel, Jr.	Dayton, Ohio	VW	1192
42	Edward Hancock	Ypsilanti, Mich.	VW	1192
47	Herman Emmert	Cleveland, Ohio	VW	1192
48	Hank Becker	Shaker Heights, Ohio	VW	1192

Third Race

1:15 p.m. 8 laps (24.8 miles),
Class H, up to 750 cc; G 751 to 1300 cc; F 1301 to 1500 cc;
unsupercharged but may be modified

Car	Driver	Address	Make	Displ. CC
1	Ted Jayne	Cleveland, Ohio	MG TF-spec.	1250
2	Charlie Ellmers	Chagrin Falls, Ohio	MG-TC	1250
4	Ronald Kehl	Cleveland, Ohio	MG-TF	1250
5	Bob Shea	Cleveland, Ohio	MG-TC	1250

Car	Driver	Address	Make	Displ. CC
8	Mike Caparon	Cleveland, Ohio	MG	1250
11	Jack Arter	Marion, Ohio	Porsche Amer.	1488
13	J. Edward Hugus	Pittsburgh, Penn.	Porsche Speeds.	1486
14	Franz Hannig	Wheeling, W. Va.	Siata Spyder	1098
26	Norman Bradley	Euclid, Ohio	Crosley	748
29	Dale Emich	Canal Fulton, Ohio	MG MKII	1250
30	Dick Gent	Cleveland, Ohio	Siata	742
31	Chuck Dietrich	Sandusky, Ohio	Lester MG	1289
32	Pete Kramer	Sandusky, Ohio	Porsche Amer.	1500
35	Dane Burgess	Ada, Mich.	MG	1299
37	Harry Rice	Columbus, Ohio	Allard 21G	1490
38	Dick Gates	Cleveland, Ohio	Gates	1299
39	Jack Manting	Big Rapids, Mich.	Porsche Speeds.	1499
44	Jack Wilson	Louisville, Ohio	MG-TF	1466
50	Bert Lisicki	Cleveland, Ohio	Crosley	749

Fourth Race

1:45 p.m. 12 laps (37.2 miles),
up to 1500 cc supercharged; 1501–2000 unsupercharged

Car	Driver	Address	Make	Displ. CC
3	Bob Lossman	Rocky River, Ohio	Triumph	1991
10	Ralph Ziegler	Pittsburgh, Penn.	Doretti	1991
22	Edwin E. Hebb, Jr.	Pontiac, Mich.	Morgan	1991
23	Ben Hall	Willoughby, Ohio	Morgan	1991
24	Chuck Dietrich	Sandusky, Ohio	MG TC	1466
25	Earl H. Uhr	Lakewood, Ohio	Porsche	1488
28	James Campbell	E. Cleveland, Ohio	Triumph TR2	1991
43	Thomas Payne	Ypsilanti, Mich.	Arnolt Bristol	1992
44	Theodore Kessel	Louisville, Ohio	MG TF	1466
49	Herbert Kouns	Columbus, Ohio	MG TC	1376
51	Jim Brooks	Lansing, Mich.	Triumph TR2	1991
55	Joe Bojalad	Pittsburgh, Penn.	AC Ace	1991

Put-in-Bay 1955 Results

First Race

10 laps (31 miles), all-MG race;
G to 1300 cc and modified to TF-54 specs

1. Ron McConnell, Lakewood   MG
2. Ralph Durbin, Birmingham, Mich.   MG
3. Charlie Ellmers, Chagrin Falls, Ohio   MG

Second Race

10 laps (31 miles), H-Mod, G-Mod, F-Prod

1. Jack Manting, Big Rapids, Mich.   Porsche Speedster
2. Chuck Dietrich, Sandusky, Ohio   Lester MG
3. Ed Hugus, Pittsburgh   Porsche Speedster

Third Race

8 laps (24.8 miles), stock Volkswagens

1. Ed Hancock, Ypsilanti, Mich.   VW
2. Hank Becker, Shaker Heights, Ohio   VW
3. Ralph Durbin, Birmingham, Mich.   VW
4. Don Black, Ypsilanti, Mich.   VW

Fourth Race

12 laps (37.2 miles), up to 1500 supercharged; 1501 to 2000 unsupercharged

1. Joe Bojalad   AC Ace
2. Jack Manting   Porsche Speedster (late entry)
3. Bob Lossman   Triumph
4. Ted Kessel   MG-TF
5. Chuck Dietrich   MG-TC s/c
6. Jim Brooks   TR2
7. Herbert Kouns   MG-TC s/c
8. Ralph Ziegler   Doretti
9. Tom Payne   Arnolt-Bristol
10. Ben Hall   Morgan
11. Ed Hebb   Morgan
12. Jim Campbell   Triumph
13. Jack Uhr   Porsche s/c

1500 cc = about 90 cubic inches.
Source: Entry list from John Comey.

CHAPTER 7

1956: A Likeable Little Race

June 9, 1956

What people liked about Put-in-Bay was the atmosphere. There was just nothing like it. I've been to about 30 racing venues—road courses, airport courses and purpose-built circuits—and there was nothing like Put-in-Bay. Between the races, you could walk across the track to the paddock and look the cars over—those cars that were so intriguing, cars you'd never seen before: Siatas, Bandinis, AC Bristols, Porsche Spyders; the list goes on. People were working on them; they had the hoods or engine hatches open. When there was a break in the activity, you'd venture a question: "How fast will it go?" The owner of an MG would reply, "Ours will do about 78 miles an hour." Now it doesn't seem like much, but then it seemed perfectly reasonable.

In comparison to my generation, graduating from high school in 1956, most of the drivers were ten or fifteen years older. They all had their college educations by then. Many had been in World War II. In combat. We didn't know it then, but only a few years prior to this wonderful race they had been huddled down in foxholes, in a stinking jungle or German forest, popping up once in awhile to take a shot with their M1 rifles. Or fending off a kamikaze attack on a ship out in the Pacific. Or flying cover for bombers on a mission–the fighter planes that the bomber crews used to call "our little friends."

All of the races were memorialized with a brass dash plaque like this one. They measured 3" × 1½" and were usually riveted to the instrument panel of your car. This one, from Cal Gleason, says "driver"; there were others for the race officials (Cal Gleason).

If they were lucky, they made it home from that. Not like the 9,000 of the First Marine Division killed on Peleliu in 1944. Close to their last moments on earth had been spent at a Bob Hope show that he put on for them at Banika Island before the attack. Hope said, "They were people starved for a normal life and a little entertainment." His show schedule was particularly heavy in December, when he would end each one by saying, "Have a Merry Christmas and God bless you."

Betty Henn pours on the steam in her Jag XK140 pace car to bring the MG field up to speed (Stu Kerr).

Here were the survivors, back in the States and in civilian jobs—they were engineers or car salesmen or stockbrokers—and they had these little cars and they were racing other little cars, and having the time of their lives. You could sense this, and you knew even at the time that it was temporary and something very, very special.

And then it came time for their race. Let's say it was the Porsche-MGA race. As the MG T-series race finished, they would shut the hoods of their cars, put on their helmets—such as they were—and get ready to go to the starting grid, according the positions they had drawn by lot.

They would form up out on the course, behind the pace car. Five-minute gun, one-minute gun, then off behind that pace car, and when they came by the start-finish they would get the green. The adrenaline would kick in, and off they would go.

The First Race

The first race on the schedule at Put-in-Bay in 1956—the MG race—was an all-star list of drivers. Harry Constant was in his TD. It was his second race; he would later go on to a Siata and an Alfa at the 'Bay, a borrowed Morgan at Road America and a long career as a Detroit race official, including the Formula One race. In 1956, Harry had trouble with the TD. His pit crew had put the leads on the wrong plugs and the engine ran roughly. By the time they figured it out, the race had already started. Bill Staufer was a well-known mechanic at Lossman Motors on Cleveland's west side, and a very fine driver. Doc Curran, with his MG-TD, was just beginning to race, and would later drive Porsche, Alfa and Elva. Chuck

The MG race is bunched up in the early laps, going through Cemetery Turn. In the first race of 1956, 24 cars took the green flag (Stu Kerr).

As the field opens up, we see only three cars at Cemetery Turn. The racing surface there was a slippery macadam and some cars, such as the one of the left, failed to achieve the necessary adhesion and went, as if drawn by a magnet, through the hay bales and into the graveyard (Stu Kerr).

Henry was an outstanding driver in his TC. Ted Jayne and Charlie Ellmers were co-conspirators in the Funny Face Auto Racing Team. Art Brow was another outstanding driver. Ralph Durbin from Detroit had been the MG national champion. Cal Gleason, also from Detroit, was a very experienced driver, as was Ralph Cadwallader of Cleveland, with his TC. Then there was Ronald McConnell, the lawyer from Lakewood in his blue MG-TD.

Prior to competing in wheel-to-wheel races, Bill Staufer ran his 1953 MG-TD in several hillclimbs. These included Sewickley, Pennsylvania, and the Ohio hillclimbs at Milan, Lucas, Youngstown, Boston Mills and Akron. His wife Pat recalls that he also competed in the 2nd and 3rd annual Old Smokey hillclimbs in Pennsylvania, and in the 1st, 4th and 5th annual hillclimbs at Mohawk near Youngstown, Ohio. Art Brow quips: "They are housing developments now." In 1956 Bill Staufer began racing at the legendary Put-in-Bay races. He also raced there in 1957, 1958 and 1959.

MG-TF pilot Ralph Durbin was known around the Detroit Region SCCA as the World's Fastest Bus Driver. Besides driving a Greyhound, he drove a variety of cars, and all of them well. He was 3rd nationally in F Production in 1954, with his MG in the Porsche class. He was 5th nationally in G Production in 1955, with his MG-TF. He was 3rd nationally in 1956, still with an MG, in the Alfa class. Then he got an Alfa and slipped to 22nd in points in 1957. He only raced a couple of races with the Alfa. He sold it to Ken Askew that year. The rest of the season was with an Austin-Healey, 23rd in D Production. Then he went back to 3rd nationally in 1958, again with an Austin-Healey. He got an 8th in E Production in an Arnolt Bristol in 1959. In 1960 he was 3rd in an Arnolt Bristol in D Production. Then, in 1961, he was 4th in C Production in an Arnolt Bristol, and he seemed to get out of racing after that.

The #19 MG-TD of Jack Wilson from Louisville, Ohio, cruises down Cooper Straight, past the stores before town and past tufts of hay that have sacrificed themselves to this event (Stu Kerr).

Heading out of town is the #41 MG-TC of longtime Put-in-Bay racer Ralph Cadwallader (collection of Ralph Cadwallader).

In the #40 TD, Cal Gleason had a number of interesting road cars, including a Vignale-bodied 4.1 Ferrari Mexico, one of three coupes; the one roadster had been raced by Bill Spear. The coupes were raced in the Panamerican road race by Chinetti, Viloresi and Ascari. Cal's car was s/n 0224, the Chinetti car. Number 0226 had been recently restored by the Marriott family, and brought a sale price of $3,685,000 at the 2011 RM Auctions. The no. 0228 car is in California with a Chevy engine, last he heard. Cal had two other Ferraris, a 1961 250GT with a Farina body (not a short-wheelbase) and a 1965 275 GTB coupe.

As if all this were not enough, Gleason had a lifelong affinity for Corvette, having bought his first one in 1953. He had 17 of them in all, including a blue 1965 coupe that he used to surprise the owner of a short-wheelbase Ferrari. "What have you got in that car?" asked the Ferrari driver. He couldn't believe that the car was stock. But it had a fuel injection engine and a 4:01 rear axle ratio—the last year for FI, the first year for disc brakes.

Chuck Henry in his well-prepared MG-TC was building a reputation as a very fast driver. In '56, the Bellevue, Ohio, resident ran the Put-in-Bay road race. In the #6 TC, he competed against well-known area drivers including national champion Ralph Durbin, Detroiter Harry Constant, Cal Gleason, Bill Staufer, Charlie Ellmers and Art Brow. However, hampered by a poor grid position (drawn out of a hat, as was the custom), he was unable to move up to the front before the end of the 10-lap race.

During the years that the Put-in-Bay road races were run, very few of the area residents were among the spectators. The people of Sandusky, Port Clinton, Huron, Norwalk, Belle-

The aluminum-bodied H-Modified Special of John Allen sits in the paddock, awaiting its turn in the second race (Stu Kerr).

vue, etc., were usually just interested in being on beautiful Sandusky Bay in the summer—whether fishing, water-skiing, sailing or just cruising around. For the most part, they only liked racing if it was circle track; Keith Kreager of Lakeland Import Auto in Sandusky notes that the only kind of racing they liked was the stock car tracks at Fremont and Sandusky Speedway. The popular drag strip in Norwalk had not been built yet. In the north-central Ohio area there were only two drivers of note: Chuck Dietrich of Sandusky and Chuck Henry of Bellevue. Two other drivers would have been Robert Beverly (TD) and Paul Woodruff (TF), both of Sandusky. But after '56 they never raced again.

Although he started from the second-to-last row, Art Brow managed to work his way up to third by the end of the 10-lap event. Second was Chuck Henry's TC and first was Ralph Durbin in his TF. And the other Detroit driver, Cal Gleason? "I started eighth," he quips, "and I finished eighth." Of Put-in-Bay, Cal said, "That place was a pain to get to. But it was my favorite race."

The Cleveland Sport Car Club kept adding new race workers. One of them was Bob Morrison, who explains how he got into it: "I had just finished saving democracy on the Korean peninsula, finished my USAF enlistment with 6 months in SAC and went to work for GE at Nela Park. I bought a '51 MGTD from Jaguar Cleveland in July '55 and traded it for a new '56 TR3 from Bob Lossman the next year. About that time I started attending CSCC meetings. Went to my first PiB that year with no idea what I was getting into. They gave me a flag and posted me at the sweeping left-hander at the end of the straight into town from the cemetery, with directions to keep spectators away from the outside of the corner. Talk about the blind leading the blind. But nonetheless, I was hooked."

The Second Race

The second race, for H-Modified cars, had a small field—only ten cars. George Durbin from Detroit drove a Renault. George was the brother of Ralph Durbin, the MG racing champion. We don't know if his Renault was the high-tech Alpine or a garden-variety Dauphine. William Pickrel was a Volkswagen dealer from Dayton who also drove a Renault. Clevelander Dick Yares had a Bandini, of course, from Tony Pompeo in New York. This car made the rounds to Mel Sachs, who drove it to a national championship. and then to Jim Eichenlaub, who drove it to a 1958 second in national points before winning the 1959 championship in a 750 OSCA sponsored by the Stop-n-Shop grocery chain. Ted Kessell was notorious for a car they called "the Screen Door Special." It was basically a Crosley Hot Shot with the body replaced by door screen stretched over a frame, plastered and painted. It was much lighter than the stock Crosley. It was entered as the Kessel-Taylor, with a 730-cc engine. Then there was a pair of Crosley-powered Siata Spyders. One belonged to Chuck Stoddard and the other to Joe Blaser, who was at the time a counterman at European Automotive on Mayfield Road—a treasure trove of hard-to-get parts for obscure imports. Joe later worked at Stoddard Import Motors. Three other Crosley specials wrapped up the entry.

Stoddard came by his Siata in this convoluted way: When he was a student at MIT, he got an MG-TD. In his senior year of college he raced it several times at Thompson Raceway in Connecticut. He liked it, but it wasn't quite the car he wanted, so in 1956 he got a Siata, a racing car from a character at Wright-Patterson Air Force Base, where he was an aircraft maintenance officer. This was a lightweight machine with no engine that Chuck finished off with a tuned Crosley engine and a set of Stewart Warner gauges.

The second race starts off rather normally, with Chuck Stoddard in his Siata Spider, seen here diving into the corner into town (Joe Brown).

In the second race, the Kessel-Taylor Special of Ted Kessel unexpectedly rolls at Cemetery Turn (Stu Kerr).

By now Ted Kessel's car is completely upside down, the corner worker quickly brings out the red flag to stop the race, and bystanders run to help the driver (Stu Kerr).

Avoiding yet another accident at Cemetery Corner, Chuck Stoddard finishes the 10-lap race in first place and collects his victory flag at the start-finish line (collection of Chuck Stoddard).

The little black car was decorated with a Tweety Bird cartoon and successfully raced at the Put-in-Bay and Akron airport sports car races. Stoddard drove to a first in H-Modified at the 'Bay in '56 and a second in '57. He recalled, "I would get up at 4 a.m. in Willoughby, drive to Marblehead, go over on the boat to Put-in-Bay, go through tech inspection, practice, drive the race and get back on the boat. It made a pretty full day."

The Bandini, one of the more promising cars in the race, did not finish. Joe Blaser, in the other Siata, was a good guy but not a great driver. The second-place car, we think, was Ted Kessel in his Crosley special, and the third was John Allen in another Crosley special.

The Third Race

As usual, there was an interesting cast of characters in the third race. It was the first race that Charlie Ellmers ever drove in the Lester MG he and the Funny Face Auto Racing Team had bought from Chuck Dietrich.

The Funny Face Auto Racing Team (FFART, for short) included Meach and Ben Hitchcock, Frank Floyd, Ted Jayne and Charlie Ellmers. The team had been running a TD and a TC. Ted and Charlie later drove the Lester at venues including Watkins Glen, Akron Airport, Cumberland and Dunkirk. Charlie also drove the Giants Despair hillclimb near Brynfan Tyddyn. The wives were enthusiastic supporters of the team. "We were married on the Ides of March," says Ruth Ellmers, "and we went to the 1958 Sebring race for our honeymoon.

Preparing for the third race at the 1955 Put-in-Bay event are Don Black, foreground, putting numbers on his Siata Spyder, and Jack Downey, whose striped Alfa coupe will be driven by Ken Askew (collection of Don Black).

Early in the third race, with starting positions drawn from a hat, Bob Shea's TC leads the pack, followed by two more MGs and a Porsche (Joe Brown).

Two Porsche Speedsters pursue the Lester MG of Charlie Ellmers in the third race (Stu Kerr).

At the end of the race I was almost run over by Stirling Moss." Ruth adds, "We were true MG aficionados. Over the years we had three T-series MGs and three B-series MGs."

People confuse the Lesters with the Listers of Brian Lister, which usually had Jaguar or Corvette engines and were built a few years later. This one was built by Harry Lester and had an MG 1250 XPAG engine in a prewar MG-TA frame with a light aluminum body. It was thought to be one of the original Monkey Stable cars raced back in the mother country. Don Marsh had it before Dietrich and put a different nose on it. Ellmers and the others replaced the cycle fenders with ones of fuller shape, molded out of fiberglass. It looked like a different car.

Having sold the Lester MG and not yet bought an Elva, Chuck Dietrich drove his old supercharged MG-TC this year.

FFART in the new car was rewarded by an almost-first-place by Charlie in the modified race at the 'Bay, according to Meach Hitchcock. After coming from last place, he was leading the final race when he had to retire with an overheated engine. Moral to the pit crew: the oil reserve tank was put there for a purpose.

Bob Shea, the Lossman Motors service manager, was there with his MG-TC. Very few better prepared TCs were on the track. For this driver, it was his last race. Bob Shea was consistently fast in the MG-TC that he tuned himself, expertly. After the 1956 race, Bob's doctor told him, "You've got to stop racing, Bob. That shrapnel you have in your back could move up and, if it does, you'll be paralyzed." Bob was a veteran of the Battle of the Bulge and had some souvenirs of the experience. After that, Bob still stayed in racing but he had other people driving his cars, which included the TC, a Sprite and, later, a Lotus Formula Junior.

Michael Caparon was there with his MG-TD. He lived in Cleveland at the time and later moved to Detroit. Caparon was notorious for driving off the south dock in his MG into Lake Erie. He claimed the mayflies made the dock slick. Walter Kern trailered his G-Modified Siata Spyder all the way from Boston. Don Black drove his 1089-cc Siata (s/n ST*446*BC) down from Detroit. It was later featured on the first Bob Colazzi poster of the Put-in-Bay road race reunion.

"I found out about the Put-in-Bay race through the Michigan Sports Car Club," Don says. He continues,

> In 1956, we didn't have anywhere to race, so we went down into Ohio and into Canada—we raced at Harewood Acres too. But the Michigan club later built Waterford Hills and set up the Oakland County Sportsman's Club. A friend of mine, Ed Lawrence, did a lot of the work on that. Ken Askew was also in that race. For a few years there he was a minister, with two parishes in southern Michigan. He drove an Alfa that he borrowed from Jack Downey. He originally drove a TC. I have a picture of him with the Alfa and me with my Siata taken while they were loading cars on the ferry boat. We

Ken Askew powers out of Cemetery Corner in the Alfa coupe entered by Jack Downey, ahead of an MG-A (collection of Don Black).

would usually put the car on the ferry and then fly over in the Ford Tri-Motor. They had three or four of those planes and used them to fly children over to school in Sandusky and fly grapes over to the mainland.

That was a great event, a small version of Watkins Glen—actually nicer than Watkins Glen. But there was that odd turn at the cemetery—if you made a mistake all they needed was a shovel.

There were several other Michigan drivers. Jack Manting was a Porsche dealer in Big Rapids, over near Lake Michigan. He had a 550 Spyder. Chuck Sherman was a customer of Tom Payne's, and he drove a Porsche Speedster. Ed Hancock was from Ypsilanti, and he drove Tom's Speedster. Another customer was Eugene Annabel, also driving a Speedster and also a customer of Payne's. All those people had yellow racing stripes that went from side to side over the front of the car. It was actually lane marking tape. It was a club called the Ypsilanti Yachting, Road Racing and Marching Society. They had a crest for it on their helmets, those cardboard helmets we used.

The last driver I want to mention was Tom Hallock, driving an MG-TF. I knew him well. The next year he got a Cooper Bobtail with a Coventry Climax engine. He was entered in a race at the Graying Airport but couldn't get there on Saturday. He asked if I would trailer the car up and get it qualified. I wore his driving suit and his helmet and got the car qualified. Then he came up on Sunday and raced it.

That Cooper, by the way, had been driven at Le Mans the previous year and was sold to him by the driver, Ed Hugus. With co-driver John Bentley, they finished a remarkable eighth overall.

Racing in the same class as the Tom Hallock and Ralph Durbin MG-TFs was Charles Allen in the #66 Siata Gran Sport, a car later bought by the author. These cars were

Charlie Ellmers hits the corner at the Colonial Ballroom, coming into town (Joe Brown).

unmatched for handling but were somewhat underpowered for their weight. The best finish for a Gran Sport was a third overall at Sebring in 1952—a long race on a long course. Mr. Allen did not fare as well.

Another contestant in the third race was Alfa driver Ken Askew. "I had a red Giulietta coupe with silver stripes," Ken says. "It was borrowed from Jack Downey. The night before the race, I took Ralph Durbin around the course in the Alfa to show him that it was the car to beat in the 1300 class. Ralph won the MG race the next day, but I had a faster time than his in the third race. I used 7000 for the redline. Later in 1956, Ralph got an Alfa dealership, which included four Giuliettas. After the race, I did not go back to Put-in-Bay. I drove in Canada. I went to Harewood Acres in Don Black's Siata in 1956. I drove my own Alfa in 1957, I drove an MG in 1958 and I drove a Chrysler Allard in 1959."

Ken adds,

> Your comment about classing by displacement was interesting according to my experience. I entered a 1300 Production Alfa [coupe] and requested that I could be put in the race with the 1300 MGs. I was then notified by the organizers that I had a sedan and must run in that class (with VWs, of which there were many).
>
> Then there were practice sessions. On the downhill toward the airport I was able to hit about 100 mph. I passed a couple of VWs at that speed. After the practice session, I was moved into 1300 Modified. In the 1300 Modified race I finished second to Chuck Deitrich, but we also were in with the 1500 Production cars; we beat two MGAs and all but three of the Porsches, including some Sports Car Ypsilanti customers.
>
> What made it especially satisfying was the Ed Hancock (a co-owner of SCY) had told Jack Downey that the Alfa was a pretty little car, but would never be a good race car. Jack was angry

Jack Manting's Porsche Spyder took the win in the third race at Put-in-Bay in 1955 (Joe Brown).

Sitting in the paddock waiting for its race is the lucky #13 Porsche Spyder of Ed Hugus from the Pittsburgh Steel Cities Region of SCCA (Stu Kerr).

about that and also that when asked about putting yellow stripes on the car, like others from Detroit (to look like Ralph Durbin, Tom Payne), Tom Payne refused to accept Jack as qualified to use the yellow stripes.

We had a lot of interesting little issues going in those days. Don Black and I have had many pleasant evenings in retrospect of the times. David E. Davis sold me an Austin A-40 Sports that started the relationship with Don. But, that is another story. It was a fun time.

The finishing order for the third race was Jack Manting first, Charlie Ellmers second, Chuck Dietrich third, Ken Askew fourth and Ralph Durbin fifth. The program announced, "Following this race there will be an intermission of one hour." This gave the corner crews and drivers time to get a bit to eat, and it gave the spectators and their friends an opportunity to get over to Heineman's Winery. They say the island's soil and climate are perfect for growing grapes—and wines of the Ohio islands are rated high among domestic *fermenti*.

The Fourth Race

Entrants of note in the fourth race included Tom Payne in the #54 Arnolt Bristol. "Tom was a dealer for Wacky Arnolt of Chicago," Don Black says. "The car was light and well-prepared and Tom was an excellent driver, so it just flew. Ed Lawrence was driving a Morgan that year and it might have been that Canadian car that Don Broadbent prepared. It wasn't completely stock—none of those Canadian cars were. Bill Bradley was there with his Siata 208S. It was a beautiful car. He bought it from an architect, Howard Preston in Birmingham. Bill was a good driver but he didn't push the car. He didn't want to damage it.

The starting grid for the feature race included modified cars up to 1500 cc, 2-liter production cars, and the winners of previous races. Seen are the #62 Morgan, #63 supercharged MG-TC, #20 AC Ace, numerous Triumphs and one Porsche Spyder (Lorrain and Manfreid Holder).

"Norman Wintermude is on the entry list too. He was a friend of Tom Payne's and he drove a TR2. There was a story that he had been a monk, but I don't know how true that is. He was quite a skirt-chaser in 1956. Mike Ward came down from Lansing to race at the 'Bay. He drove an MG-TD but later had a Speedster."

There were quite a few Triumphs in the race this year. Another of the TR2s was driven by Reed Andrews of Cleveland Heights. He'd gotten interested in racing in 1955. He and his wife Barbara were vacationing in Canada in their Austin-Healey, and they drove up to Harewood Acres, where they saw a sports car race. "It was in the pouring rain," Reed recalls, "and I said to myself, I'm going to come back here and race." With such an inviting setting, who could resist it? In 1956, Reed bought a TR2, and he did race at Harewood Acres. Then he raced at Watkins Glen and then at Put-in-Bay. He soon learned the ins and outs of racing: "That mechanic who worked for Lossman, what's his name? Quay Barber—he would bump you off the course."

The fourth race was a 12-lap event, with Ed Hugus coming in first in the red #13 Porsche Spyder, Tom Payne coming in second in the #54 Arnolt Bristol and Ben Hall of Willoughby coming in third in his #20 AC Ace. "Ben Hall was a great driver," Reed Andrews remarked. In fourth place was Chuck Dietrich in his #24 MG-TC, behind the four-cam Porsche and the Bristol-engined cars.

Final Notes

The 1956 Put-in-Bay race followed the inaugural race at Road America the previous year. Then, in '56, the new Watkins Glen course—the permanent course that would essentially be the current one—became a reality and held its first race. The energy and excitement that Put-in-Bay was a part of would help to create racing venues the following year at Lime Rock, Connecticut; Bridgehampton; Virginia International Raceway; and Riverside, California. It was part of a growth in the sport that would soon create Waterford Hills, Michigan; Wilmot Hills, Illinois; Blackhawk Farms, Illinois; and Brainerd, Minnesota.

CS 80

For those interested in the minutiae of the racing, there was a nine-point list of driver requirements that the race committee posted at most of the Put-in-Bay races. As supplied by race worker Bob Satava, here they are, with a few remarks:

1. All drivers must attend drivers' meeting—any driver who absents himself from meeting may be summarily disqualified. [At the drivers' meeting, important new information was mentioned by the race chairman. This might include warnings that some of the pavement was crumbling or to be careful not to go into the filling station and hit a gas pump.]
2. Pump fuel only may be used. Fuel in winning cars is subject to analysis. [Some of the cars, not to mention whose, were inclined to use alcohol fuel or AvGas. These were the same ones that used Castrol-R oil to mask the characteristic smell of AvGas or alcohol.]

Battling it out for an E-Production lead is Tom Payne with his #54 Arnolt Bristol, followed by a Morgan (collection of John Payne).

Making the turn at Colonial Ballroom is Ed Hugus and his lucky number 13 Porsche Spyder (Joe Brown).

3. Cars finishing 1, 2, and 3 in any race are subject to inspection at the discretion of the race committee. [Even in the early days of the sport, there were certain contestants who would take advantage with a higher compression ratio, a non-stock camshaft or larger carburetor venturis. The top three finishers were awarded trophies, and the organizers wanted to make sure they were legal.]
4. Helmets and goggles of accepted quality must be worn. Safety belts are required and must be fastened securely to car. [The helmets of the day, such as Cromwell helmets or the notorious Machpi helmets, which some believed were made of cardboard, would have to serve until the helmets tested by the Snell Foundation arrived on the scene. The goggles were reasonable good. Either they were war surplus—same thing the bomber crews and fighter pilots had worn—or they were real racing goggles from Europe. The main concern about seat belts was that they be supported in a wide area underneath the car so they wouldn't pull though under stress.]
5. No individual who has been drinking on day of race will be permitted to compete or to frequent the pit area. [Self evident: Who wants to be out on the track with someone who has been drinking alcohol?]
6. Only drivers will be permitted in car during practice and race session except with express permission of the chief starter. [The organizers wanted the drivers who were listed in the entries as responsible to be the only ones driving. A logical exception would be if a mechanic needed to drive the car in practice to dope out some problem ... or for a would-be purchaser to test the car at racing speeds. Leaving this decision to the chief starter was an excellent idea since, if it were the race chairman, it might not be possible to find him on short notice.]

7. Pit crews will be limited to three in addition to driver. [That's certainly a fair number.]
8. No advertising will be permitted on competing car or clothing of crew or driver. [The idea here was to emphasize the importance of the Corinthian sportsman and de-emphasize commercialism in racing. In point of fact, however, many of the entrants were car dealers or somehow connected to the car business. They didn't have to have a sign on their car, because everybody knew who they were, and if they were racing as a dealer that was an extra plus—not only were they supporting the organizing club but also they were endowed with extra abilities that would ultimately benefit the customer.]
9. All cars and crews must present a neat and clean appearance. [The organizers did not want cars with ersatz paint jobs or dents, and the spectators preferred not to see them either. So most of the cars looked as though they had just come out of the showroom.]

This is what they're all driving for—the golden trophy of the racing driver. In this case, it's the one earned by Chuck Stoddard for his win in the Siata Spyder (Chuck Stoddard).

The Cleveland Sport Car Club was a great organization to run these races. They were really ahead of the Sports Car Club of America at that point in time. They had an A-1 race, with frequent flag stations, a very fine communications system, good safety regulations and management that was thorough but fair.

June 9, 1956, Entry List

First Race

10:15 a.m., 10 laps (31 miles), all MG;
class G to 1300 cc and modified to TF 54 specs

Car	Driver	Address	Make	Disp. cc
2	Harry Constant	Grosse Pointe, Mich.	MG-TD	1250
3	William R. Staufer	Parma, Ohio	MG-TD	1250
4	John P. Curran, M.D.	Cleveland, Ohio	MG-TD	1250
6	Charles A. Henry	Bellevue, Ohio	MG-TC	1250
8	Ted Jayne	Cleveland, Ohio	MG-TD	1250
9	Charlie Ellmers	Chagrin Falls, Ohio	MG-TC	1250
12	Thomas K. Kramer	Huron, Ohio	MG-TD	1250
15	Art Brow	Cleveland, Ohio	MG-TC	1250
19	Jack Wilson	Louisville, Ohio	MG-TD	1250
21	Allan W. Hess	Westlake, Ohio	MG-TD	1250
22	Ralph Durbin	Detroit, Mich.	MG-TF	1250

Car	Driver	Address	Make	Disp. cc
25	Richard J. Kennedy	Detroit, Mich.	MG-TF	1250
33	Robert H. Beverly	Sandusky, Ohio	MG-TD	1250
35	Paul Woodruff	Sandusky, Ohio	MG-TF	1250
40	Calvin R. Gleason	Detroit, Mich.	MG-TD	1250
41	Ralph S. Cadwallader	Cleveland, Ohio	MG-TC	1250
44	Orlie C. Ward	Lincoln Park, Mich.	MG-Mk. II	1250
49	James F. Dever	Lorain, Ohio	MG-TC	1250
53	Fred Reynolds	Irwin, Pa.	MG-TD	1250
55	Ronald H. McConnell	Lakewood, Ohio	MG-TC	1250
58	Harry L. Keeler, Jr.	Detroit, Mich.	MG-TD	1250
67	Thomas I. Richardson	Cleveland, Ohio	MG-TD	1250
68	Robert J. Barsantee, Jr.	Ann Arbor, Mich.	MG-TD	1250
108	Robert Kron	Titusville, Pa.	MG-TD	1250

Second Race

10 laps, up to 750 cc, class H; unsupercharged but may be modified

Car	Driver	Address	Make	Disp. cc
23	George Durbin	Detroit, Mich.	Renault	748
26	John D. Allen	Cleveland, Ohio	Crosley Spec.	724
28	Charles A. Stoddard	Mentor, Ohio	Siata Spyder	750
30	William G. Pickrel, Jr.	Dayton, Ohio	Renault	750
31	Dick Yares	Cleveland, Ohio	Bandini	748
46	Theodore M. Kessel	Akron, Ohio	Kessel-Taylor	730
47	Peter M. Dawson	Birmingham, Mich.	Crosley	750
48	Bert Lisicki	Cleveland, Ohio	Crosley	749
71	Joseph R. Blaser	South Euclid, Ohio	Siata Spyder	750
73	Earl C. Dow	Canton, Ohio	Crosley Spec.	750

Third Race

10 laps, two classes: 751 to 1300 cc and 1301 to 1500 cc, unsupercharged, may be modified

Car	Driver	Address	Make	Disp. cc
1	Franz J. Hannig	Wheeling, W. Va.	MG-A	1500
10	Charlie Ellmers	Chagrin Falls, Ohio	Lester MG	1300
14	Jack F. Manting	Big Rapids, Mich.	Porsche Spyder	1486
15	Robert Shea	Fairview Park, Ohio	MG-TC	1250
17	Charles E. Sherman	Detroit, Mich.	Porsche	1500
18	Michael Caparon	Cleveland, Ohio	MG-TD	1250
22	Ralph Durbin	Detroit, Mich.	MG-TF	1250
27	Edward J. Hancock	Ypsilanti, Mich.	Porsche Speedster	1500
34	Walter P. Kern	Boston, Mass.	Siata	1090
37	Donald D. Black	Oak Park, Mich.	Siata	1089
39	Eugene E. Annabel	Detroit, Mich.	Porsche	1499
42	Neil G. Dever	Cleveland Hts., Ohio	MG-A	1500
45	Dale E. Smith	Canal Fulton, Ohio	MG-A	1500
51	Henry Dahl	Warren, Pa.	MG-A	1500
52	Barnie Burnette	Akron, Ohio	Porsche	1488
59	Thomas Hallock	Grosse Pointe Farms, Mich.	MG-TF	1500

Car	Driver	Address	Make	Disp. cc
66	Charles W. Allen, III	Maple Hts., Ohio	Siata	1395
69	Kenneth Askew	Ypsilanti, Mich.	Alfa Romeo	1300

Fourth Race

12 laps (37.2 miles), up to 1500 supercharged; 1501–2000 unsupercharged

Car	Driver	Address	Make	Disp. cc
5	Earl F. Kornfeld	Cleveland, Ohio	Triumph TR3	1991
7	Robert K. Rippel	Avon Lake, Ohio	Triumph TR3	1991
11	Robert Lossman	Rocky River, Ohio	Triumph TR3	1991
13	J. Edward Hugus	Pittsburgh, Penn.	Porsche 550	1488
16	Ralph B. Wilson	Princeton, New York	Triumph TR3	1991
20	Ben Hall	Willoughby, OH	AC Ace	1991
24	Charles H. Dietrich	Sandusky, OH	MG-TC s/c	1466
29	Earl H. Uhr	Cleveland, OH	Porsche s/c	1488
32	Quay C. Barber	Lakewood, OH	Triumph TR2	1991
36	Fletcher R. Andrews Jr.	Warrensville Hts., OH	Triumph TR2	1991
38	William E. Bradley	Detroit, MI	Siata 208S	1996
41	Mike Ward	Lansing, MI	MG-TD	1250
46	Jack Taylor	Barberton, OH	Kessel-Taylor	730
50	Eugene W. Gettig	Ellwood City, PA	Triumph TR3	1991
54	Tom Payne	Ypsilanti, MI	Arnolt Bristol	1971
56	Edward B. Eichenlaub Jr.	Ellwood City, PA	Triumph TR3	1991
61	Norman P. Wintermute	Detroit, MI	Triumph TR2	1991
62	Robert J. Shaver	Grosse Pointe, MI	Morgan Plus 4	1991
63	Herbert H. Kouns	Columbus, OH	MG-TC	1250
70	Ronald B. DeBruin	Dearborn, MI	Triumph TR2	1991
72	Edwin P. Lawrence III	Detroit, MI	Morgan Plus 4	1991

Results

First Race

1. Ralph Durbin	Detroit	MG-TF
2. Chuck Henry	Bellevue, Ohio	MG-TC
3. Art Brow	Cleveland	MG-TC
8. Cal Gleason	Detroit	MG-TD

Second Race

1. Chuck Stoddard	Mentor, Ohio	Siata Spyder
2. Ted Kessel	Akron, Ohio	Kessel-Taylor Spl.
3. John Allen	Cleveland	Crosley Spl.

Third Race

1. Jack Manting	Big Rapids, Mich.	Porsche Spyder
2. Charlie Ellmers	Chagrin Falls	Lester MG
3. Chuck Dietrich	Sandusky	MG-TC
4. Ken Askew	Ypsilanti	Alfa Romeo
5. Ralph Durbin	Detroit	MG-TF

Fourth Race

1. Ed Hugus   Pittsburgh   Porsche Spyder
2. Tom Payne   Ypsilanti   Arnolt Bristol
3. Ben Hall   Willoughby   AC Ace
4. Chuck Dietrich   Sandusky   MG-TC

Source: Don Black, G-Modified #37 Siata Spyder, 1100 cc

CHAPTER 8:

1957: A Typical Day at Put-in-Bay

June 8, 1957

It's Friday, June 7, 1957, the day before the race, and the entrants in the sports car race at Put-in-Bay are streaming across the waters of Lake Erie from Port Clinton, Marblehead, Sandusky and Catawba. Miller's Ferry is taking them and their little cars to the docks next to the children's park in the crescent of the bay.

Friends of the racing drivers meander around the cars, looking them over with interest. Besides what seem to be a thousand MGs in various kinds and colors are the more unusual machines: Siatas, Porsches and Alfa Romeos. They learn from owners that the Alfa's second name is pronounced "Row-*may*-oh." The more astute of them observe that the tachometers of the Carerra-engined Porsches go to 8000 rpm, whereas the normal ones only read to 6000.

There's not much wave action on the lake today and, at any rate, most of our passengers are people accustomed to the big water of the third-largest Great Lake. Soon the dock comes into view, and they crowd forward as if to get there sooner. The boat approaches its slip and the engine goes into reverse, revving up and quickly slowing the boat. Then back into forward as a deck hand throws a line around the bollard, then into reverse again for the stern line.

Once settled in, the gangplanks are fitted for off-loading the cars. Down the ramp they come: the ivory MG-TC with green upholstery, the red Siata with black seats, the silver Porsche with red door panels. About ten of these small racing cars will fit on one ferry boat. Relatively few spectator cars are among them.

Betty Henn has the registration desk set up, and that is the first stop for the drivers. All of the drivers are amateurs, though the skill of some equals the professionals.

Nineteen fifty-seven was a very different time than 2013, the year in which this book was completed. People young and old wanted to be active. So they raced sports cars, raced sailboats, fished, hunted, camped, canoed, played baseball, went to art museums, and so on. They had no computers or related instruments for sedentary pursuits. Obesity in children was almost unheard of. Jazz was a popular form of music, with the big-band sound of Stan Kenton lapsing into the modern sound of Jerry Mulligan and Chet Baker; rock and roll was taking over in popularity. A gallon of gasoline cost 24 cents. The average car price was $2,749. The cost of the average house was $12,220. And the average income was $4,455. Jobs were plentiful for those who wanted to work; there was a good choice of jobs as well.

Two months after the Put-in-Bay race, Juan Manuel Fangio won the German Grand Prix at the Nürburgring, driving for Maserati, to earn his fifth World Driving Championship. It was his greatest race, a come-from-behind effort after a bungled pit stop. Citroen ceased

Many people coming to the island yearned to fly on the magnificent old Ford Tri-Motor. Here is a great pen-and-ink drawing of it by artist, illustrator and advertising art director Herb James (Herb James).

production of the Traction Avant, produced from 1934 to 1957. A 1957 Plymouth Belvedere was buried in a time capsule to be opened 50 years later, June 15, 2007, six years after Plymouth's final year in production. *On the Road,* by Jack Kerouac, was published. *Atlas Shrugged* by Ayn Rand went on sale. *The Music Man,* written by Meredith Willson, starring Robert Preston, opened on Broadway. In it, the barber shop quartet sings *Lida Rose,* a very sweet Midwestern song, to Marian the librarian. The Boeing 707 took to the air. Ultrasound scanning was pioneered in Scotland. The laser was invented by American Gordon Gould.

But enough of the back-in-time snapshot and back to the races. After registration, the drivers headed for various hotels and rooming houses on the island. By name, they were the Bayview Inn, the Park Hotel, the Friendly Inn, the Victory Park, the Fox Motel, Airport Motel and a few others.

Early in the day Saturday, race organizer Dick Henn, a colonel in the army reserves, supervised the laying of the land line around the 3.1-mile course, as an assignment for the national guard, with walkie-talkies at the station of each corner worker. It was literally a life-or-death assignment. The soldiers took it seriously and, with their Midwestern work ethic, they did it well.

Saturday was a day for tech inspection, too. Fred Troyan recalls, "The inspectors were Bob Shea, Steve Ivanyi, Whitey Tyrone and myself. I was a year out of school but I had been going to Put-in-Bay for years, for the sailing regattas. I crewed on a boat called *Cotton Blossom.* It was Lee Wilson's R Boat, basically a 10-meter boat—I was on it for 5 or 6 years. The road race at the island motivated me into sports cars and the sports car business. Before, I was interested in hot rods. I knew the people who had Lakewood Chassis. They built Cad-engined 1940 Fords and Olds-engined Studebakers. We raced them on the street. We were always the fastest car. Then I remember seeing a Porsche 550 in tech inspection. I remember looking at that car. Bob Shea, bless his soul, called them 'German junk.'" Bob may have had his own point of view. He had been an army officer in the Battle of the Bulge. He had been shot by the Germans, and still had shrapnel in his body from their artillery fire. But Fred Troyan later owned a Porsche dealership.

Early Sunday morning, June 8, the streets were blocked with hay bales in preparation for the race. There was a 7:30 a.m. drivers' meeting in the town hall in which Dick Henn gave them particulars of the course, such as the off-camber road at Cemetery Corner and, as always, cautioned them, "You will race like gentlemen or you will not race at all." Since

Instead of taking a plane, you could go over on the ferry boat. This day—June 8, 1957—was unusually calm on Lake Erie. No upset stomachs for landlubbers; everybody had a good ride (Joe Brown).

there was no time for qualifying, positions on the starting grid were decided by the luck of the draw—each racer took a ticket out of a hat for the number of his grid position.

And now for the report from the Funny Face Auto Racing Team. It's a short one. "In 1957, we bid a sad farewell to Ted Jayne's TD," says Meacham Hitchcock. "The Lester continued to do well with Ted coming in a close second to one of the first Spyders that invaded the Bay, and Charlie [Ellmers] had himself a very close second to Dietrich in the TC."

The First Race

At about 8:00 a.m. the first race formed up out on Main Street in front of the Roundhouse Bar. Because a rolling start was safer than a standing start, organizers John Birchfield and Dick Henn decided to use a pace car. In this case, it was a TR3. Twenty-four cars were ready to race, all of them MGs—TCs, TDs and TF 1250s. Drivers included national champion Ralph Durbin, west side standout Ralph Cadwallader, Bill Malion and John Curran (these last two later to be Porsche Meisters), Sandusky VW dealer Chuck Dietrich, telephone executive Chuck Henry and several more. MG driver Harry Constant sat this race out. His wife Lois was pregnant with their second son. They did go up as spectators, though, and managed to make the last car ferry before the race.

The drivers went to the grid on Main Street, assisted by the grid marshals. Once in line, they got the five-minute gun—a real gunshot—and the drivers raised their arms. In the case of a car that wouldn't start, there was time to push it off to the side. Then the one-minute gun; after 60 seconds, the field moved out, in this case behind Dave Weisenburger's Triumph. Dave was a funny character. Always had a good story to tell. Always pitched in for the car club.

They'd been told to stay even, in their own rows. All were good sportsmen and when they came around to the start-finish line, they got the green flag. For some mysterious reason, the best drivers had drawn starting positions well back in the field. Drivers who were dedicated but perhaps not fully proven—Thomas Richardson, Norman Harrison and William Whistler, for example—led the first lap, as Chuck Dietrich sped through the field. Charlie Ellmers saw him going through the pack and tagged along, with Don Wolf and John Tame.

Proving once again that everyone has to start somewhere, Don Wolf began his racing career in 1957 at Put-in-Bay in the #56 MG-TD that finished 15th among 25 entrants in the first race. Don was the proprietor of his father's shop, Ed Wolf Garage, in East Cleveland. You could see the most interesting cars there—300SL Mercedes, AC Bristols, Porsche Carreras and so on. Don and his crew could fix them all, with a very high standard of workmanship. On the side, the garage was a Saab dealer, a Mom-and-Pop enterprise selling only about five cars a year. The service his Saab customers got was usually far better than the big dealerships could offer. After owning MG and Porsche race cars, Don got an Elva Mk. V sports racer, which he ran during 1960, '61, '62, and '63. He raced it with his friend Doc Curran and pit crew Tim LaGanke, at Connellsville, Pennsylvania, Dunkirk, New York, Cumberland, Marlboro and other venues. He was successful racer, but it all came to an end at Road Atlanta in 1963, where he had a heart attack while racing. Don pulled the green Elva over to the side of the course and waited out the heart attack, which he survived. Six years of racing ended there in Georgia. He drove back to Cleveland and sold the Elva.

An MG-TC driver backs his car down the ramp from the ferry boat *Challenger* (Joe Brown).

The start of the first race, as seemingly all the MGs in the world roar by the Crescent Bar under the banner of the start-finish line (Charlie and Ruth Ellmers).

But back to the MG race. There wasn't much that could be done to prepare these production cars, though you could change wheels and some of the TC drivers had fitted 16-inch wheels that were wider than the original 19-inchers. The ones on Chuck Henry's car were from a Ferrari. Then, too, the TCs were lighter by nearly 200 pounds than the TD and TF. Charlie Ellmers took advantage of the close-ratio gear-set in his TC to stick with Dietrich, the leader. This was a ten-lap race but the leaders were up at the front by the third lap. Chuck Dietrich in first, Charlie Ellmers second and Al Weaver from Columbus in third place. Chuck Henry had been expected to do better than fourth, as well as Ralph Durbin (eleventh) and Ralph Cadwallader (twelfth).

Chuck Henry was an outstanding driver with an excellent car. In the 1957 season, he entered both the Put-in-Bay race (placing fourth in Race #1, as car #5) and the Akron Airport sports car races, as car #85. In 1958, he again ran at Put-in-Bay, as car #17. By this season, he had switched to 16-wheel rims, as some of the other TC drivers did, for better acceleration and higher cornering forces. He strung these together himself using the TC centers and 5 ½" wide Ferrari rims. 1958 was the beginning of the Milan Hill Climb, which Henry used to compete in. That year he set the fastest time of the day with the rapid TC.

The Second Race

As early as the 1955 race, Chuck Dietrich had taken two cars to the 'Bay race. He had competed successfully in a supercharged MG-TC and a Harry Lester–built MG. In 1955 he

The back of the MG field is seen as they head out of town toward the airport (Dave and Sheila Bly).

placed third in SCCA national points in the Lester. This year, he took the MG-TC and his new Elva Mk. II. He had discovered the Elva while reading a magazine. "Then I read an article in an English car magazine by John Bolton—it was on a car called an Elva," Dietrich said. "It sounded interesting, so I got in touch with Frank Nichols, the builder. It just so happened that Nichols had a car available." The car had been sent to a Canadian driver who asphyxiated himself in his garage. It had a lightweight, small-diameter tube frame and an advanced suspension design. It was supposed to be for the Sebring night race, but it had no headlights! Dietrich bought the Elva and began winning races almost immediately. This was the beginning of the front-engined era for the new wave of English cars. "Compared to the Lester and the Italian cars," Dietrich said, "they were much quicker. They cornered better, had better brakes and were totally different. They were superior cars. The early Elvas had special aluminum brakes, and they also had magnesium wheels." It was in 1957 that an Elva was first raced in the United States.

In the second race of the day, we saw an interesting collection of cars that included Dietrich's new Elva, the G-Modified Cooper Climax of Tom Hallock, the H-Modified national champion Bandini of Mel Sachs, the recently-acquired Siata 750s of Chuck Stoddard and Al Beasley, and the Siata 1100 of Richard Brown, as well as some capable racing specials.

The Cooper was the car previously owned by Ed Hugus and John Bentley that had run at Le Mans the previous year, taking eighth overall. "That was the first two-passenger Cooper," Hugus said. "I asked John Cooper how long it had taken to develop. He told me, 'Pops and I sat down at the pub one night and drew it up, and then we built it the next day.'"

At the start Betty Henn drove them around in her black XK140 Jag, then waved the

Bob Shea in TC #12 sets up to take the dog-leg into town, followed closely by Charlie Ellmers in the Funny Face Auto Racing Team TC and a string of MGs coming down from the cemetery (Charlie and Ruth Ellmers).

green at the start-finish line. Again, by some unexplainable quirk, the faster cars were behind the slower ones. It didn't take long for them to move to the front, past the home-built specials by John Allen and Ted Kessel. It was a train of cars led by the Cooper. Then the Elva and Mel Sach's Bandini—as entered by his father-in-law, Dick Gent. Stoddard's Siata was next after the faster Bandini, followed by Al Beasley's Siata. The Bandini was about 800 pounds, vs. 1,000 pounds for the Siata, so it accelerated better although it did not corner better. A battle began between the Cooper and the Elva; they traded places four times until the Elva held onto the G-Modified class lead. The Cooper had not gained a following in America, because only a few were sent by the factory. As Chuck Dietrich noted, "The Cooper might have been more successful in racing if there'd been more Coopers. People would have developed the car and they'd have won more." In winning the race and finishing first in G-Modified, Dietrich also set the fastest time of the day and one that would not be improved upon until the following year—not until Manny Holder and his Porsche Spyder.

Spectator Jon Clifton drove up from Fort Wayne, Indiana, to see the race. He would later race a Bugeye Sprite at Mid-Ohio when Oak Tree Bend was a part of the course, but in 1957 he was still in high school. "I went to a lot of races while I was in high school," Jon says. "We went to Lockbourne SAC Base, Chanute, Stout Field and the first race at Road America in 1955. Then in '57 we went to Put-in-Bay. It was very enjoyable. But you had to dodge the wine bottle corks. It was the last road race. There was snow-fence crowd control. People leaned in to see the cars and then jumped back when they came. You were close to the actual racing. You had to use your horse sense so as not to be run over! It was an exciting time in a person's life. That race was unique. I wish I had gone to more of them."

The Third Race

Another new car made its appearance in the third race at Put-in-Bay. It was the Alfa Romeo. Technically it was not new, since the company had been making cars since 1910 and had won two Formula One world championships, but the Giulietta model was new to American racing. Car dealer Ed Houlihan test-drove one at the Ypsilanti sports car emporium and said, "It leans too much. It will never win a race." The next weekend, Ken Askew of Detroit won in an Alfa, at Road America, putting all but the fastest G-Modified cars behind him. Yes, Alfas did roll a little, but they were well-balanced cars, they had huge, 13-inch brakes and, best of all, they had that great little twin-cam engine. The order of horsepower in 1250-cc cars was: Volkswagen, 36; MG, 54; and Alfa Romeo, 88. Well, actually, Alfa was

John Tame and his gray MG-TF takes the left-hander at the end of Cooper Straight, in front of Tony's Place, with about 20 people watching (Joe Brown).

1290 ccs, so it looks like they got 34 more horsepower out of that extra 40 ccs. Three drivers had these Alfas: Harry Gendelman, John McMasters and Ralph Durbin. Starting an Alfa-vs.-Porsche rivalry that would last to this day were the Porsche Supers of Gene Annabel and Charles Sherman. Three MG-TDs and several Volkswagens completed the field. With the Jag 140 again the pace car, off they went. It wasn't long before the Alfa of MG champion Ralph Durbin took the lead. He was able to hold off the Porsche of Charles Sherman for the remaining seven laps, with McMasters in another Alfa following closely, then the Porsche driven by Eugene Annabel. In fifth, ahead of the other Alfa, was Art Brow in an MG-TD he had borrowed from Bill Staufer. It was a great race, and one that introduced the Alfa Giulietta to American racing.

Mixed in with the Alfas, Porsches and MGs, in the third race, were a passel of Volkswagens, six of them to be exact, including two Ghias. Their owners were largely VW dealers who wanted to get some exposure for the cars. One of the drivers was a man named Bob Snider, from Lancaster, Ohio. Triumph guru Tom Householder tracked him down for us.

Here's Bob's reply to the contact:

> I've been cogitating my little brain re: PiB—a little dim at this point—at 88, and that was some 55 years ago. Actually I was racing jalopy stock cars in Columbus when the local VW dealer [Bob Fergus] asked me to drive a VW sedan in an all-VW race at Louisville, Kentucky, that was organized to promote the then-new VWs. Great fun with some 40 cars on the street of Derby Park. I finished third and then purchased the car from him and ran several other races in Indiana and Ohio, including Put-in-Bay. I had many fun memories but always remember the PiB races.

Tom Hallock in the white Cooper Bobtail sets up to pass Chuck Stoddard in the black Siata Spyder, at the Colonial Ballroom (Stu Kerr).

Chuck Stoddard in the #1 Siata Spyder with the Tweety Bird cartoon on the side takes the last corner into town (Joe Brown).

A nicely panned photo by Stu Kerr catches Chuck Dietrich's Elva speeding along and leading the Cooper of Tom Hallock (Stu Kerr).

Stu Kerr's high angle shot captures the Cooper Bobtail of Tom Hallock from Detroit, engaged in a close race with Chuck Dietrich (Stu Kerr).

Ralph Durbin speeds past the downtown bars on his way to a win in the third race (Stu Kerr).

I do remember starting on the front row with Vaughn Miller, then getting spun off course by Ralph Durbin in an Alfa at the cemetery corner. I remember hoping that none of us got bumped off into the crowd going down the front straight in town. I did get a little trophy—for the VW class, along with Vaughn.

I remember the great wineries. We stayed at the old hotel on the main straight and watched some of the practice from a balcony off our room, just like Monaco. We did meet and drink with all the other drivers and their wives—Dietrichs, Durbins, Stoddards, Beasleys and Sam-the-Man Sheppard—guess he eventually became "The Fugitive."

My crew member, Byron Kohn, and his lovely wife Millie were both well known to the racing clan in Ohio. Byron was a water colorist in Ohio and elsewhere, and had a gallery at German Village in Columbus. They were a fixture at Put-in-Bay for several years and traveled to many of my races both in Ohio and Wisconsin. He did a number of paintings of sports cars, including one of my old TA, and had several MGs of his own.

Like many Midwesterners, Bob was in the manufacturing business. According to racing historian Tom Householder and his brother-in-law D.G. Wood, he was a draftsman for Anchor Hocking, and worked for the Metallizing Company, a plater, Combination Bait Box, which made tackle boxes, and Lancaster Mold, as an engineer. Shortly afterward, he moved to Milwaukee to start Snider Mold in nearby Mequon, where he continued his racing.

The finish of the third race was Alfa, Porsche, Alfa, Porsche and Snider was the second VW, after Vaughn Miller (see details at the end of the chapter).

Right on the tail of Lee Beck in the #26 Speedster is Ed Lidgard in the #59 Porsche coupe (Joe Brown).

The Fourth Race

It was the second year in racing for the popular MG-A, and there were four of them in the fourth race. Multiplying even faster were the Porsches, with ten of their number, including some of the new Speedsters. There were several well-known names in this event, starting with the skilled racing mechanic Neil Dever, then Edward Eichenlaub, a champion in his own right (his brother Jim would notch a national championship two years later in an OSCA). Continuing the list were car dealer Tom Payne, the renowned Barnie Burnett, celebrated Korean War veteran Fred Quartullo, and car dealer Ed Hancock.

At the checkered flag, we found, to no one's surprise, Barnie Burnett in first, followed by Ed Hancock and then Ed Eichenlaub. Down a bit in the standings were Fred Quartullo in his MG-A and, unexpectedly, Tom Payne in twelfth place. Tom was driving a Volvo, a car line he sold. This would have been the 544 model, the one that looks like a shrunken 1946 Ford sedan. Not a bad driving car, though.

The Fifth Race

In the fifth race, the Triumph TR3s introduced the previous year continued their popularity, with nine of them entered. There were four AC Aces and Bristols—a lot, considering their expense. Only two Morgans sat on the starting grid, along with two Siatas with unusual

Heading for the apex on the last turn into town is Marcel Dupont in the #83 Porsche Speedster, one of the few we've seen with whitewall tires! (Joe Brown).

And here comes Fred Quartullo in his wire-wheel MGA. The driver of car #64 was a notable Korean War hero (Joe Brown).

engines—Herb Swan's Offenhauser and Bernie Keller's Porsche-powered machine. Only one MG was in the race, the TC of Bill Bradley from Detroit. Bill had a photograph finishing service in the city and later was the distributor for Merlyn racing cars, including the terrifically light 600-pound Mark 6, an H-Modified car, and the later Merlyn Mark 11 Formula Ford, a great-handling machine. Anyway, his wife Sophia went to all of these races with him and she particularly remembers the TC. "It was a pretty fast TC," she said. "It was competitive with some of the Cleveland TCs. He raced it at Put-in-Bay and then sold it to someone in the east." The car finished fourth in the F-Modified class, as #78. But we're getting a little ahead of ourselves.

One of the nine Triumphs was that of Bob Parsons. You remember Bob, don't you? "I had always heard about Put-in-Bay," says Bob:

> I went up there with a buddy in '54 or '55. In '57 I got a TR3 and decided I've got to race there. I joined SCCA to get a racing license. They had a driving test at Akron Airport. The head of the Contest Board was Charlie Ellmers. We were supposed to drive a course out on the airport. Then Charlie said, "Next." I went roaring down this hairpin turn to the right, onto the dirt, sliding around in my TR3. All of a sudden I'm upside down. I hit one of the ruts and rolled my car. I scrambled out through one of the cut-down doors. Then I went back to see Charlie. I thought that was it for my competition license. He said, "Ahh, don't worry about it, Bob. We're not going to let a little thing like that keep you from racing."
>
> Put-in-Bay was the first place I'd ever driven anywhere really fast. I remember the back stretch from town out to the airport. The telephone poles are going by me so fast. I remember thinking, "Don't look at the phone poles." There was one guy in my race who went up the hill at Cemetery Corner and into the graveyard. In the first race, a guy in a TD got clipped by another one and

John Comey's Bugatti gets ready to start the 1957 feature race (Joe Brown).

Ben Hall in the #29 AC Ace leads a Morgan and a Triumph in the fourth race (Joe Brown).

rolled right as he was coming into town, at the 25-degree turn. In about the middle of my race, the engine blew up [it was a head gasket]. My dad was at the race and he rope-towed me all the way back to Lakewood.

That's not down the block, it's about 60 miles.

"In the very early days of the sport," Hank Becker noted, "MG-powered racing cars fielded Classes F and E. But that was in 1954. Three years later," says Becker, "Terrible Tom Payne came in with his Porsche Spyder, then it was the Holder brothers with theirs. Then we had an OSCA at the Akron races. We took second in the Keift. Jimmy Carroll went to the Canadian races and saw the so-called production classes. They put an Alfa engine in a TC. Some highly-modified MGs were seen at the Dunkirk hillclimb, as well as a Volkswagen with a Porsche Spyder engine.

"The boys who were running superchargers used Castrol R—it covered the smell of alcohol or AvGas, which was illegal for racing and which they had to use to avoid cooking the cylinder head. They would mix it with the fuel, and it had a very distinctive smell. Bob Shea was looking for some AvGas, but the little airport at Put-in-Bay didn't have it. Bob ran 12-to-1 compression in his MG and blew his engine without the AvGas."

There was a late entry in the field, as Becker noted; that of Tom Payne in his new Porsche Spyder. He won the race. The Funny Face Auto Racing Team had just purchased the Lester MG from Chuck Dietrich and, with Ted Jayne driving, they finished second, very close to the Porsche Spyder. Bill Jackson, driving a Morgan, was third overall and first in E-Production, ahead of all those TR3s and ACs. Quay Barber, a notorious Triumph driver,

An unusual playing-card motif decorates the #86 AC Ace coupe of Ed Lawrence from Detroit (Joe Brown).

Ted Jayne passes the stores going into town with the #10 Lester MG. It finished a close second to the Porsche Spyder of Tom Payne (Joe Brown).

A beautiful array of racing trophies ornaments the table in the park, all ready for the post-race prize-giving (Joe Brown).

had to settle for second this time. Little-known driver William Hutchinson of St. Clair Shores, Michigan, in a TR3, finished third in EP. Third in F-Modified was Bernie Keller in his hybrid Siata Porsche, followed by the fast MG-TC of Bill Bradley from Detroit.

The Funny Face Auto Racing Team was organized so that Ted and Charlie alternated driving the Lester. Charlie Ellmers also drove Ben Hitchcock's MG-TC, as did Ben occasionally; it was his car, after all. Meach Hitchcock raced later and drove a bugeye Sprite. Meach's wife was Robin, and they lived in Bratenahl. Ben's wife was nicknamed "Spook"; no one remembers what her real name was. She was from the Augustus family and lived in Waite Hill. Besides Put-in-Bay, they raced at Akron Airport, Watkins Glen and Lockbourne Air Force Base—that was one of the races that General Curtis Le May was involved with. John Tame, who drove a TF, says, "We also raced at Cumberland, Maryland. There was a cliff at the end if you didn't make the first turn. Race officials advised you to spin your car to avoid going over the cliff. We also raced at the Dunkirk, New York airport in '57, '58, '59 and, I believe, 1960.

Chuck Dietrich, left, receives a first-place trophy from race chairman Dick Henn for his win over Tom Hallock in the dramatic contest of Elva versus Cooper (collection of Chris Kintner).

"Charlie was the cheerleader of the team," Tame continued. "He was the one who came up with all the ideas. At the races, we always started out with a happy face on the car. Then, if something happened, we could change it. When Charlie blew the engine up, we turned down the corners of the mouth on the face. I blew my car up too. Not in a race but on the way to Watkins Glen. I left it at a gas station in Erie, Pennsylvania. I was operating on a pretty low budget. The head came off a valve and it holed a piston. If you used the heavy springs it put a strain on the valves. After that I put in new valves every year. I got them from Chuck Stoddard. He sold the BAP line of British parts when he was working out of the garage at his house."

As race organizer Dick Henn awarded first-place trophies to Chuck Dietrich, Ralph Durbin, Barnie Burnett and Tom Payne, we closed the books on another wonderful race at Put-in-Bay. Lots of excitement, good competition, no accidents and the camaraderie that only racing can offer. They'd be back next year.

Meanwhile, the growth of purpose-built racing circuits took a major leap in 1957, with construction of the 1.5-mile Lime Rock course in northwest Connecticut, the 2.8-mile Bridgehampton course out on Long Island, the 3.2-mile Virginia International Raceway down at the Virginia–North Carolina border, the classic Riverside Raceway in southern California, and 2.2-mile Laguna Seca in northern California. The permanent course at Watkins Glen had already been built in 1956, and the Road America circuit at Elkhart Lake, Wisconsin, had been built in 1955. As these and other closed-course facilities multiplied, of course, there was less need for a road racing circuit like Put-in-Bay.

June 8, 1957, Entry List

First Race

10:15 a.m., 10 laps (31 miles), all MGs—Class G-Production

Car	Driver	Address	Make
4 GP	Ronald Kehl	Lakewood, Ohio	MG-TD
5 GP	Charles Henry	Bellevue, Ohio	MG-TC
9 GP	Theodore C. Ley	Euclid, Ohio	MG-TC
12 GP	Robert Shea	Fairview Park, Ohio	MG-TC
14 GP	William Staufer	Middleburg Heights, Ohio	MG-TD
22 GP	Ralph Cadwallader	Lakewood, Ohio	MG-TC
23 GP	Charles Ellmers	Lyndhurst, Ohio	MG-TC
31 GP	Walter Hemann	Cleveland, Ohio	MG-TC
33 GP	John Leeson	Poland, Ohio	MG-TD
37 GP	Peter Owen	Detroit, Mich.	MG-TD
39 GP	Martin Alperstein	State College, Pa.	MG-TC
44 GP	John Curran, MD	Cleveland Heights, Ohio	MG-TD
52 GP	Roger Riley	Springfield, Ohio	MG-TD
56 GP	Donald E. Wolf	Cleveland, Ohio	MG-TD
63 GP	Charles C. Tipton	Lakewood, Ohio	MG-TD
67 GP	Ralph L. Durbin	Detroit, Mich.	MG-TF
76 GP	Norris Hartshorn	Cleveland Heights, Ohio	MG-TF
79 GP	Thomas Richardson	Cleveland, Ohio	MG-TD
81 GP	Al Weaver	Columbus, Ohio	MG-TF
85 GP	John Thompson	Ecorse, Mich.	MG-TD
87 GP	Allan Hess	Center Ridge, Ohio	MG-TD
95 GP	J. William Edwards	Ann Arbor, Mich.	MG-TD
153 GP	Henry J. Dahl	Warren, Pa.	MG-TD
Alt. 97 GP	Norman Harrison	Pontiac, Mich.	MG-TD
Alt. 101 GP	John Tame	Cleveland Heights, Ohio	MG-TF

Second Race

10 laps, Classes—I-Production, 500–750 cc;
G-Modified, 750–1100cc; H-Modified, 500–750 ccs

Car	Driver	Address	Make
3 GM	Richard Brown	Lyndhurst, Ohio	Siata Spyder
54 GM	Charles Dietrich	Sandusky, Ohio	Elva Mk. II

Car	Driver	Address	Make
69 GM	Ned E. Kamp	Dayton, Ohio	Morris Minor
158 GM	Thomas Hallock	Grosse Pte. Farms, Mich.	Cooper Climax
1 HM	Charles Stoddard	Mentor, Ohio	Siata Spyder
2 HM	Al Beasley	Mentor, Ohio	Siata Spyder
17 HM	Melvin Sachs	Cleveland, Ohio	Bandini
24 HM	William Pickrel, Jr.	Dayton, Ohio	Renault
27 HM	Theodore Kessel	Cuyahoga Falls, Ohio	Dow Special
35 HM	Arthur Brennan	Bloomfield Hills, Mich.	Crosley
43 HM	John D. Allen	Cleveland, Ohio	Crosley Spec.
55 HM	Col. Newt Norris	Fort Knox, Ky.	Crosley Sup. Spl.
77 HM	Herb Whiting	Cleveland, Ohio	Siata Crosley
98 HM	William Lindsay	New Carlisle, Ohio	Renault
99 HM	Clark P. Turner	Yellow Springs, Ohio	Crosley Sup. Sp.
45 IP	Richard Dohman	Detroit, Mich.	Renault '49
46 IP	George Durbin	Detroit, Mich.	Renault '56
73 IP	Joachim Kammer	Pittsburgh, Pa.	Renault Alp.

Third Race

10 laps, Class—H-Production, 750–1000 cc; G-Production, 1000–1300 cc

Car	Driver	Address	Make
10 GP	Charles Sherman	Detroit, Mich.	Porsche Super
14 GP	Arthur Brow	Cleveland, Ohio	MG-TD
16 GP	William Cowan	Lakewood, Ohio	VW Ghia
28 GP	John Morrison	New York City, N.Y.	Alfa Rom. Giul.
36 GP	Vaughn Miller	Columbus, Ohio	VW
47 GP	Robert Newman	Akron, Ohio	VW
51 GP	James B. Torbon	Poland, Ohio	VW Ghia
53 GP	Eugene Annabel	Detroit, Mich.	Porsche Super
66 GP	Eugene Shanahan	Vandalia, Ohio	VW
74 GP	James E. McNally	Pittsburgh, Pa.	Renault Dauph.
79 GP	Thomas Richardson	Cleveland, Ohio	MG-TD
82 GP	Robert Snider	Lancaster, Ohio	VW
84 GP	J. Edward Hugus	Pittsburgh, Pa.	Alfa Romeo
92 GP	Joe Gillespie, Jr.	Bellefontaine, Ohio	VW
93 GP	J.R. McMasters	Sewickley, Pa.	Alfa Rom. Giul.
97 GP	Norman Harrison	Pontiac, Mich.	MG-TD
101 GP	John Tame	Cleveland Heights, Ohio	MG-TF

Fourth Race

10 laps, Class F-Production, 1300–1600cc

Car	Driver	Address	Make
15 FP	Neil Dever	Rocky River, Ohio	MG-A
21 FP	Edward Eichenlaub, Jr.	Ellwood City, Pa.	Porsche Cpe.
26 FP	Lee Beck	Allen Park, Mich.	Porsche
41 FP	Barnie Burnett	Akron, Ohio	Porsche
57 FP	Ronald A. Royal	Youngstown, Ohio	MG-A
59 FP	Edward J. Lidgard	Royal Oak, Mich.	Porsche Cpe.
61 FP	Richard H. Dittus	Taylor Center, Mich.	Porsche

Car	Driver	Address	Make
62 FP	Charles Kelsey, Jr.	Shaker Heights, Ohio	MG-A
64 FP	Fred Quartullo	Euclid, Ohio	MG-A
65 FP	John J. Sheridan	Lakewood, Ohio	Porsche Speedst.
71 FP	Robert Lower	Kent, Ohio	Porsche
75 FP	Edward Hancock	Ypsilanti, Mich.	Porsche Super
83 FP	Marcel Dupont	Mt. Clemens, Mich.	Porsche Speedst.
94 FP	Martin Edwards	Ann Arbor, Mich.	Porsche
113 FP	Tom Payne	Ypsilanti, Mich.	Volvo

Fifth Race

12 laps, Classes—E-Production, 1600–2000cc;
F-Modified, 1100–1500cc

Car	Driver	Address	Make
6 EP	Richard J. Kennedy	Detroit, Mich.	Morgan TR3
7 EP	Robert K. Rippel	Detroit, Mich.	Triumph TR3
8 EP	Fletcher R. Andrews	Cleveland Heights, Ohio	Triumph TR3
11 EP	Robert Parsons	Lakewood, Ohio	Triumph TR3
13 EP	Tom Payne	Ypsilanti, Mich.	A.C. Bristol
19 EP	James W. Whitlow	Springfield, Ohio	Triumph TR3
29 EP	Ben Hall	Willoughby, Ohio	A.C. Ace
32 EP	Eugene Gettig	Akron, Ohio	Triumph TR3
34 EP	Robert Lossman	Rocky River, Ohio	Triumph '57
38 EP	Quay Barber	Lakewood, Ohio	Triumph '55
42 EP	Edward Houlehan	Detroit, Mich.	Morgan
48 EP	Norman Von Wintermute	Detroit, Mich.	Triumph TR2
49 EP	Alfred D. Miller	Akron, Ohio	Triumph TR3
72 EP	John Petrone	Youngstown, Ohio	Triumph '56
86 EP	Edwin P. Lawrence III	Wyandotte, Mich.	A.C. Ace Cpe.
91 EP	Robert Franklin	Jackson, Mich.	A.C. Ace
96 EP	William Hutchinson	St. Clair Shores, Mich.	Triumph TR3
10 FM	Ted Jayne	Cleveland, Ohio	Lester MG
25 FM	Herb Swan	Cleveland, Ohio	Off. Siata
78 FM	William Bradley	Detroit, Mich.	MG-TC
89 FM	Bernard L. Keller	Mansfield, Ohio	Siata Porsche
126 FM	Carl A. Haas	Lincolnwood, Ill.	Porsche Spyd.

Source: Bob Satava, Put-in-Bay race worker

Results

First Race

Finish	Car No.	Driver	Make
1	12	Charles Dietrich	MG-TC
2	23	Charles Ellmers	MG-TC
3	81	Al Weaver	MG-TF
4	5	Charles Henry	MG-TC

8. 1957

Second Race

Finish	Car No.	Driver	Make	
1	54	Charles Dietrich	Elva Mk. II	GM1
2	158	Tom Hallock	Cooper Climax	GM2
3	17	Melvin Sachs	Bandini	HM1
4	1	Charles Stoddard	Siata Spyder	HM2
5	2	Al Beasley	Siata Spyder	HM3

Third Race

Finish	Car No.	Driver	Make	
1	68	Ralph Durbin	Alfa Romeo	GP1
2	18	Charles Sherman	Porsche Super	GP2
3	93	J.R. McMasters	Alfa Rom. Giul.	GP3
4	53	Eugene Anabel	Porsche Super	GP4
5	14	Arthur Brow	MG-TD	GP5
6	102	H. Gendelman	Alfa Rom. Spyder	GP6
7	103	William Mallion	DKW	HP1
8	36	Vaughn Miller	VW	GP7
9	82	Robert Snider	VW	GP8
10	97	Norman Harrison	VW	GP9

Fourth Race

Finish	Car No.	Driver	Make
1	41	Barnie Burnett	Porsche
2	75	Edward Hancock	Porsche Super
3	21	Edward Eichenlaub	Porsche Cpe.
4	94	Martin Edwards	Porsche

Fifth Race

Finish	Car No.	Driver	Make	
1	13	Tom Payne	Porsche Spyder	FM1
2	10	Ted Jayne	Lester MG	FM2
3	104	William Jackson	Morgan TR3	EP1
4	38	Quay Barber	Triumph TR2	EP2
5	96	William Hutchinson	Triumph TR3	EP3
6	89	Bernie Keller	Siata Porsche	FM3

Source: NE Ohio Region SCCA

CHAPTER 9

1958: The Year of the Lap Record

June 7, 1958

There was a big entry list in the 1958 'Bay races: one hundred cars. There were even sixteen alternate drivers, hoping to get in the race. But many of the drivers from previous years had registered early. There was a greater variety of cars than in the past, and it reckoned to be another terrific event.

Of course you had to go through tech inspection before you could race. One of four tech inspectors was Walt Jarmain. He eventually worked for Lossman Motors for 35 years, first as a sales rep, then a parts manager, and then service and parts manager. We'll let Walt tell you about it:

I arrived from England in April of 1958. I had been an apprentice mechanic there, but Bob Lossman made me a sales rep. There were about a dozen Lossman employees sent to the Put-in-Bay races in June. Many of the mechanics were drivers—Art Brow, Charlie Barber, Bill Staufer, Bob Shea, Ralph Cadwallader and others.

We would go up on Wednesday and run tech inspection up to Friday night. We would inspect them all—the Italian cars, MGs, Elvas, everything. We would make sure the seat belts were anchored—as long as they had large washers underneath—and the driver's suit was flameproof. Usually the driver's suits were white coveralls soaked in buckets of Borax and then dried. Each of the tech inspectors carried a Zippo lighter. To test the fire resistance, we would pull one of the pockets inside out, and flip open the top of our lighter. The driver would usually have a look of surprise and then concern when this happened. Then we would light up our Zippo lighter and see if his driving suit would catch fire. If it didn't, the suit was reasonably fireproof and they were approved to race. One time a driver showed up in a London Fog raincoat. We said to him, "What the hell are you doing in that?"

We would check the roll bar and check the car for brakes. In one test, they would floor it and then pull the emergency brake. In another test, they would accelerate through the garage and then hit the brakes with their hands off the wheel. It was supposed to test whether the car would swerve. We checked under the hood to make sure everything was secure. They had to have the headlights taped and the windshield off with a racing screen for open cars. We checked wire wheels to see if the spokes were loose.

If the exhaust was loose we sent them off and told them to fix it and come back. Same with dripping oil or a leaking radiator. If they came back with no repairs, they didn't race. Once a guy busted a radiator on his TR3 and had a new one flown in from Detroit. He didn't get it repaired until very late, but we waited. We wanted to give him a second chance, and we were there after midnight. Tech inspection was done at Parker's Garage, across from City Hall.

For the people from Lossman's it was just like another day of work. Bob would pay for our accommodations and other expenses. He was a very good employer. He let us run our departments the way we wanted to. He said, "Run it like it was your own business—if an incident

The sign in the window of MG Motors announces the shop's closure for four days for the races. Usually before the 'Bay races the sports car dealers would get a truckload of cars, all of which would be sold by the time of the races (Chris Staufer).

occurs with a customer, I'll back you up." He had four stores, Renault, VW, Sunbeam-Hillman and MG Motors. MG included Borgward, Triumph, Jaguar and Austin Healey. On each of the cars entered to race by Lossman or an employee of his, behind the racing number was sticky paper with a tartan motif.

"The year 1958 was the first to require roll bars, I think," says corner worker Jim Etzkorn. "Bob Rippel was a good friend of mine. He had an immaculate TR3. He said they weren't going to make him put in a roll bar. But they didn't let him race without it." There was a certain amount of resistance to the roll bars, and the Lester MG of Charlie Ellmers and Ted Jayne just squeaked through tech inspection with a "roll pipe" in the car—only an upright tube.

And now, for those who like to keep tabs on the Funny Face Auto Racing Team, Meach Hitchcock offers this report: "In 1958, the team's TC was put out to pasture, and John Tame joined us with his TF. Lucky for the team that he did, as he was the only winner of the year, finishing third in several races. Reed Andrews added his wealth of mechanical experience as a technical advisor from time to time. Fred and Gerry Steger, numerous friends, girlfriends and wives continued to gather round to offer help and advice. The Lester, having finished third at the 'Bay, picked up a strange sickness that was not cured until Akron. Meach Hitchcock, who could stand watching from the sidelines no longer, ran the Lester as a novice at Akron and had the honor of being the only driver who finished in it for the year. (However, he needed a push to start.) The Glen saw Ben Hitchcock in a new Veloce and we all saw signs of better things to come."

The First Race

By 1958, there was a regular group of drivers who always came to Put-in-Bay. This year they included Bill Staufer, Ralph Cadwallader, John Tame, Ted Ley, Chuck Henry, Al Weaver, Ralph Durbin, Bill Malion, Bo Miske and a not-so-well known entrant named Elvadore Cranage, Jr. One member of the Put-in-Bay Reunion committee, Manley Ford, likes the fact that his name began with the car name Elva, even though Mr. Cranage actually drove an MG-TC.

Ralph Durbin must have gotten held up by traffic in the early stages of the race, because he was nowhere in the top three at the end. Instead it was Chuck Henry first, in the well-prepared TC, Bill Staufer second in his rapid TD (it's still fast, I can personally attest) and Al Weaver from Columbus in his TF, later to be an ace Alfa driver.

The Second Race

A large field of G- and H-Modified cars, along with a few of the I-Production group, greeted the starter of the second race. There were three of the new Elva Mark III cars, with Burdette Martin, Bill Bradley and Chuck Dietrich as their drivers. According to Sophia Bradley, Bill bought his car directly from the factory. These were the latest and greatest from the mind of Frank Nichols in the mother country. Add to these an 1100-cc Siata and a Fairthorpe Electron, and that was it for the GM class. Moving to H-Modified we had the vaunted Martin T of Martin Tanner from Saginaw, Michigan and the ex–Marvin Sachs Ban-

The harbor at South Bass Island with Chris Craft Constellations, Lymans and Thistle class sailboats (Stu Kerr).

Four MGs take the dog-leg at the end of Cooper Straight, the last turn before the corner into town. Ralph Cadwallader's blurred TC leads, followed by Charlie Ellmers with the Funny Face Auto Racing Team TC, then a TD and a TF (Lorrain and Manfreid Holder).

dini, now driven by Jim Eichenlaub, plus Al Beasley's 750 Siata Spyder. A number of Crosley Specials filled in the entry in HM. The I-Production cars were Renaults, and the Isetta driven by Chuck Stoddard, and Willis Grant's Saab. Three Berkeleys were on the alternate list, with one of them, driven by Clark Turner, getting in the race.

In addition to the "store-bought" H-Modifieds, there were four Crosley Specials. One of them, the #95 car, was driven by Bob Snider. We tracked Bob down through the auspices of Doretti expert Tom Householder. Here are a few recollections from Bob:

> The next year [1958] we ran a Devin Crosley that was a committee built by someone in Dayton, Ohio. It was a pretty quick in HM in practice, but had a carb came loose and died on me. I sold it to Harvey Seel in Cleveland and he ran it the next year. I will send you a picture of it. Don't seem to be able to find any other pics of the Bay races yet.
> One of the fun things about Bass Island was the quaint hotel-winery—and the taxi cabs, which were almost all old Packard and Lincoln convertible town cars. I always wondered who brought them over and what happened to them—fun times. I moved to Wisconsin and ran one of the very early races at the then new Road America. First few laps on the 4 mile course made me wonder if I was still on the race track—few corner workers—open country, and very cold. Was fun to be a part of, and run so many races there for another 20 years. Kind of the same thing with Road Atlanta—but starting in 1970 instead of 1958.

Bob Snider's humble Devin-bodied Crosley began a sequence of H-Modified cars that were best-known in and around Road America after he moved to Milwaukee and started Snider Mold Co. The Crosley was followed by a DB Panhard, then a Giaur powered by a

Chuck Henry, winner of the MG race, drifts beautifully through the corner into town in the well-prepared #17 MG-TC (Betty Henn).

Mercury outboard engine, then a Jabro-Merc, a Martin T-7 and finally an Ocelot-Saab. In this car, he set records at seven different road racing circuits one year, with the number 52 on the side. Fast-forwarding to 1971, he went to the American Road Race of Champions in the Ocelot. He competed for 25 years, mostly in "real" races and some in vintage car events.

It is no surprise that the first four cars were the five G-Modified machines, minus the Elva Mk. III of Burdette Martin. The order was Chuck Dietrich, Bill Bradley, Dick Brown in the Siata 1100 and Al Miller in the Fairthorpe.

Dietrich won handily, although his right arm was in a cast from his wrist to his elbow. Chuck had fallen off a ladder while working at Dietrich Motors, his dealership in Sandusky. Prior to Put-in-Bay, he took a fourth place with the broken elbow in the national race at Cumberland, and after the 'Bay he won the Kenneth Ahr trophy at Dunkirk, New York, still in a cast. That's what you call determination.

Then the leader in H-Modified was Al Beasley. Al is a great guy and a great sportsman and his mother, the famous Ma Beasley, was loved throughout the sport. Then Will Grant, with that popcorn-popper Saab, was the winner in I-Production, with Clark Turner taking first in K-Production with his Berkeley.

The Third Race

The third race was a mix of H-Production, G-Production and some sedans. The new Alfa Romeos looked promising, and they had become more available than in the past, due to dealers Chuck Stoddard in the Cleveland area and Tom Payne in the Detroit area. Where there was one Alfa in the 1956 race, there were nine in 1958, including those driven by Chuck Stoddard, Bill Bradley of Detroit, Len Morrisett of Grosse Ile, Michigan, Russ Smith and Harry Constant of Grosse Point, Michigan. When Stoddard became a car dealer his car-lines did not include Siata, which he had raced in 1956 and '57, so he began racing an Alfa Romeo, which is what he sold—a light blue Giulietta Spider. That's in the G-P class.

"I was doing crowd control at the end of main street," notes Jim Etzkorn. "The Alfas made a chirping noise there. At one point in the race, three Alfas went off—two into the hay and one down the escape road."

At the finish of a tightly fought G-Production race, it was Chuck Stoddard ahead of Ivan Trofimov, both in Alfa Giuliettas. Stoddard won both the G-Production race and the Blow-up Trophy. Rounding the last corner of the last lap, his engine blew up in a cloud of white smoke. Fortunately, Chuck thought to stick in the clutch and coast over the line. In third place was the winner of the distance award, Norris Hartshorn, who had driven all the way from Brentwood, Mississippi.

One of the other drivers in the G-Production event was Russ Smith from Cleveland. He had been a flight engineer and gunner in a B-24 bomber during World War II. He recalls,

> I usually manned the top turret, but I was sometimes at the waist gun or the nose gun. I flew 50 missions [with three kills]. I lived in Connecticut in the '50s, and the guy in the apartment

In the paddock waiting for the second race is the Elva Mk. III of Bill Bradley, with bare aluminum bodywork (Stu Kerr).

The Elva Mk. III #96 of Chuck Dietrich leaves the paddock to head for the starting grid (Joe Brown).

Bill Bradley from Detroit drives this Elva Mk. III, neatly taking the corner into town (Stu Kerr).

Friends racing together: Art Brow in the #21 Turner has a slight lead on his pal Bill Staufer in the #3 MG-TD as they speed through the left-hand dog-leg coming into town in the third race (collection of Art and Dutch Brow).

above me had an Austin Healey 100/4. One day I was in the parking lot washing my Dodge and this guy comes out.

We were talking and he said, "You like racing?" I said, "I go to the midget races all the time." He said, "No. I mean sports car races." And I replied, "You mean you race those things?"

I had an Alfa in '58—what you would call a Normale. I raced at Put-in-Bay and then I joined SCCA the next month. Then I sold the Normale and ordered a Veloce. I sold the car to a sales representative for Goodyear Tire and Rubber Company, or actually I traded it to him for a completely perfect MG-TF 1500—black car with red interior, plus some money—then I sold that to buy the Veloce, which I raced for a few years. I originally got interested in all of this by hanging out with that crowd at Akron Sports Cars—Bo Miske, Bill Malion, Barnie Burnette, the Hier brothers, and some others.

Malion and I went to Port Clinton but it was just after the last ferry boat left. We tried to sleep in the Giulietta—fortunately the Giulietta has wonderful leg room. Then the next morning we went over and went through tech inspection. There were a bunch of us at a winery Friday night, drinking and listening to people testing the course, usually with a police car right behind them.

When I first raced at Put-in-Bay I got a Cleveland Sport Car Club "license," which was no license at all—just the tech inspection. SCCA drivers, they said, were in danger of losing their licenses, but that was never enforced. They had a decent tech inspection—they were SCCA workers—and the corner workers were from Lake Erie Communications [also SCCA].

In '58, the car ran well. We started way back but we had a good finish. A lot of the people in the field were club drivers, not racers. Neil Dever totaled a brand new Conrero Alfa that year. He lost it and hit a telephone pole in front of the gas station. I still have the oil filler cap from that car. It says "Conrero and Company." Neil was the son of Mr. and Mrs. Dever, who ran Automotive Imports, the wholesale umbrella for Jaguar Cleveland. They were partners with John and Vince Pinote of Cleveland Trencher. They had been in the Mercury business. They also had a VW dealership. They set up Neil as the general manager of the VW place. I think 1958 was the only time he raced.

Among the H-Production entrants, we found Art Brow in a Turner, Ralph Durbin in a Sprite, Eugene Shanahan of Vandalia, Ohio, also in a Turner, and race founder John Birchfield in a Morris Minor. Durbin's Sprite was one of the first in the Midwest, but the winner of the H-Production race was Art Brow in his new Turner. And in fifth place overall, a creditable position considering his car, was Robert Rippel of Elyria, Ohio, driving, of all things, a Simca sedan.

Here is driver Art Brow talking about the Turner he drove in '58: "The first year I was at Put-in-Bay with Jack Uhr, I met a dealer who handled Turner cars. His name was Smith. I liked the car and ordered one through MG Motors. That was the year [1958] I was coming up through Cemetery Corner, a very bumpy turn, and it bounced me up so the seat cushion came out and I couldn't see anything. At 85 or 90 miles an hour I was trying to loosen my seat belt so I could put the cushion back and I finally did and I won the race." I said, "You did a good job beating Ralph Durbin in the Sprite." And Art replied, "Yes, I had to work at it."

The #21 Turner of Art Brow speeds along near the airport (Stu Kerr).

9. 1958

The Fourth Race

The fourth race was composed entirely of F-Production cars from 1300 cc to 1600 cc displacement. That included a few Porsches, several of the new MGAs and a couple of Volvos, one of them driven by Tom Payne, who, although he was usually a Porsche driver, was a dealer for Volvo; and the other one was piloted by Bob Mollman, a rallyist who usually wore a bow tie to club meetings at Linsay's Tavern, looking oh-so professorial. One of the Porsches, a Super model driven by Stephen Wilder, #50, was from New York City. A couple of the Porsches were the extremely fast Carrera model—driven by Ed Eichenlaub and Don Wolf. Don had a sports car garage in East Cleveland and could actually tear down and rebuild the crazily complex 4-cam engine with its 20 drive gears.

There were several Carerra Speedsters in this event, as there were in numerous races throughout the Midwest. There were so many of these cars at the races that it was assumed they were plentiful. Now that the collector craze is upon us, we learn there were not so many; about 151, according to Gordon Maltby at the 356 Registry. Today, we all love the T-series MGs, with their light weight and simplicity. But as soon as the MGA hit the market, they were selling like hotcakes, and they appeared at the races right away. At Put-in-Bay in 1958 there were 13 of them on the starting grid. In the driver's seats of these were veteran pilot and ex–Lotus man Bud Pell; Fred Reynolds, a driving instructor from the Steel Cities Region; Del Lance (that was before he drove the Siata); Barnie Burnett, who must have had someone else driving his Porsche; and Homer Dasey from Pittsburgh, who must have left his Corvette at home.

Before you knew it, the one-minute gun sounded—and 60 seconds later, the field moved out, in this case behind Dave Weisenburg's Triumph.

Accelerating out of the turn in the third race is #78 Al Allin from Grand Rapids, Michigan, in his red Alfa (Stu Kerr).

MGAs occupied the first three rows, with grid positions picked at random. They were followed by a Porsche coupe and a Volvo; then a Volvo and a Porsche Speedster. It wasn't long before the Porsches moved to the front, in spite of the narrow roads on the island.

As the checkered flag came down on the fourth race, it was Ed Eichenlaub in the Carrera Speedster, then Stephen Wilder in the #50 Porsche Super, and then Don Wolf in another Carrera Speedster. No Volvos were seen in the top three!

The Fifth Race

Cars in the fifth and final race of the day were getting faster and faster all the time. The 1958 field included no fewer than three of the fabulous Porsche 550 RSs. The drivers of these wondrous and mysterious machines were Sidney Baughman from the Toledo area; Bernie Keller, tinkerer, inventor and driver from Mansfield; and Manny Holder from the Holder brothers' machine shop in Cleveland. As Dick Lamport recalls, "Manny Holder drove up to the race in the Spyder, on the highway. I used to see him around town in it, and one time it was parked near the Cleveland Art Museum." Ted Jayne in the Lester MG had finished a close second to a Spyder the previous year, but there was some doubt that would be possible now. In the E-Production class we saw four cars with the fabulous Bristol engines: the AC Aceca of Ed Lawrence from Detroit, the Arnolt Bristol of William Hutchinson from St. Clair Shores, the Frazer Nash of Bo Miske from Akron and the Arnolt Bristol of Ed McBryde from Detroit. Another related car was the Ace-engined AC of Ben Hall from

A tight race between the Alfas as the red #8 of Ivan Trofimov leads the blue #25 of Chuck Stoddard (Stu Kerr).

Willoughby, Ohio. There was the Morgan of Richard Cook from Lakewood and another driven by Gordon Harrison from Detroit. Then there were a whole bunch of Triumphs, including that of the notorious Quay Barber and of Reed Andrews, both from Cleveland.

F-Modified was a close race, with Baughman pushing Manny Holder all the way. He pushed him so hard that Manny set a record that year, of 89.90 mph. He didn't even drive that fast in 1959, so the '58 record stands for all time. It will never be broken. Those who knew the Holder brothers, Manny and Lorrain, found them to be the most likeable people. They were funny and they were smart. Their wives were beautiful and witty. Then, too, both were excellent drivers. Manny would usually do the regional races and Lorrain would do the national events.

They had that Spyder set up so it was lighter than a factory car and had better gear ratios, since they re-machined the entire gearbox, making first the same as second, et cetera, so you came out on fourth that was an overdrive ratio. The ratios in their car were the same as the last four ratios of the new five-speed transmission in the RSK when it was introduced. Lorrain described the gearbox modification: "We had four fast gears in that 550. We had

At the wheel of the TR-3A pace car at the 1958 Put-in-Bay road race is early race official Dave Weisenberger. Behind is the F-Production field, made of of MG-As and Porsches, with a few Volvo 544s thrown in. This is along the back straight where speeds are kept down by frost heaves in the macadam. Since there was no time for qualifying, starting positions were drawn from a hat (collection of Betty Henn).

A trio of MG-As rounds the corner at the end of town and heads for the airport in the fourth race of the day (Stu Kerr).

changed the transmission totally. We ground down the primary shaft and put the second gear ratio where first used to be and from there we made our ratios so that we had second, third, fourth and fifth, basically. Ironically, the year after we did that the factory came up with similar ratios for the five-speed RSKs. Through the downtown straightaway we could go *boom, boom, boom, boom* through the gears. We'd just touch fourth before the corner. Manny was hitting close to ninety miles an hour before he'd start to brake—right there in town." (The Holders raced the 'Bay just two years, 1958 and 1959, and they won both years. There was no question they were the fastest.)

An entry that was getting squeezed out by the new and more powerful Spyders was one that nevertheless added color to the race and enjoyment to the team. We're speaking, of course, of the Lester MG entered by the Funny Face Auto Racing Team (FFART) of Charlie Ellmers, Ted Jayne, Ben and Meacham Hitchcock, and Frank Floyd. Today you would call it a syndicate; then it was just a bunch of people who all liked the same car. That's Lester MG, not to be confused with Lister, as in Jaguar or Corvette. It was one of the most charming little race cars you were going to see, with its long hood, rakish cycle fenders and the happy-face-before-its-time applied in yellow tape onto the grille. Ellmers quipped, "The face would be smiling if things were going well and if they weren't, well, it would be a simple matter to change it."

In E-Production class, the Bristol-engined cars that were expected to win were skunked by the garden-variety Ace roadster driven by Ben Hall, a friend of Chuck Stoddard's on the east side. Ben had a red AC with big number 31 painted on the side in tempera, and he was well ahead of everyone throughout the race.

Richard Cook recalls what led up to that race: "I walked into MG Motor Sales in 1956 and saw this beautiful, black MG-TF and bought it right away. I kept it for a year and then bought a Renault. Shortly afterward I bought a Morgan. I learned about the Put-in-Bay race from Ralph Cadwallader and Bill Staufer. I went up there for the first time as car #12. I arrived early and walked the course as you're supposed to. Early in the race, I watched Reed Andrews' car. The U-bolts for his roll bar were too long and, every time his car bottomed out it would dig up the asphalt. Later in the race I lost my steering and went into the bank at the airport. But it was a fun race."

03 80

In addition to the racing stories I have collected, there is the description by Len Griffing, a writer for *Sports Cars Illustrated* who accompanied the Porsche Super of driver Stephen Wilder from New York:

Put-in-Bay is a gentleman's race and all the gentlemen are young. Fact is, of the hundred plus drivers who entered this year, 54 were classified as novices—the official name given to all those who have never raced this course before. The informality and esprit de corps made one think of Watkins Glen ten years ago and Bridgehampton of days gone by. And the cars of the competitors reflected the attitudes of the drivers

With only one or two exceptions, all of the cars were driven to the ferry (it was pathetic to watch the slushbox oriented ferry personnel lug highly tuned small bore equipment up the ramp) and to the pit area under their own power. At the "pit" (an open field), spark plug changes and last minute tire gauging constituted normal pre race attention. But then the production cars were production cars exactly as they left the showroom of the local dealer.

All of the races had one factor in common—a lot of cars didn't finish. Since almost all of the cars in any race were really stock, many drivers felt that the edge had to come from them person-

The Porsche Speedster of Don Wolf tracks out after Cemetery Corner and hits the gas for a quick trip down Cooper Straight (Lorrain and Manfreid Holder).

ally. Thus, they bore into every corner like it wasn't there, knowing that they were going too fast but just hoping and praying that they'd make it anyway. Then again there was the one-mile-long straight. Spectators could watch the expressions on the faces of the MGA and Alfa drivers as they thought, "I'm five hundred over the redline now, but if I back off he'll take me. I'll hold it until the valves crash."

And of course there was a "biggest blow-up trophy" for the driver whose pistons crashed the loudest before his valves, awarded to Chuck Stoddard who blew up his Alfa on the last lap, sputtered across the finish line anyway, and had to substitute a little fire extinguisher work for his victory lap.

The course itself was no creampuff; it was outright scary in spots. The black-topped roads were always narrow, and many of the turns were set up to take disadvantage of reverse banking. The mile-long straight was choppy—the kind of chop that makes the rear wheels do as much steering as the front wheels; another three-quarter-mile straight had two skyline rises that made 100 mph cars airborne; the start-finish straight was fully curbed and exceedingly rough at the braking area before the turn. Several cars lost their shocks completely at this point on the first lap, and severe braking became a series of rabbit-like leaps. All but the best were "bottoming."

Our entry was a tired-looking but really quite potent Porsche Super that took tech inspection in stride—except for the hand brake. Steve (Wilder) explained that if he tightened it the rear wheels would lock on the course. "Tighten it anyway"—so we did.

The cars line up for the feature race, with Manny Holder in the #54 Porsche Spyder and Norm Clark in the #62 Triumph TR-2. Just ahead of the TR is the tail of Ted Jayne's Lester MG (Ed Cavan).

Arriving at T.I. for the second time, an audible buzz went through the crowd, "He has no emergency brake." Steve backed the entire length of the wall, spun rubber half the length of the shop, jumped the handbrake, and slid the back wheels right out of the doors. Applause greeted this one.

The staff, remembering Corvette's 1957 Sebring debut, in which the styling department was brought along just to paint on the numbers, could do no less. We brought along our Art Department. And along with handbrake trouble, T.I. couldn't read our numbers! Forbes fixed this with Kem-tone, which defies solvent, and to this day the police still show interest in the big yellow-and-black #50 on the side. Oh well, the car needed paint anyway.

Our pit operation consisted of changing wheels, backing off on the handbrake (yes, the rear wheels did lock up), and changing shocks (seems we were always changing shocks). We finally settled on the original pair that got the car from New York.

Drivers Meeting in Town Hall spelled out the rules. An accident would probably put an end to this annual race, so safety comes first. Everyone races first for fun, to win secondly. No-passing signs are located 50 yards before each corner, and in the NP area the corner belongs to the outside car that has the line.

Question: "What happens if he doesn't give it?"

Dick Henn, who officiated: "If you're racing here you're assumed to be a gentleman."

But these gentlemen really did put on a race. Everyone who put rubber to road was out to win, and though the rules were perfectly adhered to (not one car was black-flagged) clusters charged down every straight and somehow—though I don't know how—managed to single out either through the corner or down the escape road. The only accident was in practice when a 4-CV Renault rolled on a turn, was righted, and continued to circulate. However, after the day's racing all but a handful of the haybales fell casualty.

Cornering at the Colonial Ballroom is Richard Cook in the #12 light blue Morgan Plus 4 (Joe Brown).

The first race was a nostalgic contest between TCs, TDs and TFs that finished one each in that order, settling no arguments.

The next race was a walk-away for the Elva driven by Chuck Dietrich, who's been a regular at Put-in-Bay since its inception, although the Berkeley team and Lone Isetta and SAAB entries provided more interest.

The Alfa race was the hairiest of the day. The two leaders, Stoddard (best blow-up trophy) and Trofimov were way ahead, as they cornered and shifted smoothly throughout. The continuous over-extension of the mad pack that followed had everyone but themselves waiting for the crunch of metal.

We had a personal interest in Race Four—Porsche #50. The local papers said it was a closely contested race but Ed Eichenlaub's Carrera passed Steve on the first lap at the second turn, and Steve actually didn't see him again until the Wilkes Barre Hill Climb!

The last race was a close finisher, but Holder's Spyder edged out Baughman and McBrydes Arnolt Bristol showed the Triumphs the quick way home. And after the race there were the awards.

Since we had a Super running against 13 MGAs, we (SCI) offered a trophy for the fastest one. Deciding to give something now, instead of something better later, we bestowed on Bud Pell, with apologies to cartoonist Lichty, a large white shop coat emblazoned front and rear "Hero Driver." It was worth parting with the jacket to watch the grin on his face.

The crowd had complete freedom to watch the race from any vantage point they wished, and

Ben Hall's AC Ace opens up a lead on the field of Triumphs behind him (collection of Betty and Dick Henn).

while none of the cars were running on alcohol many of the spectators were. One in particular, who wanted to get a free ride to the mainland, hobbled across the track about 150 feet from a fast bend. Since his right leg was in a cast and he needed crutches, we just assumed he'd tried the same thing at a previous meet.

If he had misjudged, a nudge from one of the speeding machines would have sent him to the mainland without an assist from the ferry, that is, if he didn't just plain orbit. But once the police decided to control the crowd, they acted with finesse akin to the blade of a guillotine. Within a flash, one spectator who wouldn't move was escorted away in handcuffs by two burly officers.

But a race is only a race without the little things that make it different from every other one. This one had Lonz' Winery, where everybody consumed many liters of champagne, vintage '58 air-ferry service to the island via Ford's literally very first T-birds—corrugated tri-motor aircraft, vintage '27; taxis that took everyone who could find a place to sit at a quarter a head, vintage '32 and '34; a Ferrari "America" whose prosperous owners had to sleep on the grass on the town square because the hotels were full; the flat-rate $58.50 for unofficial moonlight pre-race practice; and only two American cars on the island, brought by the Fury-driving associate editor of SCI and by a Buick-driving Volkswagen sales manager from Ohio.

Lots of fun at Put-in-Bay? Yes, but don't get too excited about coming next year, unless you're willing to catch a Thursday ferry, probably sleep on the grass, and help clean up the champagne bottles around the edge of the course. There's never a beer can in sight. Mr. Lonz sees to that.

03 80

Manny Holder drives the victory lap with Barbara in the seat beside him holding the checkered flag as it snapped in the wind, with the wonderful sound of the four-cam engine resonating behind them. His record speed was an 89.9-mph lap average (Lorrain and Manfreid Holder).

Later that summer, approximately 103 days later, beginning September 20, 1958, a noted racer engaged in a major contest. Briggs Cunningham, driver, patron and contestant at Sebring, Le Mans and most national races in the USA, this time sailed the yacht *Columbia* in the America's Cup regatta, against the British boat *Sceptre*. There were four races, on the 20th, 24th, 25th and 26th. Usually, these are decided by a matter of seconds. Cunningham won each of the races, with times from 7 to 12 minutes. Newspaper reporter and sports car racing driver Denise McCluggage was also at the races. She noted: "This is something only Briggs would say: when he found out how slow the British boat was, he said, 'I think we should switch boats with them and make it a better race.'"

The same weekend that Cunningham won the America's Cup, his sports car team of Lister-Jaguars was racing at Watkins Glen, managed by Alfred Momo, proprietor of Cunningham's race shop. As soon as Briggs got in after beating *Sceptre* for the last time, he called Momo from a telephone on the dock. He was delighted to hear that one of his Listers had placed first, with Ed Crawford at the wheel, and another placed second, driven by Walt Hansgen. As he hung up the phone, a newspaper reporter came up to him and said, "Congratulations on winning the race," to which Cunningham replied, "Yes, I only wish I'd been there."

June 7, 1958, Entry List

First Race

10 laps (31 miles), 10:30 a.m., all MGs, Class G Production

Car	Driver	Town	Make
3 GP	William Staufer	Middleburg Hts., Ohio	MG-TD
4 GP	Ralph Cadwallader	Lakewood, Ohio	TC
7 GP	John Tame	Cleveland Hts., Ohio	TF
10 GP	Ted Ley	Euclid, Ohio	TC
11 GP	Charles Tipton	Lakewood, Ohio	TD
16 GP	Martin Alperstein	State College, Penn.	TC
17 GP	Charles Henry	Bellevue, Ohio	TC
22 GP	Ralph Durbin	Detroit, Mich.	TF
44 GP	Ronald Kehl	Lakewood, Ohio	TD
47 GP	Al Weaver	Columbus, Ohio	TF
49 GP	Bill Henry	Wayne, Mich.	TD
74 GP	Allen Hess	Westlake, Ohio	TD
80 GP	Willard Whisler	Mansfield, Ohio	TC
82 GP	Thomas Kersey	Grand Rapids, Mich.	TD
86 GP	Jack Hargreaves	Detroit, Mich.	TD
91 GP	William Malion	Cuyahoga Falls, Ohio	TD
98 GP	Bernard Miske	Cuyahoga Falls, Ohio	TD
101 GP	Elvadore Cranage, Jr.	Cleveland, Ohio	TC
102 GP	Richard Reihm	Oak Park, Mich.	TF
103 GP	John Bernard	Warrensville Hts., Ohio	TF

Second Race

10 laps; Classes: I-Production, 500–750 cc;
G-Modified, 750–1100 cc; H-Modified, 500–750 cc

Car	Driver	Town	Make
1 HM	Al Beasley	Willoughby, Ohio	Siata Spyder
2 GM	Richard Brown	South Euclid, Ohio	Siata Spyder
6 GM	Robert Lossman	Rocky River, Ohio	Morris Minor
26 IP	Charles Stoddard	Mentor, Ohio	Izette
28 GM	Alfred Miller	Akron, Ohio	Fairthorpe
35 IP	Gene Tyrone	Westlake, Ohio	Renault
36 GM	Burdette Martin, Jr.	Northfield, Ill.	Elva Mark III
43 HM	Martin Tanner	Saginaw, Mich.	Martin T
48 IP	William Pickrel, Jr.	Dayton, Ohio	Renault
51 IP	Willis Grant	Canton, Ohio	Saab
58 GM	William Bradley	Detroit, Mich.	Elva Mark III
71 HM	James Eichenlaub	Ellwood City, Penn.	Bandini
75 HM	Vince Morency	Ferndale, Mich.	Crosley
83 IP	James Whitlow	Springfield, Ohio	Renault
94 KP	Don Drensky	Cleveland, Ohio	Berkeley
95 HM	Robert Snider	Lancaster, Ohio	Crosley
96 GM	Charles Dietrich	Sandusky, Ohio	Elva Mark III
99 IP	Bernard Miske	Cuyahoga Falls, Ohio	Renault
106 HM	Bruce Townsend	Hudson, Ill.	Crosley Sp.
119 HM	John Allen	Shaker Hts., Ohio	Allen Crosley
Alternates:			
105 KP	Clark Turner	Yellow Springs, Ohio	Berkeley
107 KP	William Seeley	Yellow Springs, Ohio	Berkeley
122 KP	Edwin Weatherup	Yellow Springs, Ohio	Berkeley
123 HM	Herman Emmert	Cleveland, Ohio	Crosley

Third Race

10 laps; Classes: H-Production, 750–1000 cc; G-Production, 1000–1300 cc

Car	Driver	Town	Make
3 GP	William Staufer	Middleburg Hts., Ohio	MG-TD
8 GP	Ivan Trofimov	Cleveland, Ohio	Alfa Romeo
18 GP	Edward Lidgard	Royal Oak, Mich.	Volkswagen
21 HP	Arthur Brow	Lakewood, Ohio	Turner
23 HP	Ralph Durbin	Detroit, Mich.	Sprite
24 HP	John Birchfield, Jr.	Wicklilffe, Ohio	Morris Minor
25 GP	Charles Stoddard	Mentor, Ohio	Alfa Romeo
27 GP	Robert Rippel	Elyria, Ohio	Simca
32 HP	Eugene Shanahan	Vandalia, Ohio	Turner
33 GP	Norris Hartshorn	Brentwood, Miss.	Alfa Romeo
46 GP	Joe Diamond	Detroit, Mich.	Alfa Romeo
52 GP	J.L. Chausee	Dearborn, Mich.	Volkswagen
56 GP	William Bradley	Detroit, Mich.	Alfa Romeo
59 GP	Harvey Seel	Avon Lake, Ohio	Simca
60 GP	Robert Watson	Detroit, Mich.	VW Ghia
63 GP	L.D. Morrisett, Jr.	Grosse Ile, Mich.	Alfa Romeo
64 GP	Leslie Smith	Detroit, Mich.	VW Ghia

Car	Driver	Town	Make
77 GP	Richard Cremer	New Hudson, Mich.	Alpha Spyder
78 GP	Al Allin	Grand Rapids, Mich.	Alfa Romeo
84 GP	Harry Constant	Grosse Pointe, Mich.	Alpha Spyder
Alternates:			
92 GP	William Malion	Cuyahoga Falls, Ohio	Alpha
108 GP	Paul Woodruff	Sandusky, Ohio	Volkswagen
109 HP	Dale Smith	Canal Fulton, Ohio	Turner
110 HP	Henry Dahl	Warren, Penn.	Morris

Fourth Race

10 laps; Class: F-Production, 1300–1600 cc

Car	Driver	Town	Make
13 FP	Tom Payne	Ypsilanti, Mich.	Volvo
15 FP	Bud Pell	Detroit, Mich.	MGA
20 FP	Roland Payne	Lakewood, Ohio	MGA
30 FP	Fred Reynolds	Irwin, Penn.	MGA
45 FP	Robert Mollman	Bedford Hts., Ohio	Volvo
50 FP	Stephen Wilder	New York City, N.Y.	Porsche Super
53 FP	Robert Wheaton	Cleveland, Ohio	MGA
61 FP	John McManus	Cleveland, Ohio	MGA
67 FP	Don Wolf	E. Cleveland, Ohio	Porsche
68 FP	Albert Close	Detroit, Mich.	Porsche
69 FP	Hank Handley	Detroit, Mich.	MGA
76 FP	Clement Mendham	Roseville, Mich.	MGA
79 FP	Howard Johnson	Mayfield Hts., Ohio	MGA
81 FP	William Strand	Brecksville, Ohio	Porsche
85 FP	Del Lance	Dearborn, Mich.	MGA
88 FP	Barnie Burnett	Akron, Ohio	MGA
93 FP	William Mallion	Cuyahoga Falls, Ohio	MGA
97 FP	Philip Forsythe	Elyria, Ohio	MGA
117 FP	Edward Eichenlaub, Jr.	Ellwood City, Penn.	Porsche Speed.
121 FP	Homer Dasey	Pittsburgh, Penn.	MGA
Alternates:			
90 FP	Robert Floeck	Greenville, Ohio	MGA
113 FP	Leland Beck	Allen Park, Mich.	Porsche
104 FP	Dudley Deimel	Columbus, Ohio	MGA
114 FP	Richard Dittus	Taylor Center, Mich.	Porsche

Fifth Race

12 laps; Classes: E-Production, 1600–2000 cc; F-Modified, 1100–1500 cc

Car	Driver	Town	Make
9 EP	D. Keith Whaley	Willowick, Ohio	Triumph
12 EP	Richard Cook	Lakewood, Ohio	Morgan
19 EP	Quay Barber	Cleveland, Ohio	Triumph
22 EP	John Tewich	Cleveland, Ohio	Triumph
29 FM	Ted Jayne	Cleveland, Ohio	Lester MG
31 EP	Ben Hall	Willoughby, Ohio	Ace
34 EP	Gordon Harrison	Pontiac, Mich.	Morgan

38 EP	Thomas Munson	Lathrup Village, Mich.	Triumph
39 EP	John Petrone	Youghstown, Ohio	Triumph
41 EP	Charles Markman	New York City, N.Y.	Triumph
54 FM	Manfred Holder	Cleveland, Ohio	Porsche 550
55 EP	Robert Samm	Monroeville, Penn.	Triumph
57 FM	Bernie Keller	Mansfield, Ohio	Porsche 550
62 EP	Norman Clark	Xenia, Ohio	Triumph
65 FM	S.L. Baughman	Lucas, Ohio	Porsche 550
72 EP	Edwin Lawrence	Detroit, Mich.	Ace
73 EP	F. Reed Andrews, Jr.	Cleveland Hts., Ohio	Triumph TR3
87 EP	William Hutchinson	St. Clair Shores, Mich.	Arnolt Bristol
100 EP	Bernard Miske	Cuyahoga Falls, Ohio	Frazer Nash
167 EP	Ed McBride	Detroit, Mich.	Arnolt Bristol
Alternates:			
89 EP	Fred Quartello	Euclid, Ohio	Triumph
111 EP	Raymond Baldwin	Hamburg, N.Y.	Triumph
115 EP	Forbes Howard	Grosse Pointe, Mich.	Triumph
116 EP	Ron Alexander	Youngstown, Ohio	Triumph

Results

First Race—G-Production MGs

Driver	Address	Make
1. Charles Henry	Bellevue, Ohio	MG-TC
2. Bill Staufer	Middleburgh Hts., Ohio	MG-TD
3. Al Weaver	Columbus, Ohio	MG-TF

Second Race—H-Modified, G-Modified, I-Production

Driver	Address	Make
1. Charles Dietrich	Sandusky, Ohio	Elva Mk 3, G-M
2. Bill Bradley	Detroit, Mich.	Elva Mk 3, G-M
3. Dick Brown	Euclid, Ohio	Siata, G-M
4. Al Miller	Akron, Ohio	Fairthorpe, G-M
5. Al Beasley	Willoughby, Ohio	Siata, H-M
6. Willis Grant	Canton, Ohio	Saab, I-Prod.
7. Clark Turner	Yellow Springs, Ohio	Berkeley, K-Prod.

Third Race—H-Production, G-Production, Sedan

Driver	Address	Make
1. Charles Stoddard	Mentor, Ohio	Alfa Romeo, G-Prod.
2. Ivan Trofimov	Cleveland, Ohio	Alfa Romeo, G-Prod.
3. Norris Hartshorn	Brentwood, Miss.	Alfa Romeo, G-Prod
4. Art Brow	Lakewood, Ohio	Turner, H-Prod.
5. Robert Rippel	Elyria, Ohio	Simca, Sedan

Fourth Race—F-Production

1. Ed Eichenlaub   Ellwood City, Penn.   Porsche Speedster, F-P
2. Stephen Wilder   New York, N.Y.   Porsche Super, F-P
3. Donald Wolf   East Cleveland, Ohio   Porsche, F-P

Fifth Race—F-Modified, E-Production

1. Manfred Holder   Cleveland, Ohio   Porsche 550, F-M*
2. S.L. Baughman   Lucas, Ohio   Porsche 550, F-M
3. Ben Hall   Willoughby, Ohio   AC Ace, E-P, 1st in EP
4. Reed Andrews   Cleveland Heights, Ohio TR3, 3rd in EP

*Course record: 89.9 mph, Holder brothers' Porsche Spyder

Source: *Sandusky Register* 6/9/58, *Cleveland Plain Dealer* 6/8/58; race entry list from John Comey, Art Brow and Ralph Cadwallader

CHAPTER 10

1959: The Last CSCC Race

June 6, 1959

Demonstrating the difference between entry lists and result sheets, Harry Constant was listed for 1959 in the second race, driving a Siata Crosley. He bought it from Bud Dayler in Buffalo—it was probably the former Ken Ahr machine. He and Tom Payne went to pick it up with Payne's VW camper. That was the focal point of the Detroit gang at many races. As Harry puts it, "We all hung out and had a good time." But the racing would have to wait, as Harry's new car broke a camshaft in the ferry boat parking lot at Marblehead.

For those following the fortunes of the Funny Face Auto Racing Team, 1959 appears to have been a better year. Meach Hitchcock reported that the Lester MG still ran under Charlie Ellmer's guidance; Ben Hitchcock still had the Veloce; Ted Jayne entered a Berkeley with a new windscreen he had designed, guaranteed to increase its speed by 15 mph (duplicates were for sale); Meach Hitchcock tried his luck in a Sprite, and John Tame ran against the TFs as long as there were any around, then raced his Isetta. Meach concluded philosophically, "Maybe we'll win some hardware, but even if we don't, the Funny Face Auto Racing Team will have a lot of good fun at a great sport."

First Race

Russ Smith recalled his entry in the previous year, at the 1958 Put-in-Bay race: "I bought my first sports car from Bill Malion and Bo Miske at Akron Cars. It was an Alfa Giulietta, Normale. They talked me into going to Put-in-Bay. I was so excited that I went to the Statler Hotel and joined SCCA. You had to have sponsors at that time, and Bill and Bo were my sponsors. I stood up at the meeting and Father Henn asked me, "Why do you want to be in SCCA?' I said, 'I want to be a hero driver.' The room was silent. Someone at my table whispered, 'You shouldn't have said that.' All the same, at the next meeting I got my membership card. I didn't need it for Put-in-Bay, though. I started 18th in 1958 and finished there too. I didn't know how to drive a race car."

Russ proceeded to get some more experience by going to the 1958 Akron airport race, Labor Day weekend. He talked to competition chairman, Barnie Burnett. Barnie said, "Do you have a GCR?" (For those not in SCCA, that is the book of General Competition Rules.) Russ said he did, Barnie asked him a few questions, and then he said, "Put three pieces of tape on your car and race. "I didn't know enough to brake before the corners," says Russ, "so I over-revved the engine and dropped a valve. That was a big bill. I raced three more times—

Tech inspection sometimes ran after dark and included the brake test, braking straight with your hands off the wheel. As Mickey Mishne once noted, a lot of people learned to keep the steering wheel straight with their knees. Here we see Willard Whisler of Mansfield, Ohio, successfully completing the test at the 1959 race (Rollin LaFrance).

Marlboro, VIR and Meadowdale. By then it was evident I needed a Veloce. I put my order in and put the Normale up for sale. A fellow who worked for Goodyear traded a black TF and money for the Normale, then I sold the TF and got the Veloce for practically nothing.

"So by the time 1959 rolled around, I had a Veloce. That was the year Bill Malion had the great idea to have carburetor jets made by a machinist in Cuyahoga Falls, but he didn't number them. He would hold them up to the sunlight and guess what the size was. He'd say, 'Let's try these.' The jets were wrong and the car ran terribly. That was the race where Stoddard was passing me on the outside in the right hand turn at the hotel. The picture was taken from the balcony."

As Alfa driver Dave Elder recalls, "I found out 1959 was the last one. Stoddard might have told me about it. I was ten years from my high school graduation in 1949 but I skipped that and I'm glad I went. It was a nice day. My permanent SCCA number was 19, but they gave me number 94. They weren't SCCA. They had a bunch of MGs when we lined up and a classy guy ahead of me in an MG said, "would you like to change places with me?—I know you'll be passing me anyway.' There were two Conrero-tuned Alfas and one of them hit a telephone pole. The phone company charged him $200 to replace it. When I was coming into town and pulling over 7000 rpm, a guy with a picnic basket crossed the road in front of me. It was kind of informal that way. It seemed like all the turns were no-passing zones, so there weren't a lot of opportunities for passing. I knew I was second and that's the way I finished—second to Stoddard. I was in the electrical business, so I had to leave early to get back to Rochester, so I couldn't stay for the trophy presentation. Then I had a terrible time getting my trophy, but finally did."

In the east, crossing the course during the race was strictly forbidden. At Bridgehampton in 1950, they said: "The public is requested not to cross the highway and to remain at a safe distance during the trials and the running of the races. Any person crossing the course during a race will be subject to immediate arrest." Holy smokes, the result of people living in too close a proximity to each other—and this at a race that was far less safe than the 'Bay.

One of the MG drivers was John Tame. John was a club racer. In the mid-fifties he got a gray MG-TF 1250 and, at first, rallied the car successfully, in events from the Ohio 24 to the Chateau Chevalier, the Photo Rally and the Red Leaf Rally near Kane and Bradford, Pennsylvania. "I navigated and Bob Meyer drove—he was a classmate of mine from Case Tech," John notes. Then he entered the TF in some races. The Kirtland, Ohio, resident joined the Cleveland Sport Car Club and raced at Put-in-Bay in 1957. He raced there in '58

The #103 black Alfa Giulietta gets the once-over by the crew while the driver's guests discuss whether it would be best to use 1.10 or 1.25 main jets in the carburetors (Rollin LaFrance).

as well, then came back in '59 to post a solid second place in the usually tough MG class at the 'Bay. "The last year I couldn't get past Bill Staufer's TD. I had more top speed because the TF was more streamlined, but he had more acceleration." John was the archetypal amateur driver—"I drove my race car to the track, stripped off mufflers, bumpers, windscreen, etc., raced, put the car back to street condition, drove it home and drove it to work on Monday," he said.

Second Race

As one of the entries in the second race (for H-Modified and I-Production), Kaye Hier was driving his first race, in a red Siata Spyder. Naturally, his brother Alan and his mother were there with him. His mother became popular with the H-Modified drivers for the cookies she baked and passed out on race day. As with the first race for most drivers, he didn't win or even come close to winning. But this great little race set him off on a driving career that lasted many years. He kept the Siata until 1962, when he went to see local fabricator Gerry

A great Rollin LaFrance photograph of the town, the front straight and the old water tower. The starting field for the first race is ready to go. It's a mixture of Alfas, VWs, MGs and Berkeleys. Suzy Dietrich is driving the pace car, a supercharged TC (Rollin LaFrance).

Mong about one of those new mid-engined cars. As Mong describes it: "At that point [1962], independent suspension and rear engines were the thing to do in a race car. I had previously built a special pattern after a Porsche 550, with a large diameter perimeter frame, VW engine turned around, upside down transmission and an aluminum body. Then I made a pair of identical hobby cars for two brothers, Kaye and Alan Hier. Their mother was there and she said, 'Oh, they look like the Bobsy twins.' I never liked the name, but it stuck. By the time the cars became popular it was too late to change it." Going back to the Siata that started this all, the Hier brothers drove it four years until it was time to move up to the exquisitely fabricated, aluminum space-frame Bobsy.

Third Race

By 1959, there were enough Austin-Healey Sprites to have a complete race for them, and for the few Turners also in the H-Production class. These popular, low-cost cars handled well and attracted drivers including Jack Uhr (Sprite), Art Brow (Turner), Meach Hitchcock (Sprite), Harry Griebling of Lexington, Ohio (a Sprite driver related to Les Griebling, who would soon build the Mid-Ohio road racing course), Gene Tyrone of Westlake (a Sprite driver and employee of Lossman Motors), Judge Herb Whiting in a Sprite, and for a change of pace, Steve Ivanyi in a Morris (Steve was the brother of George Ivanyi, a well-known advertising art director and illustrator).

After quitting the racing scene as a driver, Shea owned a few cars that he let others drive. "In 1959, Jack Uhr drove Shea's Sprite at Put-in-Bay," says Art Brow. "Positions on the

Here's a classic battle between Russ Smith in the #17 Alfa and Chuck Stoddard in the #22 car (Stu Kerr).

grid were drawn out of a hat, so Jack was on the back row and I was there in my Turner. I went from second-to-last to third in three laps. Then I brushed a haybale and when I looked back, my helmet visor flew off. I tried to get a pair of goggles that was in the side pocket. While I was trying to get them on, I buzzed the engine on the Airport Straight, I had low oil pressure, and the camshaft seized. Jack Uhr was third but he overheated. Ron Miller's intake manifold blew a plug out, and Whitey Tyrone's exhaust system fell off. What a race!" Uhr also drove the Sprite at Akron. Somewhere in that timeframe, Shea had a Morris Minor pickup truck, which he let Bob Lossman race at Put-in-Bay. "It was modified," says Walter Jarmain, "and it had a straight pipe—it was very fast."

Fourth Race

One of the figures in the fourth race was Doug Wearn from Columbus. In about 1956 he got interested in sports cars. "I started with a TD," says Doug; "then I got a couple of Jags, and then a TC. I wanted to do some racing, and through a friend of my brother-in-law I bought a Mark 1 from Chuck Dietrich. He helped me along in the racing. I went to Indy, Louisville, Cumberland and Vineland in 1958. Then I bought a Mark II Elva from Chuck. We drove it together at the Road America 500 in 1959.

Another classic contest, this one between Bill Staufer in the lead TD and John Tame closely following in his TF (Rollin LaFrance).

"The year before I raced at Put-in-Bay I went up as an observer. Then I took the Elva in 1959. We started on Main Street at the park and took the 45-degree right to the airport. Dietrich was in front on the way out to the airport. A couple of Carreras went by like we were standing still. Dietrich spun at the cemetery and I got off the gas to give him some room. Coming down from the cemetery there's a slight left corner and a bump. I think I was in the air about 70 or 80 feet there. He was still in front when we went through town. At the end of the straight through town, Dietrich lost control of his car and hit a tree where the course turns 90-degrees right, and I got by him there. He did not get back on the course."

Wearn must have passed the other Carrera Speedster at some point during the 10-lap race, because he is listed second overall and first in G-Modified, with the Porsche of Paul Vollmar from Sandusky in third overall. First overall and first in F-Production was the Carrera Speedster of John Curran. Doc Curran had his car race-prepared at Stoddard Import Motors and was a good driver.

In addition to the G-Modified Elvas, the fourth race turned out to be a Porsche benefit, with a preponderance of the lightweight 1600 Speedsters. It was a feast for the ears as the hollow, turbine-like exhaust note of the German cars bounced off the buildings along the start-finish straight. The field also included MGAs and Volvo P544s, the ones that look like shrunken 1946 Fords.

On his way out of town is Ted Jayne of the Funny Face Auto Racing Team in the #21 Berkeley (Rollin LaFrance).

Fifth Race

The vast majority of the 23 cars starting the fifth race were E-Production cars, and the largest number of those were Triumphs: 8 of them. Others included the Morgans of Richard Cook, Curt Gifford (an early flat-radiator model), Gordon Harrison and William Schwendler; the Frazer Nash of Bo Miske; the Arnold Bristol of Chuck Dietrich; and Leo May's AC Bristol. In F-Modified was last year's winner, Manny Holder, in his Porsche 550, and Jack Manting in another one; Bud Pell in the Lotus Mk. VI; and Charlie Ellmers in the Lester MG.

One of Charlie Ellmer's many friends, Triumph driver Bob Morrison, shares this story relating to the Lester MG: "Of course the Lester was rapidly outclassed by the Porsche Spyders and then the Elvas and Lolas as they came along, but Charlie had an interesting philosophy. He told me this at Cumberland: 'When I race, I consider that I'm racing only two people, the guy in front of me and the guy behind me. If I pass the guy in front of me, then I have a new race, but it still only involves two cars. The same is true if the guy behind passes me.'"

A little-known fact about Ellmers is that he was the head of the contest board of the NE Ohio Region of the Sports Car Club of America. He was responsible for approving and

The vast panorama of South Bass Island lies before us in this high-altitude shot taken by Rollin LaFrance. We can see most of the field of the first race, right after the start (Rollin LaFrance).

Suzy Dietrich in her pace car, a supercharged TC that the drivers found hard to keep up with (Stu Kerr).

issuing competition licenses to the drivers. Not long after the 'Bay race, he gave Roger Penske his first competition license. "We just wanted to have a look at whoever's applying, see if they can drive and maintain a car in a safe condition," Charlie said. "Well, here was Roger Penske and he's got a shiny gold Jaguar with wire wheels. I asked him to drive me around the block and then I said, 'I think we can sign off on this,' Roger."

Back to the fifth race of 1959: "When I got to Put-in-Bay in 1959," Morgan driver Richard Cook recalls, "I was met with an unwelcome sight. There were two of the new AC Bristols. One of them was owned by a driver I knew from the Mansfield Hillclimb, Lt. Leo May. At Mansfield there was a good jog halfway up the hill. May was stationed at Lockbourne Air Force Base. At the end of the 'Bay race, he was behind a Triumph, a Morgan and an Arnolt Bristol." Richard Cook, on the other hand, finished second in class after Quay Barber and fifth overall.

During the race, there was at least one little contretemps. "In 1959 I had an accident at Put-in-Bay," says longtime racing driver Reed Andrews. "I went off course between the airport and the cemetery. I almost hit John Clark. He wasn't a driver, just an interested spectator. I went between a tree and a fence post. John ran over and said, 'Are you all right, Reed?' I said, 'Yes, was anyone hurt?' When John told me no one was, I said, 'Help me get all of this stuff out of the car.' There were sticks and weeds in the car. We cleared them out and I said, 'I've got to get back on course.' It was like getting back on a horse after you've been thrown off."

Russ Smith remembers that the incident happened in a corn field instead of a thicket and gives this account of it: "After my session in the 1959 race, a few of us went out to walk the course—Bo Miske, Bill Malion and myself. We're walking along the road from the airport to the cemetery and here comes Reed Andrews in his TR3. Reed lost control of it and disappeared into a corn field, then he came out fifty yards later with his car full of corn. It was hilarious. Bo later sold his Frazer Nash to Reed Andrews."

In the modified class, Manny Holder was again the fastest Spyder. And Charlie Ellmers came in after Bud Pell's Lotus. Bill Bradley's Elva did not finish, and a Maserati that was supposed to come from Connecticut never arrived.

Betty Henn noted that her husband Dick was serving his fourth term as CSCC president and said, "This year saw the final run of our famous Put-in-Bay Road Races, due to circumstances beyond our control, and hopefully some day to be revived. Our entries had risen from the original 30 to our saturation point of over 100. We had many 'alternates' hopefully standing by and were turning away a goodly number of hopeful entrants. The crowd of spectators was estimated as high as 15,000 and, as was a fitting accolade, the course was included in *Road and Track*'s 'Map of Famous Road Racing Circuits in the United States and Canada' as well as a description of the race in Charles Markman's beautiful *Book of Sports Cars*."

Bob Morrison, originator of the CSCC newsletter, adds a note to the crowd size: "There were times when we actually tried to avoid publicizing the race to the general public in advance, for fear the island might be overrun."

Tony's Place, the little café just before town. Faces inside are looking for the cars. Al Beasley in the #1 Siata Spyder is driving by, and there's a postwar Packard in the alley (Rollin LaFrance).

10. 1959

Nobody really thought this would be the last Put-in-Bay road race. People went to the trophy presentation; they put the windshields back on their MGs; they went to get a drink with their friends; all the while talking about what a great race it had been and saying that next year might be even better. TR3 driver Bob Parsons was about to get out of the army. He was already thinking forward to the 1960 Put-in-Bay Race. "I couldn't wait to get back to Put-in-Bay," is the way he put it. He was mustered out in August 1959. Some people who had been too young to race were already planning to bring a car. Those who had neglected to take the Ford Tri-Motor over said, "Next year I will for sure." But next year didn't come. That was pretty much it for the 'Bay races.

⊗ ∞

In addition to my own collection of stories of the race, there is a description by Bob Karol who accompanied the photographer Rollin La France from Philadelphia. There's a story of its own about the adventure. Bob and Rollo went to prep school together at Western Reserve Academy outside of Cleveland. Bob lived in Hollywood and was employed as a draftsman for an engineering company. He had decided on going back east to the Put-in-Bay road races. He thought he might get a magazine to pick up some of the expenses and called *Road and Track*:

> They took me to lunch. They knew all about the race and were glad to find someone else who did too. I had a Nardi Fiat 600 that I'd bought from Ken Miles at North Hollywood Motors. He was a salesman there. I was looking at this car and he asked if I wanted a test drive. He took it

The #84 Bandini of Jim Lang breezes by the snow-fence crowd in town, with the Al Beasley Siata next to him (collection of Jon Clifton).

Norm Bradley's #41 Fiat-Abarth Zagato tracks out on the corner past the Colonial Inn, toward the start-finish line (Stu Kerr).

Bob Samm makes the turn at the Colonial Inn in his Lotus Mk. VII, ahead of all the other cars in the second race (Stu Kerr).

out on Angels Crest Highway toward Big Bear Lake. At one point he passed an old lady on the inside of a right curve, off the road, on the gravel. A cop was coming the other way and saw this. He turned around and pulled us over. He looked at Miles' license and said, "Do you always drive that way?" and Miles replied, "Yes. How else can I keep my superb reflexes in condition?" Then the officer said, "Just don't let it happen again." He must have known who Miles was. Naturally I was sold, and I bought the car.

I was going back to get Rollo. He was finishing classes at architecture school. He was going to go to California and get a summer job. On the way back, the car kept blowing head gaskets. I bought a bunch of them and carried a canvas water bag slung on the front bumper. I got to where I could take off the head, replace the gasket, reassemble everything and be on my way again, in an hour. After I got to Philadelphia we went to the Fiat dealer in Manhattan, where they discovered the radiator core was clogged up. They replaced that and another head gasket and we were headed to the Midwest.

Before going to Put-in-Bay, they stopped at Western Reserve Academy, where Rollo borrowed a 4 × 5 Speed Graphic camera, tripod and film holders from Mr. Moos, his art and photography teacher. Up at the island they got to the ferry boat dock and decided to take the car over with them.

Rollo La France comments, "Bob ferried the '600 to PIB so we could plan the views around the course and map out how we could travel between locations during the race."

With the Perry Monument in the background, the Sprite of Meach Hitchcock leads the Turner of Art Brow in the third race of the day (Rollin LaFrance).

To which Bob adds, "We had all our gear to make a non-stop pilgrimage back to LA after the race, so leaving everything in the car parked on the dock wouldn't have been prudent."

They arrived at the island in the daylight and drove around trying to plan track locations for photography and race-watching. By the time they were done on Saturday, Rollo had taken pictures from 18 locations.

"On Friday night we went to Joe's Bar up near the cemetery," says Bob. "We were staying in the same place as the Holder brothers. I knew them and later did some engineering work on a motorcycle they were developing.

"I don't recall that we knew in advance about night practice. I think we discovered it as a consequence of going to Joe's Bar, maybe 100 yards from Cemetery Corner. This turned out to be a convenient pit stop for the spectators who did know—probably from previous years—what was going to happen late in the evening. I recall walking from the bar to the corner with other knots of people ahead of and behind us."

"We enjoyed a six-pack," says Rollo, "while waiting for the approaching whine of each engine and the shine of the headlights. It was a gas, seeing the looks on the driver's and passenger's faces when the flash went off in the dark. I don't think anyone made a second lap!"

Doug Wearn goes over his Elva Mk. II in Parker's Garage just after tech inspection (Rollin LaFrance).

"Of course," Bob adds, "the Put-in-Bay cop waiting at the end of the straight entering town might have had something to do with it!

"I recall Cemetery Corner was surrounded by spectators long into the night," Bob continues. "Low conversations could be heard in the pitch blackness with an occasional glimmer of a cigarette lighter seen here and there. When a car with its bright headlights approached the corner, you could make out the silhouettes of people everywhere.

"When Rollo shot his flash, the spectators in the vicinity of the car were illuminated in addition to the driver and passenger. I was totally surprised to see so many people, standing not too far from the road, practically shoulder to shoulder—most of them with a beer or wine bottle in their hand."

Rollo missed some of this because he was concentrating on getting the camera ready for the next shot in the dark. "It was great fun waiting for the next midnight driver to come along," he remarks. "I think the beer helped."

"When the cars successfully, if not skillfully, slid around the corner and accelerated away," Bob goes on, "everyone would cheer. As the taillights faded, the blackness returned, the brief excitement settled and the quiet murmuring began again. Not too many minutes later, the next set of headlights would appear in the distance, approaching from Airport Corner.

Speeding by the Round House Bar in the middle of town is Chuck Dietrich in the #31 Elva Mk. IV, in the fourth race (Rollin LaFrance).

"I felt, then, that particular spectating experience was exceptional. The mood felt very special, if not romantic in its character—somewhat like a scene of the Mille Miglia. Maybe that's why I remember it so well."

Usually, on Saturday, Rollo would set up for a certain location and Bob would go off to a viewing vantage-point and take notes for the article, then return to go to another location. Rollo had limited mobility because of all the photograph equipment he had. However, at some points, Rollo had to cross the track during the race with his 4 × 5 camera, tripod, film, lenses, etc. Bob would occasionally help with setups for the more difficult shots, such as the one where Rollo is lying on the edge of the roof with film holders, lenses and the change bag for reloading the film holders in the daylight. Rollo was one of the few photographers using a 4 × 5 view camera. Rollin La France remarks: "Actually, using a 4 × 5 format to cover a sports car race is slightly insane. But being somewhat of a fanatic I wanted to get as much detail as possible, and with the large format I could enlarge and crop like hell with minimum graininess."

On race day some unusual and excellent shots were taken, including a few at high elevations. Rollo explains: "I was scrounging for ladders before the race. One shot I wanted was to get along the start of the race from an elevated height to have a clearer view of the

Going through tech inspection is the Holder brothers' Porsche 550 RS. Note the tubular framing for the fiberglass rear deck they made, lighter than the factory piece (Rollin LaFrance).

On the pace lap for Put-in-Bay's last race weekend in 1959, Bud Pell's #29 Lotus and Charlie Ellmer's #37 Lester MG lead the 18-car field (Rollin LaFrance).

cars. The second shot was to be able to climb up on a roof—which I think was a narrow roof—over the open wood walkway in front of some of the buildings on Main Street in town. I thought Bob took a photograph of me lying along the edge of the roof, but I could not find anything in my file."

After watching and covering all of the day's five races, Bob recalls, "Saturday night we took a ferry boat to Lonz Winery, at Middle Bass island. There were a million people there. We drank wine all night and caught the last ferry boat back to Put-in-Bay to get some sleep."

"The next morning we went back to Western Reserve Academy, where we returned the camera and processed and printed the photographs using the school's photograph darkroom," Rollo notes.

Then they headed for California. Rollo was driving. He was a good driver; friends used to call him Juan Manuel Fangio. He was drafting semi-trucks, two feet off their bumpers. You have to be pretty alert when you're doing that. If he didn't draft, they'd be stuck in the headwinds and could only go 55. There's only so much you can do with a Nardi Fiat 600, even if it was Ken Miles' car. Bob had an Olivetti typewriter on his lap, writing up the race report. Arriving on the coast, he turned in the article, and that paid for some of the expenses.

As an aside, Bob sums it all up: "After the race, we drove back to LA together in the Fiat. We both got a job with Danish architect Svend Peschardt designing houses on drawing boards set up in his Hollywood apartment. Great gig: free drinks and swimming pool breaks. I sold the Fiat and we both bought matching Ducati Elites and spent Sundays racing on Mulholland Drive above Malibu. At the end of the summer, Rollo rode his Ducati back to Philadelphia." That was an adventure too, but it's a story for another time.

Anyway, here is Bob Karol's *Road and Track* article on the 1959 race at Put-in-Bay:

> Once sheltering Commodore Perry's fleet, South Bass Island now harbors the last remaining true U.S. road race which speeds through the hay-baled town of Put-in-Bay. Originally conceived in 1952 by vacationing members of the Cleveland Sport Car Club, the event has grown from a scant 30 entries to over 100, now considered to be the saturation point. Such notables as Ed Hugus, Colonel Kuhn, and Bob Fergus have competed in this haven for small displacement cars.
>
> The roughly rectangular course follows the only four connecting roads on the island; from the start/finish line the road narrows abruptly at the square right turn and, past a slight kink, stretches over a mile toward Airport turn. Over the shorter, bumpy back stretch the course climbs sharply to negatively cambered Cemetery corner and from there returns down another mile-long straight, through a fast left-handed dogleg and a sharp right, to the finish line.
>
> The day before the race, as usual, Parker's Garage was the center of social activity as well as tech inspection headquarters; however, the seemingly endless task of processing cars and drivers was not without its lighter moments. Accelerating the length of the garage during the handbrake test, Frazer Nash driver Bo Miske disappeared, speed unchecked, out the back door. Returning from his trip around the building, he explained, "I knew I forgot to connect something!" Fur-

After passing the Morgan, Jack Manting in the #95 Porsche Spyder gets a little flying time and concludes it's only a bump in the road (Rollin LaFrance).

Bud Pell in the Lotus Mk. VI drives up the hill to Cemetery Corner with a horde of interested spectators looking on (Rollin LaFrance).

Reed Andrews, a popular driver the from NE Ohio Region, hustles his TR-3A through Cemetery Corner on his way down Cooper Straight into town (Ed Cavan).

ther inspection proceedings were temporarily disrupted when a propane tank exploded in the next block and race personnel and spectators were treated to a demonstration of volunteer fire department efficiency.

The long, hectic day ended with the mandatory drivers' meeting in the town hall, resembling a PTA function more than the usual trackside muster, after which everyone retired. Well, almost everyone. Well past midnight an occasional whining and squealing emanated from distant Cemetery corner as a driver unofficially practiced in the moonlight. If apprehended, the driver first received a warning, and, if he persisted in his efforts, his car was impounded until race time next morning. Surprisingly, the majority of speeding cars stopped turned out to be townspeople having a go at it in their big sedans.

Even without pre-race publicity, word spread quickly, and on Saturday an estimated 15,000 spectators swarmed over the island, embarking from the three ferries and Island Airlines' Ford Tri-Motors, which shuttled back and forth to the mainland from dawn to dark. Anything with wheels was pressed into taxi service including the pre-war phaetons, once again brought out of retirement, brushed clear of cobwebs, and hurriedly put into running condition.

It was impractical to snow-fence the entire island, so additional help was recruited for the safety crew, and with the cooperation of the spectators, there were no incidents. Race communications, furnished by the National Guard, were supplemented by 14 radio cars, and a mainland mobile patrol of enthusiastic motorcyclists lent an appreciative hand.

Getting the day off to a good start, the timing stand broke, spilling officials and equipment

Pouring on the steam in the corner out to the airport is Manney Holder at the wheel of the #129 Porsche Spyder. In 1959 Manny won the feature race for the second year (Rollin LaFrance).

during the practice sessions prior to the race program. For the first time in the history of the Bay—women not being permitted to participate in the race itself—Susie Dietrich and Betty Henn had the honor of driving the starting pace cars. Susie, quite excited about pacing the first race in her blown TC, poured it on, almost losing the pursuing Alfa Veloces.

The entire race program was revised from that of last year, and although the MG's still battled for their own silverware, included with them in the first race were the diminutive class J and other G-Production machines. In the Alfa pack, Chuck Stoddard's lead was uncontested when Neil Dever lost it on the dog-leg, coming to rest on the sidewalk after literally bucking city hall. Elder and Trofimov followed respectfully behind to the finish. Bill Staufer's TD led a tightly-bunched trio of the MG's from start to finish, and except when Tame spun his second place TF, retaining his position ahead of Fela's TD, there was seldom a whisker separating them. Spectators began wagering on the Fiat-Bianchina-Goggomobil duel for last place, while Bill Pickrel set the pace for the Berkeleys.

In the second race, for H production and modified, Al Beasley's Siata Spyder rapidly pulled away from the pack, pursued by Samm's Crosley-powered Lotus VII and Will Grant's Saab, which was also fighting off the triple Fiat-Abarth threat of Bradley, Stone and Stein. Suddenly the smoke-screening Siata coasted into the pits, and the Abarths, finally passing and outdistancing even the remaining modified cars, set their sights on the leading Lotus VII. Valve trouble eliminated Bradley's Abarth while he was running in 2nd place, permitting Stone to move up; but he spun in a last-minute effort to shake tail-gating Stein, whose Abarth then grabbed 2nd

After the races, various personages and machines traverse the main street, which only moments before had been the site of speeding race cars. Here we see a military surplus amphibious Duck, a Touring 2000 Alfa and a Renault Dauphine (Rollin LaFrance).

Post-race merriment includes the traditional pole-climbing at Joe's Bar near the cemetery. Climb the pole and write your name on the ceiling, and the drinks are on the house (Rollin LaFrance).

When the wine is all gone on South Bass Island it's time to get in a boat and head for Middle Bass Island and the famous Lonz Winery (Rollin LaFrance).

position overall and a class first. Recovering in time, Stone secured 3rd overall and a 2nd in class, the not-too-far-behind Saab managing a class 3rd.

After an hour break for lunch, the program continued. The third event, reserved for 1000-cc production machines this year, was definitely a driver's race and most agreed that it was the day's most exciting. Starting from the middle of the pack, Dudley Deimel quickly wormed his Sprite into 4th position, and from there he slowly badgered his way into first place. Tom Kersey's Turner, fiercely battling for the lead, bounded up the Cemetery corner embankment toward the tombstones, fortunately halted by a sturdy fence, while Deimel bulldozed through the haybales below. Meacham Hitchcock, content to watch the fun from a safe distance, finished 3rd. It was hard to ignore Ron Ulmer's exceptional driving, his Morris sedan being the loudest car on the island.

Having to contend only with other G-modified cars in past events, the Elvas had always emerged victorious; but the revamped fourth race matched them against the formidable F-Production Porsche Carreras and twin-cam MGA's. Chuck Dietrich, driving the latest Mark IV Elva, could hold off the Carrera assault of "Terrible Tom" Payne and Doctor Curran for only 3 laps. Doug Wearn's older Mk III already having been overtaken. In his effort to catch the fleeing Porsches, Dietrich spun quite dramatically on Cemetery corner, allowing Wearn to slip past. Pulling all stops, he re-passed the older Elva, but on the first turn slid on the sticky macadam into a telephone pole, retiring the best car conveniently in front of the pits. Meanwhile, Charles Tipton, in one of the pursuing MGA's, met the same fate, as had Dever's Alfa in race No. 1.

At Put-in-Bay, tomorrow is another day. In front of the harbor, Ruth Ellmers sits in her MG-TD as two gentlemen ride by on a bicycle built for two (Rollin LaFrance).

Wearn still motoring along, captured 2nd place overall behind Curran's Carrera, and Vollmar moved up into 3rd, as a technicality later eliminated the front-running Payne.

In the fifth race, for E-Production and F-Modified, the sympathetic crowd, otherwise for the underdog, favored popular Manny Holder, whose Porsche Spyder rapidly build a commanding lead. Jack Manting's similar 550 chased from a distance while Pell's Lotus VII and Ellmer's veteran Lester MG brought up the rear. During the scramble among the production cars, Reed Andrews also went astray on the dog-leg; meanwhile a Morgan from Wisconsin completely lost a fuel line and attached hardware, but determined owner Curt Gifford coasted to a stop in front of the general store, purchased a bit of tubing, which he wired into place, and proceeded on his way. At the finish it was Quay Barber's Triumph that showed the way home to Roger's Morgan and the 3rd place Arnolt Bristol driven by Chuck Dietrich. His lead never questioned, Manny Holder led Manting's 550 and Pell's Lotus VII across the line.

So that anyone who had to return home could catch a late ferry to the mainland, the awards were presented in the town park immediately after the last race. With the important annual business completed and their cars waiting on the dock for Sunday's return voyage, everyone climaxed the eventful weekend with a tour of the neighboring islands and their celebrated wineries.

With littered sidewalks to sweep and trampled lawns to repair, the islanders are still looking to race weekend next year even more eagerly than the competitors themselves.

At least that's what everyone believed.

June 6, 1959, Entry List

9:00 until 9:45 a.m.: Practice

First Race

    10:30 a.m., 10 laps (31 miles), Classes: G-Production MGs;
    G-Production, 1000–1300 cc; J-Production 350–500 cc

Car	Driver	Address	Make
2 GP	Ralph Cadwallader	Lakewood, Ohio	MG-TC
3 GP	William R. Staufer	Parma, Ohio	MG-TD
5 GP	John S. Tame	Cleve. Hts., Ohio	MG-TF
8 GP	Ivan Trofimov	Cleveland, Ohio	Alfa Romeo
17 GP	Russ Smith	Akron, Ohio	Alfa Romeo
21 JP	Ted Jayne	Cleveland, Ohio	Berkeley
22 GP	Charles Stoddard	Mentor, Ohio	Alfa Romeo
25 JP	Robert Stewart	Cleveland, Ohio	Goggomobil
33 GP	Al Miller	Akron, Ohio	Fairthorpe
34 GP	Al Weaver	Columbus, Ohio	MG-TF
46 JP	William Pickrel, Jr.	Dayton, Ohio	Berkeley
50 GP	Willard Whisler	Mansfield, Ohio	MG-TC
51 GP	Charles Fela	Akron, Ohio	MG-TD
58 GP	Neil Dever	Rocky River, Ohio	Alfa Romeo
61 GP	Edward J. Lidgard	Royal Oak, Mich.	Volkswagen
65 GP	Earl Kulgoske	Massillon, Ohio	MG-TD
66 GP	Ralph L. Durbin	Detroit, Ohio	MG-TF
74 JP	Robert H. Johnson	Akron, Ohio	Fiat Bianchina
78 GP	James G. Farley	Marion, Ohio	Alfa Romeo
94 GP	David Elder	Rochester, N.Y.	Alfa Romeo
100 GP	William Malion	Cuyahoga Falls, Ohio	Alfa Romeo

Second Race

    10 laps, Classes: I-Production, 500–750 cc; H-Modified, 500–750 cc

Car	Driver	Address	Make
0 IP	Richard H. Dittus	Taylor, Mich.	Saab
1 HM	Alvin Beasley	Mentor, Ohio	Siata Spyder
23 HM	Vincent Morency	Ferndale, Mich.	Crosley
30 IP	Willis J. Grant	Canton, Ohio	Saab
41 IP	Norman Bradley	Euclid, Ohio	Fiat Abarth
42 HM	Ronald Dow	Canton, Ohio	Crosley Spec.
48 IP	Ben Shoemaker	Massillon, Ohio	Fiat 600
49 HM	Kaye Hier	Stow, Ohio	Siata
59 HM	Harvey G. Seel	Avon Lake, Ohio	Crosley Spec.
60 HM	Robley Jones, Jr.	Lorain, Ohio	Fiat Special
72 HM	Phillip Reynolds	Jackson, Mich.	Crosley Spec.
75 HM	Melvin L. Sachs	Cleveland, Ohio	OSCA
76 IP	David E. Stone	Shaker Hts., Ohio	Fiat Abarth
80 IP	Robert E. Stein	Shaker Hts., Ohio	Fiat Abarth
81 IP	George Squire	Fairborn, Ohio	Crosley Hotshot
84 HM	James F. Lang	Fort Wayne, Indiana	Bandini

Car	Driver	Address	Make
86 HM	Lt. L.D. Morrisett	Grosse Ile, Mich.	Renault Alpine
88 HM	Robert Samm	Monroeville, Penn.	Lotus Mk. VII
96 HM	Herman C. Emmert	Cleveland, Ohio	Fiat
155 HM	Harry Constant	Grosse Pointe, Mich.	Siata Crosley

Third Race

10 laps, Class: H-Production, 950–1000 cc

Car	Driver	Address	Make
4 HP	Jack Uhr	Lakewood, Ohio	Sprite
9 HP	Arthur A. Brow	Lakewood, Ohio	Turner
10 HP	Stephen Ivanyi	Grafton, Ohio	Morris
15 HP	Meacham Hitchcock	Shaker Hts., Ohio	Sprite
16 HP	Ecurie Elf	Wickliffe, Ohio	Sprite
20 HP	Ronald A. Miller	Lakewood, Ohio	Sprite
28 HP	Harry Griebling	Lexington, Ohio	Sprite
39 HP	Gene E. Tyrone	Westlake, Ohio	Sprite
43 HP	Robert G. Newman	Akron, Ohio	Turner
45 HP	Leslie C. Smith	Detroit, Mich.	Sprite
52 HP	Win Reed	Pontiac, Mich.	Auto Union
54 HP	George Williams	Akron, Ohio	Turner
57 HP	Marvin Schwedler	Warren, Mich.	Sprite
62 HP	Thomas E. Cones	Cincinnati, Ohio	Sprite
64 HP	Donald H. Gardner	Euclid, Ohio	Sprite
82 HP	Frank E. Thomas	Sandusky, Ohio	Sprite
83 HP	Edward Houlehan	Garden City, Mich.	Turner
87 HP	Dudley C. Deimel	Columbus, Ohio	Sprite
89 HP	Ronald L. Ulmer	North Eaton, Ohio	Morris
91 HP	Anton V. Stica	Detroit, Mich.	Sprite
136 HP	Herb Whiting	Cleveland, Ohio.	Sprite
189 HP	H. Ronald Cowan	Grand Rapids, Mich.	Turner

Fourth Race

10 laps, Classes: F-Production, 1300–1600 cc; G-Modified, 750–1100 cc

Car	Driver	Address	Make
11 FP	Charles Tipton	Cleveland, Ohio	MGA
12 FP	Howard E. Johnson	Mayfield Hts., Ohio	MGA
13 FP	Tom Payne	Ann Arbor, Mich.	Porsche Speedster
19 FP	Robert L. Bub	Gates Mills, Ohio	MGA
24 FP	Roy G. Orr	Columbus, Ohio	Porsche
31 GM	Robert D. Wearn	Columbus, Ohio	Elva Mk. III
44 FP	Ronald G. Kehl	Berea, Ohio	Riley 1.5
47 FP	John P. Curran M.D.	Cleveland Hts., Ohio	Porsche Carrera
55 FP	Robert E. Stein	Shaker Hts., Ohio	Elva Courier
56 FP	Sidney L. Baughman	Lucas, Ohio	Porsche Carrera
67 FP	Albert R. Close	Detroit, Mich.	Porsche Super
68 FP	William Hutchinson	St. Clair Shores, Mich.	Elva Courier
70 FP	Paul Vollmar	Sandusky, Ohio	Porsche
71 FP	Bill Strand	Brecksville, Ohio	Porsche

73 FP	Art Riley	Franklin Sq., N.Y.	Volvo
79 FP	Scott D. Harvey	Dearborn, Mich.	Porsche
114 GM	Bernie Keller	Mansfield, Ohio	Lotus LeMans
117 FP	Roger Many	Hamilton, Ohio	MGA
131 GM	Charles H. Dietrich, Jr.	Sandusky, Ohio	Elva Mk. IV
143 FP	Quay Barber	Lakewood, Ohio	MGA
193 GM	Alan R. Patterson	McKeesport, Penn.	Elva MK.IV
717 FP	Fred C. Reynolds	Irwin, Penn.	MGA

Fifth Race

12 laps, Classes: E-Production, 1600–2000 cc; F-Modified, 1100–1500 cc

Car	Driver	Address	Make
6 EP	Quay Barber	Lakewood, Ohio	Triumph
7 EP	Fletcher R. Andrews, Jr.	Cleveland Hts., Ohio	Triumph
14 EP	Richard S. Cook	Lakewood, Ohio	Morgan
18 EP	John H. McCann	Bay Village, Ohio	Triumph
26 EP	Curt R. Gifford	Williams Bay, Mich.	Morgan
27 EP	Gordon E. Harrison	Pontiac, Mich.	Morgan
29 FM	Bud Pell	Detroit, Mich.	Lotus Mk. VI
32 EP	Alton P. Rogers	Niles, Ohio	Morgan
35 EP	Alan K. Vogan	Canton, Ohio	Triumph
36 EP	Lt. Leo J. May	Columbus, Ohio	AC Bristol
37 FM	Charlie Ellmers	Willoughby, Ohio	Lester MG
38 EP	Robert K. Rippel	Elyria, Ohio	Triumph
40 EP	B.A. Miske	Cuyahoga Falls, Ohio	Frazer Nash
53 EP	William S. Schwedler	Detroit, Mich.	Morgan
63 EP	Walter F. Abbott	Canton, Ohio	AC Bristol
69 EP	Charles H. Dietrich, Jr.	Sandusky, Ohio	Arnolt Bristol
77 EP	Ernest G. Davis	Dearborn, Mich.	Triumph
85 EP	James Mackenzie	Cleveland, Ohio	Triumph
93 FM	William E. Bradley	Detroit, Mich.	Elva Mk. III
116 FM	E.F. Spicer	Salisbury, Conn.	Maserati
129 FM	Manfred Holder	Cleveland, Ohio	Porsche 550
159 EP	Richard Denny	Garden City, Mich.	Triumph

Alternates:

1.	95 FM	Jack Manting	Big Rapids, Mich.	Porsche 550
2.	97 EP	Arthur H. Novak	Royal Oak, Mich.	Triumph
3.	99 FM	Burdette Martin	Detroit, Mich.	Elva 1500

Source: Art Brow

Results

First Race

Position	Car No.	Driver	Make	Class
1.	22	Chuck Stoddard	Alfa Romeo	1 GP
2.	94	Dave Elder	Alfa Romeo	2GP
3.	8	Ivan Trofimov	Alfa Romeo	3GP
4.	33	A. Miller	Fairthorpe	4GP

Position	Car No.	Driver	Make	Class
5.	3	Bill Staufer	MGTD	1MG
6.	5	John Tame	MGTF	2MG
Last	17	Russ Smith	Alfa Romeo	GP

Second Race

Position	Car No.	Driver	Make	Class
1.	88	Bob Samm	Lotus	1 HM
2.	80	Bob Stein	Fiat-Abarth	1 IP
3.	76	Dave Stone	Fiat-Abarth	2 IP
4.	30	Will Grant	SAAB	3 IP
5.	86	Len Morrisette	Renault Alpine	2 HM
6.	48	Ben Shoemaker	Fiat 600	4 IP
7.	0	Dave Dittus	SAAB	5 IP
8.	41	Norm Bradley	Fiat-Abarth	6 IP

Third Race

Position	Car No.	Driver	Make	Class
1.	7	D. Deimel	A-H Sprite	
2.	98	T. Kersey	Turner	
3.	15	Meach Hitchcock	Sprite	
4.	136	Herb Whiting	Sprite	
5.	45	L. Smith	Sprite	
6.	39	Gene Tyrone	Sprite	
7.	16	John Birchfield	Sprite	

Fourth Race

Position	Car No.	Driver	Make	Class
1.	47	John Curran	Porsche	1 FP
2.	31	Doug Wearn	Elva Mk. III	1GM
3.	70	P. Vollmer	Porsche	2 FP
4.	56	S. Baughman	Porsche	3 FP
5.	717	Fred Reynolds	MGA	4 FP
6.	67	A. Close	Porsche	5 FP
7.	68	W. Hutchinson	Elva Courier	6 FP
8.	24	R. Orr	Porsche	7 FP
9.	79	Scott Harvey	Porsche	8 FP
10.	73	Art Riley	Volvo	9 FP
11.	101	P. Forsythe	Elva Courier	10 FP

Fifth Race

Position	Car No.	Driver	Make	Class
1.	129	Manny Holder	Porsche Spyder	1 FM
2.	95	Jack Manting	Porsche Spyder	2 FM
3.	29	Bud Pell	Lotus Mk. VI	3 FM
4.	6	Quay Barber	Triumph TR 3	1 EP

5.	32	A. Rogers	Morgan	2 EP
6.	37	Charlie Ellmers	Lester MG	4 FM
7.	69	Chuck Dietrich	Arnolt MG	3 EP
8.	85	J. Mackenzie	Triumph	4 EP
9.	7	Reed Andrews	Triumph	5 EP
10.	27	G. Harrison	Morgan	6 EP
11.	63	W. Abbott	AC Bristol	7 EP
12.	97	A. Novack	Triumph	8 EP
13.	77	E. Davis	Triumph	9 EP
14.	14	Dick Cook	Morgan	10 EP
15.	159	R. Denny	Triumph	11 EP
16.	40	Bo Miske	Frazer-Nash	12 EP
17.	53	W. Schweddler	Morgan	13 EP
18.	26	Curt Gifford	Morgan	14 EP

CHAPTER 11

1963: The Secret Road Race

October 5, 1963

By 1963, in sports car racing, most of the purpose-build road courses already existed. We were through the era of racing on public roads and flat airport courses, including the SAC Base circuits, and the permanent courses at Watkins Glen, Bridgehampton and Elkhart Lake were already being raced on. Lime Rock, Virginia International Raceway, Mid-Ohio, Riverside and Laguna Seca were already active, as were many other courses. Racing on the public road courses at Watkins Glen stopped in 1952. At Bridgehampton it was 1953. And at Elkhart Lake it was also 1953. Brynfan Tyddyn ran from 1954 to 1956. And Put-in-Bay went from 1952 through 1959. Or at least they thought.

The 1963 Put-in-Bay race had its own program; here is its cover (Vic Skirmants).

All of these great races had their following, from the people who raced there to people who watched the races. To people in the Midwest, it seemed that Put-in-Bay died. Many wanted to bring it back to life again. And the racing people in Detroit and Toledo did bring it back, for one precious year, 1963. The original 'Bay races were organized by the Cleveland Sport Car Club, who sent notices out to Columbus, the Steel Cities SCCA Region in Pittsburgh, the Detroit Region and, of course, NE Ohio SCCA, as well as some of the Canadian clubs. When the time came around for the 1963 event, none of the SCCA regions were involved. In fact, they were opposed to the race, believing that the course was unsafe. They were so much opposed that they threatened to take season-end points away from drivers who did participate. This left the organizing to Waterford Hills and the owner of the track, Oakland County Sportsmans' Club. In addition to road racing in the summer, they had skeet shooting in the fall. According to MGA driver Carol Henning, announcement of the race was only at the club meetings in the log house at the race course, and in the club newsletter. The main of these was a note on a 3 × 5 card pinned to a cork board in the clubhouse. The only "outside" word of the '63 race was in the form of an SCCA notice to the regional executives of the NE Ohio and Detroit regions of SCCA, asking them to oppose the event prior to its scheduling, which was not specified. Naturally, Waterford was not going to send a notice out to the other clubs saying, "Come and drive at our unapproved race."

This had to have been a 90 percent Waterford event, because I was very active in NE Ohio SCCA, I wrote for the newsletter, and I worked corners for Bill Benham's Lake Erie Communications. I still had my Abarth and it was race-ready, and I never heard anything about a 1963 race at Put-in-Bay. I wish I had heard about it—I would like to have run it. When the previous Put-in-Bay races were run, I was too young to drive in competition. Bill Donley, a longtime member of the CSCC and Alfa owner, worked the old 'Bay race a couple of years out at the airport corner, and he remembers that the club got permission from the state to have one race after the "last" race in 1959. He suspects that the same permit may have been used by the Detroit group for their event.

Jack Holth and his new bride were corner workers at Waterford Hills who volunteered to work the Put-in-Bay race in 1963 ... and here are their passes (Jack Holth).

According to race worker Jack Holth, a team, initially of three men, organized a new 'Bay race for '63: Tom Abbott from the MG Car Club in Toledo, Ed Houlehan, who was the chief starter at Waterford Hills course just north of Detroit, and Al Blumberg, who was an official with FIASCO—that would be the Fort Industry Auto Sports Club of Ohio, Fort Industry being the original name for Toledo. The group that started the 'Bay races, Cleveland Sport Car Club, was not involved, and neither was NE Ohio SCCA, which supplied many of the course workers; Northwestern Ohio SCCA was a rally club, not a racing club. All of the '63 event founders were in some way involved in racing. Tom Abbott, for instance, raced at Waterford Hills in an Alfa. "The whole race was clandestine," recalls Jack Holth.

Detroiter Vic Skirmants, best known as proprietor of 356 Enterprises, the Porsche place, sent a list of the organizational roster, which looked like this: Ed Houlehan, chief steward and chief starter; Joan Lawrence, chief timer and registrar; Art Novak, technical inspector and paddock Marshall; Dick Norton, assistant chief steward and technical inspector; Dick Bailey, flags and communications; Dick Reder, ticket sales; and Al Blumberg, crowd control and course marshal. The odd thing was, it wasn't really an organization. It

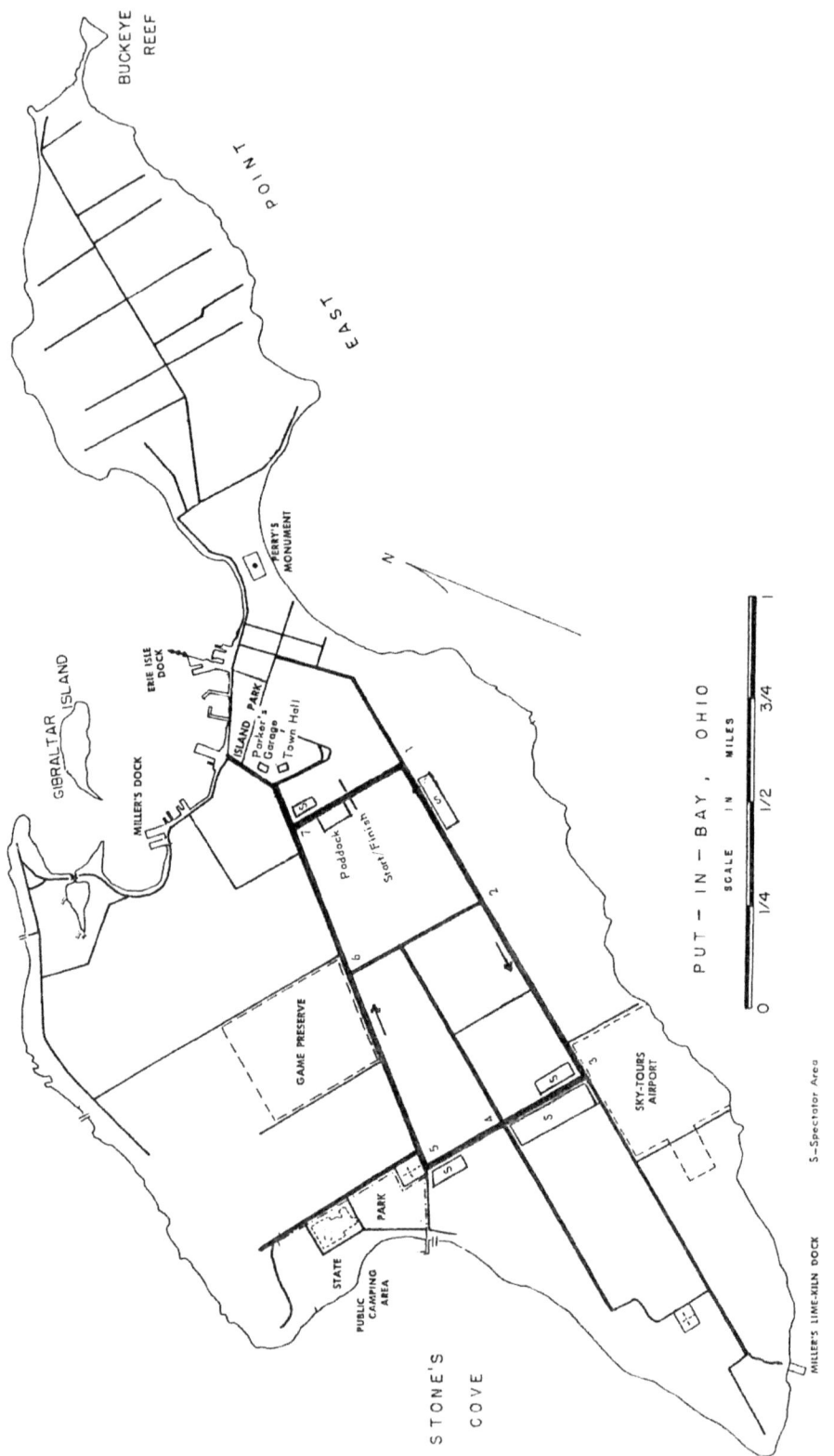

Seen in the paddock are a Fiat Abarth sedan(#15), a Fiat Abarth Zagato coupe (#152), a Porsche coupe, an MG Midget, a Volvo 1800 and an Elva Mk. IV (Jack Holth).

wasn't Waterford Hills (that is, Oakland County Sportsman's Club). It wasn't SCCA. It wasn't CSCC. And it wasn't the MG Club. The name of the sponsor was "Central Ohio and Put-in-Bay Racing Enterprises."

Some people called it "the outlaw race," because it was not run by any established club, such as Cleveland Sport Car Club as in the past. Longtime racer Reed Andrews, an official in NE Ohio SCCA, recalls, "People were using false names to enter in 1963, so their licenses wouldn't be taken away. SCCA would not have OK'd the illegal race because of the condition of the course. I was encouraged to go up and see what could be done to put it on the SCCA schedule, but I did not." Andrews knew the course and believed nothing could be done to upgrade the safety standards. As one who went to several of the earlier races, I believe it was the crowd control, not the course, that presented the problem. In other words, if you could have achieved the impossible and held a non-spectator event at the 'Bay, that would have been a safe race in the eyes of SCCA.

As "Mister Porsche," Vic Skirmants, notes, the '63 event was held on October 4 and 5, a Friday and a Saturday, rather than the first week in June, as was the practice of CSCC. Luckily, there was no rain, as there had been in 1952, when race chairman Dick Henn cancelled the racing on the seventh lap of the only race. This was counter to SCCA practice—but it was not an SCCA race. The '63 race even had a printed program, as loaned for reference

Opposite: Here's the race course outline for the 1963 event. Where the earlier races were 3.1 miles and went through town, the '63 race skipped the town and crossed over a block after Delaware Ave., making it a 2.4-mile course in a roughly rectangular configuration (Vic Skirmants).

by Vic Skirmants. Advertisers included Detroit imported car dealers and Boutet's machine shop on Grand River, as well as Rubini Motors in Toledo and Belle Tire, a Pirelli distributor.

As Jack Holth notes, Dick Bailey was the head of flagging and communications at Put-in-Bay, as he was at Waterford Hills. At the time of the race, Holth and his wife Carol were virtually newlyweds, having been married that August. They were turn marshals out at corner four. Two of the Waterford officials did not work the 'Bay race, according to Vic Skirmants. "My friend Larry Boyce and I were turn marshals at Waterford when we were 18 years old. You could also drive there when you were 18," he notes. "I raced my Porsche coupe there when I was 20 years old. I got some very good grades in school and my mother signed off for me. The way that Put-in-Bay was organized, Larry and I could not be turn marshals, so we just went down to be spectators. We drove down to Port Clinton, slept in the Porsche and went over to the island on the first boat.

"I remember the course was pretty simple," Vic recalls; "four ninety-degree turns. I knew a couple of people from Waterford—Ralph Durbin in his Arnolt Bristol and Frank Cipelle in his 1300 Porsche coupe. It was interesting to watch the cars on the island."

The course was different and shorter than the original 3.1-mile one. After the last of the races on the 3.1-mile course, in 1959, a law was passed making it illegal to conduct races on highways. Under pressure from island merchants, the Ohio congress made an exception to the law for Put-in-Bay, provided that the race course did not go through the main part of town, which it had originally. Instead, it cut across in back of the Town Hall, so it elim-

A substantially modified MG barrels down the straight at the new and modified Put-in-Bay course (Stu Kerr).

inated the two doglegs going toward and away from the park on the waterfront. It was still run clockwise and it did go out to the airport, across to the cemetery and back toward town. The new distance was 2.4 miles. The paddock was located in a field right after the turn in back of the town and toward the Airport Straight, and the Start-Finish line was right after the paddock. According to a report in the *Sandusky Register,* there were hundreds of spectators in the come-back year for the races. As *Sandusky Register* writer Jack Berkley noted, "The event was filled with thrills as drivers put their cars through the paces." Louis Heineman of Heineman's Winery remembers the new course: "The last race was on a shortened course that did not go into town."

The racing classes had essentially the same cars as those originally mandated by Dick Henn, but the list was modified to accommodate the new SCCA performance classes. As an example, an AC Bristol, which would have been in E- Production in 1959, had now been moved to C-Production by the Sports Car Club of America. An Alfa Romeo Veloce, which would have run in G-Production in 1959, was now running in D-Production. So the races ran from H- to C-Production, from H- to F-Modified, and two sedan classes: 1300 (VWs) and 1300 to 2200 cc. In other words, they kept the same displacement limits that Dick and Betty Henn had used for the CSCC races.

All of these events were overseen by a dedicated timing and scoring crew led by Joan Lawrence Voltmer. According to information provided by Don Burry, the equipment for this crew consisted of "a card table, typewriter, cigarettes, Coke bottles, piles of paper, many kibitzers and a grand total of two stopwatches."

The popular Volvo P1800 accelerates out of the corner, and it looks like he's going out to the airport (Stu Kerr).

At the start of the production sports car race, Bud Pell in MGA #1 and Carol Henning in MGA #83 get a good start after the flag drops (collection of Manley Ford).

Among the race officials listed for the event was Dick Reder, whose title was optimistically given as "Ticket Sales." Dick explains how this worked: "I tried to make the race break even financially, but I don't think it came anywhere close. Originally, we had hoped that the ferry operators would tack on an additional couple of bucks to help offset some of the expenses, especially since the summer was over and all the race visitors would be gravy for them. Naturally, they said 'forget it.'

"I built a ticket booth near the southern end of the island, tried to sell admission, which worked fairly well until the boats started bringing in people en masse. I had no help with crowd control at that point, so most simply looked at the booth and kept on walking. We couldn't have legally stopped them anyway, so I quit and went to the races. I wonder if the booth is still where I left it!"

Heineman Winery owner Louis Heineman remembers one effort to generate income: "In the last race, they wanted to put up a snow fence around our winery and charge people to watch the race, but we didn't go along with that."

In the original races, from 1952 to '59, the only way that money was made was by basically shaking down the merchants, which only Bob Lossman was able to do. He had a cottage up there and knew everyone well, including the mayor. He was one of those rare personalities that no one could say "no" to. After the races, he went around to the bars and rooming houses and said, in effect, "Well, Fred, I know you made a lot of money this weekend and you wouldn't have made it without the sports car race. Now it's time to help out the car club, so let's have a little contribution." In other words, not asking but telling. The persuasive Mr. Lossman also got some money from the ferry operators. He didn't become "the millionaire plumber from Lakewood" for no reason.

The pre-printed event program had a different schedule for different cars than the final

Carol Henning in the #83 white MGA maintains her lead on the #71 MG Midget at the last Put-in-Bay road race, October 5, 1963 (Al Bizer, collection of Carol Clemens).

one. Porsche guru Vic Skirmants provided us with the most up-to-date of the schedules. In it we see that the first race started at 11 a.m., for G–H Production and all sedans, a race of 10 laps. This was shortly after the performance classes came in, so you would have a Fiat-Abarth Zagato racing against an MG-TC. Actually, the #80 Abarth finished among the top three. Also in the class was the 948-cc Austin-Healey Sprite, with limited options, the Fiat 1200 Spider and Lancia Appia GT. From the *Sandusky Register* race results, the Sedan O Series (over 1500 cc) was won by Ed Scott of Birmingham, Michigan, driving a Volvo and the Sedan U Series (under 1500 cc) by Andre Dubel of Ferndale, Mich., Driving a Simca. The H-Production class was won by Reno Guerrieri driving a Fiat Abarth Zagato, followed by John McCarter of Ashland, Ohio, in a Sprite.

The second race, at 12 noon, was F- and G-Production. F-Production was taken by Leon Murray of Lansing, Michigan, driving a Volvo P-1800 coupe, with Bud Pell of Farmington, Michigan, finishing second in his MGA. The G-Production class was won by Gordon Harrison of Pontiac, Michigan, in an MG Midget, and in second was Bill Schwedler of Detroit in a Sprite.

Carol Henning drove her MGA in that race. Today her name is Carol Clemens. She was the only woman ever to drive in a race at Put-in-Bay. We'll let her tell you the story in her own words:

> I lived on the West side of Detroit, and I decided to join the Waterford club. I also joined the MG Car Club. I did hill climbs and gymkhanas and I crewed for an MG racer. Then I decided

I'd like to try racing. I bought an MG from Craig Pell. It was a new 1961 MGA. When I bought my car I didn't know how to drive a stick shift, but they taught me. We went over to a parking lot and I learned there. I drove it to work and I drove it to the races and raced it. Then, in 1963, I started racing at Waterford. It was my first season. We raced every weekend, May through September. I would race on Saturday or Sunday, maybe in the Feature. You had to be in the top two or three of your class; it depended on the number of people. Not to boast, but I would usually make the Feature. My unmarried name was Carol Henning, and that is what you will find in the race results.

I was at Waterford, and Put-in-Bay was announced six months before, at a meeting at the sportsman's club. And it was in the club news. Joan Voltmer was the registrar and also was timing and scoring. Joan was living in Florida and Michigan. She has a regular spot at Sebring. There are a lot of corner workers from Waterford at Sebring.

It took a while for SCCA to come on board. At first they said if you raced at Put-in-Bay all your points would be lost. They would not sanction the race. It was at the end of the season, and people did not want to lose their points. People would race under an assumed name with a different car number and a different driver's suit. Waterford had a hard time getting insurance. We might have had to get it from Lloyds of London. The insurance was mainly for the spectators, since the drivers signed waivers—I was surprised that there were so many spectators.

Ed Houlehan was the main flagman at Put-in-Bay. Ed had standing starts because a rolling start was hard to do on the little road that we started from. We were not allowed to start on the main street for some reason. The race was Friday and Saturday, and it seemed that the merchants closed their shops—there was nothing to do but prepare your car. There was a barbeque on Friday night at a church on the second straightaway, for the drivers and the race workers. My mom and dad came up with me. I walked the track with my dad. Then they had about a five-lap prac-

Carol Henning, in her #83 MGA, finished a strong third, and received a checkered flag as the only female racing driver in the last Put-in-Bay road race ever held (Al Bizer, collection of Carol Clemens).

tice, a short practice on Friday. As I recall, there was no regular qualifying because of limited time, and the grid positions were assigned by drawing out of a hat. In practice, the guy in front was hard to pass. The roads were narrow. I was 19 or 20 years old at the time—you could drive when you were younger at Waterford.

There were two taverns open. We went to one just for something to eat, and my dad had a beer—I didn't. I drove the feature race in my MGA. It was a white 1961 car, #83. I never had any trouble with it except that I hit the grille on the starting line at Put-in-Bay because they had a standing start. Houlehan would start the first group then wait a minute and start the next group. The car in front of me was Bud Pell from Waterford in the #1 MGA in British Racing Green. I think he hit someone, too.

Anyway, they gave us the flag and the corner came up fast because it was a short block, maybe a tenth of a mile. On the first lap, the cars were just sorting themselves out. I saw that my headlight was hanging so I pulled off the side of the road after the start. My dad was there and he helped me pull the headlight off. It was worth the time. I didn't want to be known as the kind of person who would hurt another driver or a spectator.

Right after the start we made a right turn, then we went out to the airport and made another right turn—went across the bumpy road next to the vineyards to Cemetery Corner and then back to the start/finish road. It was a 15-lap race on a square course. I thought it was fun—like driving around the block. I finished with a third in class.

Also in the race was a Jerry Tobin in the MG Car Club. He had an MGA. As far as I remember there were no TCs or TDs. There were some Triumphs. Jerry Latimer, a Waterford driver, had an Alpine there. Other people I knew from Waterford: I knew Bob Clift, who drove a Sprite before he had a Corvette. And I knew Frank Cipelle, who had a Porsche 1300 at Put-in-Bay and later bought MIS. He owned it four or five years and then sold it to Penske.

An Alfa Veloce waits in the paddock for its race. This is essentially the same kind of car that raced at Put-in-Bay in 1959 (Jack Holth).

Here's that Alfa Veloce out on the course, into a corner, with its weight shifting as the driver brakes. And what is that? A movie camera strapped to the roll bar? Hollywood! (Stu Kerr).

The two modified classes, F and G, ran in race three, along with C–D Production, at 1:00 p.m. This was a change from the order of earlier races, which had them in the feature race because of their speed. The course record had been set at 89 mph by Manny Holder's Porsche Spyder, and the Elva and Lotus sports racers were getting faster all the time. G-Modified was won by John Sharrigan of Watertown, Massachusetts, driving a Brama, which was a home-made copy of a Lotus 23. And F-Modified was won by Robi Roncarelli of Toronto, Ontario, in a Simca Special. In C-Production it was Jim Barron of Madison Heights, Michigan, in his AC Bristol. Then in D-Production, it was Jack Sargent of Swanton, Ohio, driving his Alfa Veloce, followed by Joe Navarro of London, Ontario, in a Triumph TR-4.

Race four, at 2:00 p.m. was called the small feature; it included F-G-H Production and all sedans. Among other things, it pitted the Porsche 1300 against the Triumph Spitfire and 1100-cc Austin-Healey Sprite. In the MG class, separate from the other G-Production machines, the #196 MG-TC led Bud Pell's #1 MGA for part of the race. Activity in the sedan class was livened up a bit when the Mini-Cooper of Gordon Brown pushed a Volvo right off the road.

And race five, the big feature, starting at 3:00 p.m. combined the top production classes (C-D-E) with G- and H-Modified. Class E grouped the Porsche 1500 and 1600, the Morgan Plus 4, the 1600-cc Elva Courier and the Sunbeam Alpine. Class D had the Alfa Romeo Giuliettas, Arnolt Bristol, MGB and Porsche Super 90. Class C included the Daimler SP-250, Frazer Nash, Morgan Super Sport, 1800-cc Elva Courier and Lotus Elite. Demonstrating that Put-in-Bay was not a tight course like Waterford Hills, the rapid AC Bristols were able to lap the Triumph TR4s, both cars having the same engine displacement.

The TR-4 roars down the straight. This is one car not seen at the earlier event (Stu Kerr).

A little contretemps with a solid tree versus a Triumph TR-3 (Stu Kerr).

The luxury of an inside garage for an Elva Mk. IV, an AC Bristol and a Fiat Abarth Zagato (Jack Holth).

Cars roll out of the paddock to line up for the feature race. The #69 car is a home-made copy of a Lotus 23, called a Brama, driven by John Sharrigan of Watertown, Massachusetts (Stu Kerr).

As spectator and later driver Bob Gustafson remembers, "Ralph Durbin had a medical condition that required him to drink a lot of water. So he would pick up a cup of water at the MG station right after turn 3. He would drink most of it and then throw the rest at Ed Houlehan as he went by!"

There was an accident during this last race, involving the #33 GM Elva Mk. IV. "Of course I remember the accident," says Vic Skirmants. "It was a front-engine Elva, which hit the telephone pole a little off-center. Instead of pushing the engine back into the driver, it sheared off the intake manifold, which probably saved him."

Of the accident, Jack Holth recalls, "The Elva went out of control trying to avoid a spectator who had run across the course. It was a terrible wreck and the car was completely demolished. They couldn't even find the driver. He was sitting at the base of a tree having a cigarette. And that was the end of wheel-to-wheel racing at Put-in-Bay."

Louis Heineman also remembers the accident: "The car went up in the church yard and that was the last race."

Dick Reder adds: "The last time I saw the Elva, it was on a trailer, the front half sitting on top of the rear half, heading back home."

By 3:30 p.m. the course was closed and the trophy presentation was held. Officials of the event decided that the least they could do for the driver of the wrecked $4,000 Elva was to declare the race finished at the time of the crash and, since Jack Garlinghouse of Lansing, Michigan, was in the lead at the time, the trophy would go to him. In second place was Jim Barron in his AC Bristol, followed in third by Ed Fischer in another AC Bristol. Class

The #63 car is the Simca Special (aka Abarth) of Robi Roncarelli from Toronto, Ontario (Stu Kerr).

winners included (in DP) Leonard Anderson from Pennsylvania, in a TR4; (in FP) Leon Murray in a Volvo P1800, and (in GP) Frank Cipelle of Birmingham, Michigan, in a Porsche 1300. "I do remember that Frank Cipelle was there in his 1300 Porsche," Vic Skirmants notes, "but I don't remember how he did." Dealer Tom Payne had brought in three of the rare 1300 cars in order to compete in the smaller displacement classes. It's interesting to note that none of the big league cars from past years—such as the Porsche 550 Spyders of the Holder brothers, Jack Manting or Ed Hugus—were present at this event.

In HP, Reno Guerrieri led in a Fiat Abarth; in Sedan M, it was Gordon Brown of Toronto, Ontario, with a Mini-Cooper, and in Sedan O, Ed Scott in a Volvo 544.

Other than the accident caused by a careless spectator, the safety record of the CSCC races had been extremely good. Dick Reder played a small role in the event, that of contacting the ferry boat companies to ask if they would raise the fares and pass the increase on to the event organizers. As it turned out, Dick recalls, "I was hoping we would make a little money off the racing, but it didn't happen." Dick's interest in sports cars began in 1957, in the army at Augsburg, Germany, where he bought a 1948 MG-TC. He went to the Maserati factory, but everyone was on vacation. Nevertheless, someone showed him the racing cars and took his picture in one of them. Then he went to Ferrari and saw the road car of the late Peter Collins. It was a black, long-wheelbase 250 coupe. "All the cars were handmade," Dick noted.

The adventures continued, as race official Dick Reder recalls: "After the racing we went out to eat at the Roundhouse Bar. We found that all of the waiters had gotten a bit tipsy and failed to show up for work. Jack Holth and I took matters into our own hands and started filling out order forms for the cook."

Here's the Brama at speed on its way to win the G-Modified class (Stu Kerr).

The #33 Elva Mk. IV is the car Chuck Dietrich drove in the 1959 race. Here it is speeding past the houses lining the race course (Stu Kerr).

A kid ran across the race course in front of the #33 Elva and it swerved to miss him, hitting a tree with the left side of the car. This is the result (Jack Holth).

Here are some of the damaged parts following the wreck of the Elva Mk. IV. Due to the way the car crashed and the impact absorption of the car, the driver was not injured (Jack Holth).

Holth adds, "There were twenty or thirty people waiting to eat. We just put white towels on our arms and took their orders. I used to do that in college, so it was easy to do."

"I don't remember if we ate that night or not," Reder concluded. "The restaurant had a pole in the middle of it, and some of us climbed the pole and wrote our names on the ceiling. The night became one huge party."

Some of the drivers and spectators, stayed over on Saturday night. They may have stayed at the lovely rooming house that featured a pattern of mayflies on the wallpaper. This way, house guests could not tell the difference between the printed mayflies and the real ones populating their room. Then, others among the Put-in-Bay aficionados just got on the next boat to the mainland and went home.

The ending of the 1963 Put-in-Bay race put paid to the idea of races on public roads. Crowd control was getting more difficult. In 1955, the worst thing that could happen was a drunk wandering across the course during a race. This happened at least twice. Once an enterprising corner crew sent one of their number to buy a six-pack for the drunk. "Sit here and drink it all," they ordered. You never saw a more agreeable drunk. But who could anticipate some nitwit kid running across the course at just the wrong moment? It must have been a change in the culture. It certainly meant a change in the way races were run. It meant no more Put-in-Bay. And that's a shame.

But this was not the last road race ever because, when vintage racing began to grow, there was a nostalgic yearning for another real road race. That was when Alan Patterson stepped in to organize the Pittsburgh Grand Prix at Schenley Park. The organizing body was the Vintage Sports Car Club of America, and many of the race workers were from the

There's one connection between the Last American Road Race at Put-in-Bay and the vintage race at Pittsburgh, and that is the man in this car, Alan Patterson, who raced at the 'Bay in 1953 and later founded the Pittsburgh vintage race (Joe Brown).

Steel Cities Region of the Sports Car Club of America. Apart from the mechanical damage inflicted by those high, unforgiving granite curbs, it was a safe race, one that drew ever-growing crowds and generated $2.5 million in donations for autistic children from event sponsors. Organizer Patterson? Who was he? The #12 MG-TC driver at the 1953 Put-in-Bay road races.

October 5, 1963, Race Results

Race One

According to the *Sandusky Register*, the Sedan O series (over 1500 cc) was won by Ed Scott of Birmingham, Michigan, driving a Volvo, and the Sedan U series (under 1500 cc) by

Andre Dubel of Ferndale, Michigan, driving a Simca. The H-Production class was won by Reno Guerrieri driving a Fiat Abarth Zagato, followed by John McCarter of Ashland, Ohio, in a Sprite.

Race Two

The second race, at 12 noon, was F- and G-Production.

F-Production was taken by Leon Murray of Lansing, Michigan, driving a Volvo P-1800 coupe, with Bud Pell of Farmington, Michigan, finishing second in his MGA; third was Carol Henning in her MGA.

The G-Production class was won by Gordon Harrison of Pontiac, Michigan, in an MG Midget, and in second was Bill Schwedler of Detroit in a Sprite.

Race Three

The two modified classes, F and G, ran in race three, along with C–D-Production, at 1:00 p.m. This was a change from the order of earlier races, which had them in the feature race because of their speed. The course record had been set at 89 mph by Manny Holder's Porsche Spyder, and the Elva and Lotus sports racers were getting faster all the time. Holder's record was not broken.

G-Modified was won by John Sharrigan of Watertown, Massachusetts, driving a Brama, which was a homemade copy of a Lotus 23. F-Modified was won by Robi Roncarelli of Toronto, Ontario, in a Simca Special. In C-Production it was Jim Barron of Madison Heights, Michigan, in his AC Bristol. Then in D-Production it was Jack Sargent of Swanton, Ohio, driving his Alfa Veloce, followed by Joe Navarro of London, Ontario, in a Triumph TR-4. There was an accident toward the end of this race and it was stopped, with winners declared as of the time of the accident.

Race Four

This was called the Small Feature; it ran at 2:00 p.m. and included F-G-H-Production and all sedans. This race was cancelled due to the accident. There were no results for this in the *Sandusky Register* and, in fact, race four was called the Feature Race in their coverage.

Chapter 12

Farewell to Put-in-Bay— It Was a Wonderful Race

The Put-in-Bay road races had a pretty good run. In nine years of racing, they surpassed the record of any other race on public roads ever run in the United States, and some of those in other countries—not major races such as Monaco, the Mille Miglia, Targa Florio or Tourist Trophy, but races such as Carerra Panamericana, Buenos Aires, Pau Belgium and Bari Italy.

It was by far the safest road race ever run, with no fatalities and no serious injuries. Despite a few spin-outs and a couple of roll-overs, no serious harm occurred; not even the accident in the 1963 race.

According to statistics compiled by Roger Linton, 120 different cars drove there over the years, with 292 different drivers at the wheel. Notable cars included the ex–Ed Hugus

Autocross Class GS car, driven by Rik Davis, by the Put-in-Bay welcome sign, in 1981 (collection of Ellen Honsperger).

Rear view of the Roger Johnson Corvette turning the corner at Lake Erie at the 1982 event and hoping to miss the autocross cones (collection of Ellen Honsperger).

The 1983 event staging area, in front of Frosty's Beer and Pizza. Seen in the middle of the street is the A-Modified formula car of Skip and Ellen Honsperger, powered by a rotary engine. Ellen set the fastest time of the day, beating well-known autocrossers Joyce and Dave Looman (collection of Ellen Honsperger).

Cooper-Climax that finished in the top 10 at both Le Mans and Sebring; the first Lotus in the United States, a Mark VI; the first Elva in the U.S. and a number of others following it; 7 ACs; a rare monoposto Kieft MG; several Siata 750s, 1100s, 1400s and 208s; Bandini drivers including a national champion; a rare high-tail 550 Porsche Spyder as well as a number of 550RS Spyders; 3 Fiat-Abarth Zagatos; and a Doretti. That's in addition to about a million MGs as well as 18 Alfas and 18 production Porsches.

Drivers of national stature were at the 'Bay races, including Chuck Dietrich, who drove in Europe on the Elva team; three-time Alfa champion Chuck Stoddard; two-time national champion Al Beasley, Sr.; one-time national champions Jim Eichenlaub, Mel Sachs and Don Wolf; Ed Hugus, a frequent racer at Le Mans and Sebring as well as the Put-in-Bay events; Carl Haas, later to be the U.S. distributor for Elva and Lotus cars and a partner in the Newman Haas Indycar racing team; and Tom Payne, who later drove for Carroll Shelby.

Of course a statistical summary of the Put-in-Bay road races falls far short of capturing the essence of this fabulous event that so many people loved. Where else are you going to find a beautiful harbor next to the race course, the friendliness, the relaxed atmosphere, and, as taken in context of the time, the novelty of the cars and of the sport itself.

Jim Bennett recalls: "When you think of it, the cars are coming down the road, spectators are sitting on the sidewalk, only hay bales in front of the fire hydrants, no roll bars. It's a wonder somebody wasn't seriously hurt." But then we remind him of the displacement limits. We didn't have the Jaguars and Allards going 150 miles an hour. We just had two-liter production cars, a liter and a half modified.

"Remember Barnie Burnett, the one-armed Porsche driver?" Jim says. Of course we

The 1984 autocross drivers' meeting, photographed past the backsides of Roger Johnson and Terry Bassett (collection of Ellen Honsperger).

Many of the well-known drivers from the original race attended the MG meeting on June 2, 1990. Organized by Bob Satava, "the MG King of Cleveland," with Dave and Sheila Bly, it brought 35 early MGs over to the island. Pictured are (left to right) Bob Satava, champion driver Charlie Ellmers, and race organizer Betty Henn (Carl Goodwin).

Well-known TC driver Ralph Cadwallader poses with a TC. Ralph drove all of the CSCC races except that of 1952 (Carl Goodwin).

12. Farewell to Put-in-Bay—It Was a Wonderful Race

Suzy Dietrich drove the pace car at Put-in-Bay and, according to most drivers, drove it mighty fast (Carl Goodwin).

Jim Dever was also a fixture at the 'Bay races, at the wheel of his MG-TC. Jim was a mechanic at Lossman's and, later on, worked on a lakes freighter. He had some mighty interesting stories (Carl Goodwin).

Bob Satava gets ready for the parade lap with Betty Henn riding in his race car. Bob competed in this car for many years at Mid-Ohio and other vintage events (Carl Goodwin).

A line of T-series MGs makes the parade lap on the original 3.1-mile course for the Put-in-Bay road races (Carl Goodwin).

A 1959 Porsche roadster leads the parade, at this point, for the 2009 Put-in-Bay road race reunion (Pat Black).

remember him. He won all the races. I had a white Porsche Speedster that I bought in Akron, and I always wondered if it was his car. "Remember the Porsches come up over a rise going into town?" Jim says. "They were in the air quite a ways—because they were rear-engined. The front-engined cars didn't sail like that." Many stories, many memories.

As to the claim of Put-in-Bay being the last road race, occasionally you hear of a vintage road race such as the late Steamboat Springs event or the current Pittsburgh Grand Prix. Not to demean the efforts of dedicated vintage racers, but they are really not the same as a "real" race.

But after 1963, people couldn't quite let go of Put-in-Bay's appeal. So there were three events that took place after the actual races.

One was an autocross held in 1981, '82, '83 and '84 on the first weekend of October, and organized by the Northwestern Ohio Region of SCCA. The primary organizers were Roger Johnson and Terry Bassett, autocross champions from Toledo; for the last two years, Skip and Ellen Honsperger co-chaired the event. They set up a pylon course around the town square. A certain number of the old cars were there, including MGs, Alfas, Porsches and Triumphs. Among the top competitors were Gary and Paulette Lownsdale of Detroit, running a race-prepared Lotus Elan.

As Roger Johnson describes it, "It was the world's worst autocross course, but the best-ever autocross event ... and party!" Roger was the regional executive of the Northwest Ohio SCCA Region and the publicist of the event. Terry Bassett ran the autocross program for the region; Roger credits him with setting up the whole event, including snow fences around the course; the course itself which, by necessity, was around the town park; and the workers,

At the 2010 reunion, longtime Put-in-Bay driver Art Brow waves from the ex–Bill Staufer MG-TD with his wife Dutch Brow, who was also a racing driver (Nancy Goodwin).

Cars more likely to have been racing at Put-in-Bay include this ivory MG-TF and the Triumph TR-3A that follows it (Pat Black).

The so-called Flat Radiator Morgan takes a time-out from the parade to visit with some admirers next to the curb at the town park at the 2009 reunion (Pat Black).

the classes and the regulations. The event met with a fantastic reception and was continued for three more years.

Recollections of the autocrosses include: the '74 Corvette with a Jimmy 6–71 blower of a certain Neil Wilson—it hit a concrete wall; a Ferrari driver going over the curb (according to the rules he had to go back to the boat and off the island); a Mini-Cooper on the sidewalk at Frosty's Bar; the antics by the Trans Am Club president in his 455 Super Duty; a Model A entered by the blacksmith shop; and, of course, the sailboat folks who "came ashore with a clean t-shirt and a $20 bill, and changed neither during their visit."

The next event was an MG meeting on the island, June 2, 1990, the 31st anniversary of the races. It was organized by Dave Bly, Sheila Bly and Bob Satava, "the MG King of Cleveland," who, at the time, was the president of the Cleveland Sport Car Club (which, of course, had run the original races). The races of the 1950s were so popular that, in the last year, 200 drivers had to be turned away. Stirling Moss planned to drive it but was prevented by a commitment to Aston Martin. Bob Satava was a corner worker. This was a great event, and Dave, Sheila and Bob did a fine job of organizing it. About 35 MGs were ferried over to the island. Many persons in the original cast of characters showed up, including Charlie and Ruth Ellmers, Betty Henn, Suzy Dietrich, Jim Dever, Art Brow and Ralph Cadwallader.

They rode as guests in the cars of other people and they spoke of the past. Many of the original racing cars were on the scene as well. They displayed the cars on the park at the harbor, and then they drove around the old course. The lead car was Satava's MG-TD racing car, with Betty Henn sitting in the back. Ahead of it was a village cop car driven by a police-

Suzy Dietrich gets ready to go in the old Dietrich racing TC, now owned by Bob Satava (Carl Goodwin).

Four cars from the early days of racing at Put-in-Bay: (left to right) the #24 Chuck Dietrich TC, the Ralph Cadwallader car owned by Ollie Emerson, the Chuck Henry TC owned by the Henry family, and the John Tame MG-TF owned by Pat Black (Carl Goodwin).

Fronting the row of spectators out at the airport autocross is Alfa club officer Joe Wehrheim with his Giulietta Spider. Wife Jeanne is sitting in the car—she's a good sport, riding long distances with the top down (Carl Goodwin).

woman, who drove around the course at a leisurely pace. Careful, you might roll those things over! Nevertheless, it was nice to see the old cars staged at the start-finish line and taking their parade lap. If you squinted your eyes, you could imagine they were racing.

During that same year, Put-in-Bay historian Bob Satava plus Dave and Sheila Bly and their cousin made a tour of several road-race participants and put it all on videotape. Drivers and race-workers recorded included Charlie Ellmers, John Tame, John Comey, Ralph Cadwallader, Art and Dutch Brow, Reed Andrews, Al Beasley and Betty Henn.

Then after the passage of a few more years, from 2009 at least through the writing of this book in 2013, there came the Put-in-Bay Reunion. The organizers included Jack Woerhle, Bob and Linda Williams, Manley Ford, Bob Colaizzi (as the poster artist) and Roger Linton, son of the 1950s OSCA and Siata racer Otto Linton. This was intended to be an ongoing event with numerous aspects, and so far it is, having gotten better every year. When it started, there was a slide show on races of the past, put on by the author and by Chris Kintner, grandson of the race chairman.

There was a car show in front of the park, accented with interviews that Bob Williams did with people who had been involved with the early races, such as Art Brow and Suzy Dietrich, followed by a parade around the old race course at a pace that you could call brisk. Lunches and dinners filled in the odd time slots, and a good time was had by all. Elements have been added since that first year, including the placement and dedication of engraved memorial stones at various places around the race course, mainly corners. Then there was an autocross out at the airport, and then the next year there was a short wheel-to-wheel race. Interest and attendance has been going up each year. MG racer Manley Ford has written and sent press releases out to the vintage sports car magazines, and the magazines have become very attentive to these each successive year.

For these and many other people, the Put-in-Bay road races will be in their hearts and minds forever.

Appendix: Special Contributors

Many people were instrumental in the writing of this book, as witnessed by the long list of names in the acknowledgments. But there were a handful without whose help the book could not have happened. Following are brief biographical sketches of these special people.

John Birchfield

According to long-time Put-in-Bay racing driver Ralph Cadwallader,

John Birchfield is a name that has become little known in the history of Put-in-Bay, so before too much fades from memory and John's contribution becomes vague and unappreciated, I think it is important to recount his part in getting the races started.

When I talked to John he was unassuming and very low key about what he did. However, I confirmed that he was asked to handle this embryonic race because he had just put on a very successful rally for the club and if he could [do] that a mere road race would be a walk in the park.

Dick Henn and Andy Zimmerman handled the politics while John took over the actual mechanics of the race. He and Norm Bradley went to the island in April of '52, drove around in Norm's XK120, laid out the course and decided, due to the rough narrow roads and sharp bends, that the course should be limited to two liter unblown and 1500 cc blown or modified. That was quite altruistic of Norm since he really wanted to run his Jag.

They decided that the old grape field was the idea spot for the pits and that Parker's Garage was the place for tech inspection.

From there John pretty much managed what became in September of 1952 the first of eight very successful Put-in-Bay races.

It was a wonderful era for a lot of us—the beginning of a time in our lives we shall never forget—and for this we thank you—John Birchfield.

"I pit-crewed at Bridgehampton for the 'round the houses race," says Birchfield, "and they paid for my motel accommodation. A bunch of people from Grumman were there. I went to Sebring to pit crew for a Jag and they didn't pay for my motel. Things must be different in different places.

ଦ ଓ

John Birchfield grew up and went to school in Cleveland. Then World War II came along. "I wanted to end up in P-38s," he said. "I didn't want a single-engine plane. I went to Lawrenceville, Illinois, where they trained P-38s, but I didn't get assigned to one. Then I went to the classification center in Birmingham, Alabama. They made me a flight engineer on a B-29 and sent me to Monroe, Louisiana. I was ready to go to the Pacific when they dropped the second bomb on Japan.

After the war, he graduated from NYU and went to work at Grumman Aircraft in Bethpage, Long Island. There were several

John Birchfield at the South Pole with penguins (collection of John Birchfield).

enthusiasts working there, and, in 1949, he became acquainted with sports cars.

"One of the crowd," John says, "had a fully-restored 1937 MG-TA (SN 635). When he decided not much later to move to California and declared he didn't want to drive the TA out there, I arranged to buy it. After that I bought an MG-TD."

He joined those deserting Grumman and decided to go back to Cleveland and work for Jack and Heintz. Coincidentally he learned about road racing, especially at Watkins Glen, which he attended almost immediately after starting work at J&H. It was at that time still an around-the-houses race using public roads. He made contact with the Cleveland Sport Car Club, probably through Bob Lossman. He got them interested in road rallies and helped them set up a couple.

"I don't know who thought of it," says John, "but there was soon a group within CSCC that was working to get a race going at Put-in-Bay. I naturally gravitated towards the group. I didn't keep records but my wife said we attended all of them, from first to last. I worked in almost every capacity."

In the mid-fifties, Birchfield bought an Austin-Healey, the kind with the folding windscreen. With this he did a few rally events with Jim Carroll:

I knew Jimmy Carroll. He was colorful and well-liked. We drove the Ohio 24 rally together, in my Austin-Healey. The screw holding the clamp for the top vibrated out and the clamp flew off. So Jim had to hold the top with his hand. It was pretty cold. With Jim, I was a co-founder of the MG Car Club. We decided we wanted one out here because it was a long way to go to Chicago.

I enjoyed everything about the Healey except its tendency to stop running in rainy weather because of the poorly-protected distributor. Then, in 1956, Chevrolet came out with a upgraded Corvette with stick shift (instead of a Powerglide automatic) and dual four-barrel carburetors. Helen and I bought it. Shortly after buying the Corvette, we learned of racing at a nearby location, Harewood, in Ontario. It was a converted RCAF base from WWII. After we went there several times as spectators, I decided I wanted to be a competition driver. The Corvette was fast enough, but racing it required a new set of tires after each race. I ordered a Sprite.

While waiting for it, I decided to enter the Corvette at Akron. As well as I can establish it, that was 1958, the last race there. The day before the race, the airport operators closed part of a runway for repairs. The announcement came late at a drivers' meeting. But neither Jim Kimberly nor Ebby Lunken (both Ferrari drivers) got the word. When we lined up for practice laps, I, the eagerest of beavers, got in line between them. One of them asked that I allow them to go together. I graciously agreed and they departed. I followed the revised course. Imagine the surprise of the crowd at the start-finish when I appeared first: they had followed the old course, which they knew well. The race was uneventful for me vis-à-vis the Ferraris, but on one lap I heard the announcer state that they had timed me near the end of the long straight at 130 mph. I found my front end making lateral eights because of the soft suspension. That unnerved me, so the Ferraris had no competition from me that day.

I returned to racing at Harewood, where I never exceeded 100 because the straights were too short. By the way, we drove the 'Vette to Harewood when we raced it because we couldn't get the top up with the roll bar in place. It got cold in Ontario those fall evenings. The Sprite had arrived and I was getting it into shape to race. That fall the SCCA held a Nationals at the Glen. I entered it. I drove to and from, having learned my lesson about roll bar clearance, the top could go up. I did well, garnering first Sprite (but there was no separate class for Sprites and I watched the Saabs lap us all). I was proud of my consistent laps (within 3 seconds) which I returned to after all the Saabs went by; I even beat Bob Lossman's dealership entry Sprite.

My last Put-in-Bay race I served as corner marshal/flagman at the left bend entering town, at the end of the long run from Cemetery Corner. The highlight of my duty at that left bend was the presence of a beer-drinking spectator on the outside of the bend who would reel across the street to restock himself whether there was traffic or not. I finally fixed that by buying him a twelve-pack and having Helen alert me when he seemed about to move.

That would have been 1959, when John took a break from his corner to drive Sprite #16 in the third race of the day.

John's racing activities were eventually curtailed, though: "About this time I was given a choice by my employer: quit taking Fridays off for tech inspection, or quit. I became a race spectator."

During the winter, John was active in the ski patrol, having worked the 1980 Olympics at Lake Placid and the 1988 Olympics at Calgary.

When he was 83 years old, Birchfield went on an expedition to Antarctica. He went in the summer, when it wasn't too cold. He flew to Buenos Aires and then took the Russian ship *Marco Polo* down to the bottom of the earth.

J.A. Brown and Georgia Brown

The Browns contributed photographs in various chapters.

Joe Brown was a racing photographer for nearly 50 years, according to Paul Weisenbach, a friend who went to races with him. "I met Brownie at Raceway Equipment, a speed shop at 77th and Madison in Cleveland," Paul says. "Brownie was a photographer of oval track events for many years. He had a press pass from National Speed Sport News. He got some of his pictures printed there and a couple of other racing publications.

"Most of all, he followed the sprints. He would go to Ashland and Dayton, Ohio; Winchester, Indiana; Cuyahoga County Fairgrounds and Milwaukee, which was run

Photographer Joe Brown sits in his Alfa Romeo on a summer's day (collection of Georgia Brown).

after the Indy 500. He also went to Powell near Columbus and Barberton Speedway. He followed the midgets, too, at Painesville, Van Wert, Greenville Fairgrounds, Toledo and Upper Sandusky."

He usually had three cameras, a 2¼ Rolliflex loaded with black and white, a 35 mm Leica, loaded with color, and sometimes another 35 with black and white. Actually, according to his widow Georgia Brown, he had 20 cameras, each one carefully stored in its own box. He did his own processing, at least of the black and white. He started taking pictures of sports car races in about 1948 or '49, when he got his MG-TC. He didn't stop taking pictures at oval tracks; he just added sports cars to his interests.

Joe joined the Cleveland Sport Car Club and was its president. He went to Watkins Glen, Akron Airport sports car races and Put-in-Bay. After the MG, he got an Alfa, in 1963. He was a watchmaker by trade and worked for Webb C. Ball and Cowell and Hubbard. Then he worked for Thompson Products and, after that, for Case Western Reserve University, designing and making electrically controlled prosthetics.

"Joe Brown was instrumental in us having lots of cameras," says Sally Carroll, the current president of the Cleveland Sport Car Club. "He was self-taught and had a darkroom because of the volume of photographs he needed to develop. We also had a darkroom. He only took pictures at Put-in-Bay, Akron Airport and Watkins Glen; he didn't go as far as Elkhart Lake. He also made a lot of things. He worked for the jeweler Cowell & Hubbard, and made my engagement and wedding ring. He did a lot of model building—cars. And he made an MG gearshift knob for Jim, made it out of walnut." At the 'Bay races, he took pictures of drivers from Cleveland, Detroit, Pittsburgh and other Midwestern locales.

Bob Satava, a corner worker at Put-in-Bay, owns the Joe Brown TC. "When Joe sold me the MG, he went to Europe and bought an Alfa Giulia. He took a lot of pictures while he was there—of the Alps and so forth—and he put on slide shows for the club when he got back. "

"All the time he was taking pictures of racing," says Georgia, "he really wanted to be a race car driver. In 1985, he went to the race at Winchester and won a race car. It was a red 1940 sprint car, won from the Williams Grove Old Timers and *The Good Old Days* magazine. Brownie had the car in the front yard. He would start it up now and then and say, 'Isn't that the sweetest sound you ever heard?'"

Joe Brown died June 23, 2001. In 2009 he was given a posthumous award for his photography and for his work on a feature article in *Vintage Motorsport* titled "When Sports Cars Flew at Akron Airport." He received both a bronze and a gold award from the International Automotive Media Competition. He was an extremely talented, popular and likeable man, and it is a shame that his ability was not recognized until after his death.

Leonard F. Griffing and Brenda Griffing

The Griffings contributed a portion of chapter 9.

The day after D-Day. Paratrooper Len Griffing is seen as the fourth from the left. He would later write about the Put-in-Bay races (from the archives of Olive Drab.com, with help from Brenda Griffing).

A member of the 501st Parachute Infantry Regiment's 101st Airborne Division, Company E, Len Griffing participated in the D-Day invasion of Normandy in 1944 and the 501st's actions in Bastogne and the Netherlands. He was awarded the Purple Heart and a Bronze Star.

A New York City native, Griffing attended St. Francis College in Brooklyn, graduated from Hofstra University, and did postgraduate work at the Bridgeport (Conn.) Engineering Institute and the Harvard Business School. He worked as a writer, photographer, editor, and engineer in New York, Los Angeles, and Miami. He was an advertising agency account executive in New York, wrote for *Sports Cars Illustrated* magazine in the late 1950s, and later drove for the Lotus factory team in California.

In 1992 he retired from the traffic engineering division of Broward County to assist in the month-long horse rescue effort in the Redlands area after Hurricane Andrew. He resumed parachuting in his sixties, making jumps in Israel, Guatemala, and South Africa. He died on November 21, 2003, when he was 78. Len Griffing is survived by his wife, Brenda, of Fort Lauderdale, and a cousin, Doris Barton, of Brooklyn.

Dick and Betty Henn

Dick Henn served as an officer throughout World War II in both the European Theater and domestically at a prisoner of war camp in Pennsylvania, detaining German prisoners. Dick and Betty's son served

Dick and Betty Henn and a wintertime tour in the MG-TD (collection of Chris Kintner).

in the Pacific Theater during World War II, while their daughters, Bettsy and Suzy, helped Betty keep things under control on the homefront. Dick subsequently served as a full colonel in the U.S. Army Reserves while also becoming a successful investment counselor. He and his wife Betty lived on Scarborough Road in Cleveland Heights. Before retiring, Betty worked as a nurse and also volunteered with the USO for over 50 years. This achievement was recognized during a segment of the popular Cleveland, Ohio, edition of the *PM Magazine* TV show. They both became interested in the sports car scene, becoming early members of the Cleveland Sport Car Club. Dick was its president in 1952, the first year of the Put-in-Bay road races, and they were the organizers of the race. Dick also served as club president in 1954, 1958 and 1959. They had a series of interesting cars, starting with an MG-TD and soon going to a Jaguar XK-140 roadster and later the E-Type Jaguar. They were well known in the Cleveland area for hardly if ever motoring with the hood, or "convertible top," in place. They much preferred open-air travel, even during the winter.

Dick and Betty Henn helped found the North East Ohio Region of the Sports Car Club of America and the Race Communications Association. In addition to chairing eight consecutive years of unforgettable races at Put-in-Bay, Dick tended flags and phones at Watkins Glen, Cumberland, and other classic races without number. In between times, Dick and Betty planned, organized and conducted such notable rallies as the Tulip Run to Holland, Michigan; the Alley Rally and Steeple Chase in downtown Cleveland; the Miniature Mille Miglia, called the "Run to the River," from Cleveland to Marietta, Ohio; the Skyline Tour over historic Skyline Drive; and then to climax this Olympic performance, they acted as chair and registrar for five great annual races at Akron Airport. It was said that "anybody who can't remember Dick Henn at the Start-Finish Line and Betty Henn in charge of the Registration Desk hasn't been to a race—or, at the worst, has missed the best of it."

At a 1972 North East Ohio Region of the Sports Car Club of America banquet held in their honor at the Crawford Automobile Museum in Cleveland, Ohio, Dick and Betty were recognized for their 20 years of involvement with the SCCA. A. Tracy Bird III, then executive director of the SCCA, wrote, "As one of the early leaders in Sports Car Club of America activities, as well as being a co-founder of the Race Communications Association at Watkins Glen, New York, in 1950, Mr. Henn exemplifies the energy which was the foundation of the SCCA. The National office of the Sports Car Club of America would like to extend its sincere gratitude for meritorious service to Richard L. Henn and his wife, Betty Henn."

At the 40th anniversary of the Put-in-Bay road races, driver Ralph Cadwallader had these words to say: "When I called Betty Henn for her reminiscences of Put-in-Bay she said, 'Oh, there were so many; but one thing stands out about the first race—it's a peculiar thing but it sticks in my memory like a photograph. At that time it was quite chic and the 'in' thing to have brightly colored racing coveralls like the big European drivers.

"So—many of our drivers had dyed their white coveralls various shades of red, blue, green and yellow. It was a beautiful sight to see them standing by their cars on the starting grid waiting for the decision to start the race on what was a very wet track. Well, it started to rain and the suits got wet and started to bleed. Now my picture is of all these drivers standing around each in his own colorful puddle of water, green, blue, red matching his coveralls! A really beautiful sight in the midst of a rain-delayed race—I have never forgotten that.

"Then there was the insurance policy incident—Dick had left the policy home in the safe but the mayor was not going to let the race start in the morning unless he personally saw the policy. Now this was late and no ferries were running, so Dick commandeered a speedboat and driver (as only Dick could do) and sped to the mainland where they jumped into Dick Gent's Cadillac and took off for Scarborough Road. They got the policy, turned around and headed back to Catawba Point where the speedboat and driver were still waiting. Betty said that as they approached Put-in-Bay island the sun had just started to rise and in spite of her weariness it became one of her most beautiful memories. Needless to say the race started on time.

"Much has been said of Dick and Betty Henn but never will all the things be known that make them so special to all of us. And each of us has his own special reason to love them. Let me paraphrase Winston Churchill," Ralph concluded, "and say, never have so many of us owed so much to these two—Dick and Betty Henn."

Bob Karol

Bob contributed a portion of chapter 10.

Bob Karol's first car, at age 20, was a Lancia B20 GT, the same model that finished second in the Mille Miglia. After developing invaluable, high-stakes roadracing experience winning numerous police chases, Bob finished third in his first and only SCCA race. Bob found the Lancia a new home and migrated to Hollywood, where he bought a Fiat Nardi 600, Ken Miles' personal beater, from the legend himself.

Bob brokered an assignment by *Road & Track* to write an article about the forthcoming 1959 Put-in-Bay race with photography provided by Rollin LaFrance, his friend back east. Bob bravely flogged the little Fiat from Los Angeles to Philadelphia to collect Rollo and his gear, then proceeded to Put-in-Bay. After the race, the two drove nonstop back to Los Angeles. As Rollo drove, Bob typed the Put-in-Bay article on an Olivetti typewriter balanced on his knees.

Bob then bought a Ducati motorcycle—the first in California—and started

A photograph of Bob Karol. The year is 1961. He says: "Riding an AJS-7R, I qualified 2nd on the grid in my first race in Europe: a street race in Germany on rough cobblestones with curbs and light posts lining the course and railroad tracks crossing it. Two German officials are standing to my left, just out of view, waiting to greet the German national champion, seen wheeling his 350 Norton Manx behind me up toward the starting line. Nodding in my direction, one pompous race official sneers to another in German, 'American piece of shit.' The instant I turned and snarled at him, the track photographer snapped my picture. Best racing photograph I ever took" (collection of Bob Karol).

racing it. He discovered that for the cost of racing his Lancia for one weekend, he could race a motorcycle an entire season. And it took twice as much skill. Two years later, after road racing in German national races while serving in the U.S. Army, he received his military discharge in Europe and in 1962 became the first American to race in European FIA motorcycle GPs, including Nurburgring and the Isle of Man mountain TT.

Bob subsequently returned to college to earn a BS in applied science, invented the Anidyne rotary engine, and pursued careers in automotive and aerospace engineering. Following a decade of California club racing, he competed in Mexico's La Carrera, a motorcycle and car race on an open road he had never seen before—a mini-version of the historic Carrera PanAmerica road race he had followed as a teenager.

Bob then concluded he'd rather be a vehicle dynamics expert witness and motorcycle racing instructor, so he began teaching the ultimate dynamics and psychophysics for winning both on the track and the open road—which he's now done for over 25 years. Still, Bob needed a better test than his jaded racing career called for of the concentration a racer needs to segregate fear from function.

He subsequently bungee dived from San Francisco's Golden Gate Bridge 200 feet to the bay: a midnight, fog-enshrouded, girder-straddling adventure that elevated the challenge of suppressing fear to a new plateau. In the process, Bob set a record by becoming the oldest person to dive from the Golden Gate Bridge and live to talk about it. Of course, the bungee cord helped to make it a two-way trip.

Today, Bob still teaches aspiring racers how to road race a motorcycle as fast as humanly possible without crashing and killing themselves. On the other hand, as an expert witness, Bob testifies in court how motorcycle street-riders crashed and killed themselves, riding faster than humanly possible.

Stu Kerr

Stu contributed photographs in various chapters.

Stu Kerr is a fine racing photographer besides being a longtime racing enthusiast and race worker. Here's how that came about.

"My father had been a B-17 pilot in Europe during World War II," says Stu. "He was in the 8th Air Force and flew 33 missions. While he was over there he became interested in European cars and particularly sports cars.

"He started bringing home early issues of *Road & Track* magazine. He bought the

Stu Kerr is a racing photographer and corner worker with Lake Erie Communications, the elite racing safety group founded by Bill Benham of NE Ohio SCCA (collection of Stu Kerr).

second Volkswagen in Cleveland—his still had the flip-up turn indicators. Then he took me to the Put-in-Bay road races. My favorite cars were the Lester MGs, the Alfas and the Elvas, especially the Dietrich and Stoddard cars."

Stu took photographs at a number of the Put-in-Bay races, and several of his photographs appear in this book.

Shortly after the 'Bay races were over, the Mid-Ohio track opened for racing. Stu camped out as a spectator at the early races with some NE Ohio SCCA members. Someone said, "Why don't you talk to Bill Benham about working the races?" So he joined Lake Erie Communications and was active until he was drafted into the army. He served from 1966 to '68. He was trained as a radio teletype operator but ended up being a legal clerk with a secret security clearance until his two years were up.

After he left the service, he took his kids to Mid-Ohio. Then he got back into working the races. "Mid-Ohio was my home track," Stu says. He also worked at Road Atlanta, Gingerman, Nelson Ledges, Cumberland and the road course events at Indy for both cars and bikes. Highlights of his experience include working as a corner marshal at the USGP in Austin Texas and being a spectator at Sebring a couple of years. "My dad had a private plane and we just landed on the runway. It was exciting to see the Ferraris and GT-40s compete."

Professionally, Stu was in the public health field for 41 years, half that time as the health commissioner for the city of Findlay, Ohio. One of his achievements was a smoke-free indoor-air program, first in Findlay and later as part of the team that worked on a successful statewide law.

After retirement he continued to work races, including the late American Le Mans series. How many races has he worked, we ask. "Probably less than a hundred," Stu remarks.

Christopher Henn Kintner

Kintner contributed various photographs and research and is the grandson of the race chairman of the Put-in-Bay events.

Chris' enthusiasm for sports cars and racing, their history, their sounds, their looks and how fun and even how frustrating they can be, runs deep, three generations deep. We've already discussed Chris' grandparents, Dick and Betty Henn. His parents, Bob and Bettsy Kintner, were almost equally as involved in the sports car lifestyle, as Bettsy was nearly always at Put-in-Bay, Akron Airport, Cumberland or the Glen to help out her parents wherever she could, whether it was sitting on the old flatbed truck near the start-finish line at Put-in-Bay to help with timing and scoring or helping to keep registrations straight at the Akron Airport races. Chris' father, Bob, served as the regional chairman for the NE Ohio region of the SCCA for several years and was also involved in the Put-in-Bay and Akron races. Bettsy even drove her MG-TD from Cleveland, Ohio, to Colorado to see one of the earliest races at Pikes Peak, with her brother along for the ride. Chris' uncle still grumbles about the fact that Bettsy wouldn't let him behind the wheel while she drove up the mountain.

Bob Kintner was a member of the Race Communication Association and volunteered annually as a flagman at the Watkins Glen Grand Prix. This is back when the Formula One race was the highlight of the racing season at the Glen, if not in the entire country. Rumor has it that Chris was conceived at one of these races. Whether that is true or not is not important, but the races certainly had an impact on his life. Chris, along with his parents, attended every Watkins Glen Grand Prix from the year he was born (and appeared in a miniature Race Communications Association uniform) until the riots and fires at the Grand Prix in the 1970s. Of course they attended other races as well and participated in many sports car related activities. When Chris was old enough to drive, he became the first third-generation member of the Cleveland Sport Car Club.

Chris' father, Bob, and his mother's father, Dick Henn, passed away in 1976. But this did not put a damper on the enthusiasm. Bettsy and Chris carried on with the Cleveland Sport Car Club and even stumbled upon an opportunity for Chris to help with the restoration of the Dean Van Lines Special Indianapolis racecar, which was originally owned by Dick Simon, built by A.J. Watson and driven by Eddie Sachs, who placed second to A.J. Foyt by eight seconds in 1961. The restoration was backed by PPG, and they used it to promote the PPG Indy Car World Series, as it was then called. Chris was able to tour with the completed car to several Indy Car races, including the week of time-trials and the Indy 500 at the Indianapolis Motor Speedway. It was his job to insert the inertia starter into the front of the car to crank the four-cylinder Offenhauser engine to a roaring start prior to the car being driven for a few parade laps at whatever venue they were visiting.

Chris entered the United States Air Force in 1983 and after basic training ended up at Wright-Patterson Air Force Base near Dayton, Ohio. He subsequently became an active member of the Dayton Sports Car Club, but it wasn't until being selected for special duty in Washington, D.C., and eventually meeting and marrying Cheryl that the

Christopher Henn Kintner, operator of the smallest of the three cars next to his mother Bettsy's MGA and his father Bob's Jaguar XK-150 (collection of Chris Kintner).

opportunity to obtain his first MG, a 1974½ MGB, came along in 1994 (for $500). Incidentally, recognizing that Cheryl shared his passion for vintage sports cars and motorsports, Chris found it appropriate to propose to Cheryl at the vintage races at the Mid-Ohio Sports Car Course. He even had a bottle of champagne hidden in the cooler. Shortly after acquiring their MG, Chris and Cheryl joined the MG Car Club Washington, D.C., Centre. Soon after, Chris volunteered to become a board member and Cheryl was named club secretary.

While on a one-year remote, unaccompanied tour in South Korea (Cheryl remained near Washington, D.C.), Chris taught himself how to build Web sites. He become the webmaster for not just the MG Car Club Washington, D.C., Centre, but also the MG Vintage Racers (MGVR) and the Chesapeake Chapter of the New England MG T Register (CCNEMGTR).

Eventually the old MGB was fully restored by Chris and friends, and the car won several awards before being sold/traded for a lovely 1957 MGA. Chris had dreamed of owning an MGA since he was a toddler, standing on the seat of his mother's MGA and pretending to race.

Chris and Cheryl donated the funds for the large stone corner marker in front of the Chamber of Commerce building, marking turn one of the original road race course at Put-in-Bay. The stone is dedicated to Chris' grandparents, Dick and Betty Henn. Chris and Cheryl are also sponsoring a second large stone to mark turn two of the original course, this one will be dedicated to their own enthusiasm for the last of the real road races, the races at Put-in-Bay.

Chris retired from the United States Air Force in 2003. He and Cheryl live in northern Virginia, about 40 miles from Washington, D.C. He now works as an information assurance analyst. Bettsy Kintner passed away in 2010. In 2013 Chris became the president of the MG Car Club Washington, D.C., Centre. Cheryl remains the Club secretary. It's certainly been a decade of new beginnings and new challenges for both Chris and Cheryl.

Rollin LaFrance

Rollin contributed photographs for chapter 2 and chapter 10.

Rollin was the class artist in elementary school and bought his first camera, a $2 Donald Duck camera, off the back of a comic book. (He remembers being excited and saying, "Mommy, mommy can I get this?") He learned photography, processing and the use of a 4 × 5 Speed Graphic with a focal plane shutter at Western Reserve Academy in Hudson, Ohio, covering sports and all school events for the school newspaper and yearbook for four years. In his junior year he attended the 14th Annual Northeastern Ohio Scholastic Press Conference with 66 competing high schools at the Kent State University School of Journalism, winning 1st place in photography in the Mass Interview category, and 3rd place in the Dramatized News Event category. He was one of only two photographers to win a pair of prizes.

Rollin spent a couple of his teenage years perfecting his brazing skills in stripping chrome from his first car, a 1941 Ford convertible. The V-8 had great sound after he put pennies in the heat risers, and the car nearly gave his father a heart attack by backfiring in the driveway. This car was fun to drive but took concentration to keep it traveling in a straight line above 50 mph; the swaying was due to inadequate suspension and shocks.

His father bought an MG-TD from an associate at work, and Rollin used it for travel from Cleveland to Philadelphia, where he studied for his architectural degree at the University of Pennsylvania. The last trip ended on I-80 north of Pittsburgh with a broken timing belt. Bob Karol was game enough to provide a tow back to Cleveland with his Lancia Aurelia GT, traveling on back roads at night to avoid being ticketed. Rollin wanted to rebuild the engine himself, and managed to disassemble it, but didn't have the tools or skill to replace the bearings. Everything went into a box and off to the shop. The following summer when jobs were scarce, Rollin's father made him sell the car to a dealer. The TD exterior and interior had been carefully maintained, including painting the underside of the fenders (in a rust color). The car was sold at a profit, but Rollin was very upset when he found the car on the lot marked up 100 percent!

In 1959 Rollin photographed the "Last American Road Race" at Put-in-Bay for *Road & Track*; Bob Karol wrote the article. Following the race they drove straight through from Cleveland to Los Angeles in Bob's Fiat Nardi 600, driving flat out and hitching tows in tractor-trailer slipstreams for an additional 5 mph. They bought twin Ducati motorcycles and practiced on winding Mulholland Drive in the Hollywood hills. On his return from Los Angeles to university and reaching Cleveland on the Ducati, his mother was horrified and made him disassemble the bike to fit in her trunk for the drive back to Philadelphia.

Following graduation and six months' active duty at Fort Knox with the Pennsylvania Railroad Army Reserves, Rollin got his dream job working for his favorite professor at Mitchell/Giurgola Architects in Philadelphia, becoming a partner in 1974. From 1962 to 1984 Rollin provided architectural photography as a sideline for nearly all office projects, and published his work in many architectural magazines, journals, and books, including covers and book jackets. The firm established an office in New York City in 1966 when Prof. Giurgola became chairman of the department of architecture at Columbia University. Rollin is licensed in Pennsylvania, New York, New Jersey, District of Columbia, Virginia, Connecticut, Australian Capital Territory, and Victoria, Australia.

Racing photographer Rollin LaFrance smiles from the door of his MG-TD (collection of Rollin LaFrance).

The firm was successful in winning major design competitions and many design awards, including the two-stage international design competition for the New Parliament House of Australia in Canberra in 1980. Mitchell/Giurgola and Thorp Architects established an office in Canberra in 1981; Rollin and family moved there in 1984 where he was partner-in-charge of furniture and interiors coordination. The Parliament building of 3,000,000 square feet cost $1.1 billion and had 4,500 rooms with 34,000 pieces of furniture costing $24 million. Parliament officially opened in May 1988 with ceremonies with the Queen.

Rollin and family returned to Philadelphia in 1990, where he joined a former partner, retiring to Washington Crossing, New Jersey, in 2000.

Bibliography

Correspondence and Interviews with the Author

Alderson, Jake. Letter, November 27, 1995.
Andrews, Reed. Letter, February 6, 2003; personal interview, May 19, 1986; telephone interviews, December 11, 2009, and October 28, 2012.
Askew, Ken. E-mail, March 8, 2012, and May 13, 2013; letter, January 7, 2005.
Barsantee, Bob, Jr. Telephone interview, January 16, 2013.
Beasley, Al. Telephone interviews, October 24, 2012, and March 23, March 27, May 3, and June 1, 2013.
Becker, Hank. Telephone interviews, November 12, 2009, and October 31, 2012.
Bennett, Jim. Letters, April 3 and May 9, 2013; telephone interviews, April 2 and May 17, 2013.
Beverly, Bob. Telephone interview, February 28, 2013.
Birchfield, John. E-mail, April 9 and October 9, 2012; letters, September 10, 2012, and May 8, 2013; telephone interviews, April 13 and August 8, 2012, and April 30, 2013.
Bizer, Bill. Telephone call, March 12, 2012.
Black, Don. Telephone interview, April 8, 2013.
Black, Pat. Telephone calls, June 11 and 12, 2013.
Bowling Green State University. Letter, June 5, 2012.
Bradley, Sophia. Telephone interview, January 2, 2012.
Brooks, Bob. Telephone interviews, January 20 and February 5, 2013.
Brow, Art. Telephone interviews, August 28, 2001, December 29, 2012, March 18, 2013, and May 17, 2013.
Brow, Art, and Dutch Brow. Personal interview, December 26, 2001.
Burry, Don. Letter, October 18, 2011.
Cadwallader, Betty. Letter, April 26, 2004.
Cadwallader, Ralph. Telephone interviews, January 5, 1997, and September 14, 2001.
Carroll, Sally. E-mail, September 3, 2006, and March 23, 2012; telephone interviews, January 13 and May 26, 2013.
Cavan, Ed. Letter, June 12, 1986.
Cavan, Grace. Letter, June 12, 1986.
Charter, Stephen M. Letters, May 3, May 10, and May 21, 2012, and March 19, 2013.
Chriss, Chuck. E-mail, March 20, 2013.
Clemens, Carol. E-mail, March 19, 2012, July 23, 2012, and June 9, 2013; telephone interviews, March 18 and 20, 2012, and March 25, 2013.
Clifton, Jon. Letter, May 13, 2013; telephone interviews, April 29 and May 21, 2013.
Clining, Dan. Telephone interview, March 21, 2012.
Comey, John. Letters, September 25, 2001, and May 3, 2003; telephone interviews, August 28, 2001, September 17, 2001, December 26, 2003, and January 5, 2004.
Comey, Joy. Letter, September 29, 2004; telephone interviews, February 20 and 28, 2013.
Constant, Harry. E-mail, November 19 and 23, 2009, and March 8, 2012; telephone interviews, July 12 and October 2, 2011.
Cook, Dick. Telephone interview, October 28, 2012.
Cook, Richard. E-mails, June 29, 2009, and October 28, 2012.
Cooper, Suzy. Personal interview, August 17, 2006; telephone interviews, March 15, 2005, and October 2, 2012.
Crawley, Dominic. E-mail, April 8 and 9, 2012.
Davison, Mark. E-mail, March 12 and 16, 2012.
De Boer, John. E-mail, March 19 and 24, 2013; telephone call, March 18, 2013.
Dennis, G. Patrick. E-mail, March 24, 2013.
Dennis, Pat. Telephone interviews, March 19 and 23, 2013.
Dietrich, Chuck. Letter, February 9, 1995; telephone interviews, May 19 and 22, 1986, and August 28, 2001.
Dietrich, Suzy. Telephone interviews, February 1, 2002, and October 22, 2004.
Donley, Bill. Telephone interview, May 6, 2013.
Donley, William. Telephone interview, May 17, 2013.
Elder, Dave. Telephone interview, October 28, 2012.
Ellmers, Charlie. E-mail, May 16, 17, and 18, 2001; January 26, 2002; and May 3, 2003; personal interview, June 17, 1986; telephone interviews, May 4 and 14, 2001; May 17, 2003; December 26, 2002; and November 14, 2004.

Ellmers, Ruth. Personal interview, June 17, 1986; telephone interview, January 19, 2009.
Etzkorn, Jim. Telephone interview, January 17, 2013.
Ford, Manley. E-mail, December 3, 2009; February 20 and 29, 2012; April 3, October 24 and 29, 2012; telephone call, February 20, 2012.
Foss, Charlie. E-mail, July 1 and 4, 2009, and June 20, 2012.
Gent, Richard. Fax transmission, March 4, 2002; telephone interview, November 29, 2001.
Gleason, Andrea. E-mail, October 31, 2012.
Good, John. E-mail, September 3, 2008.
Gorris, Bill. Letters, January 30, 2002, and January 9, 2013; telephone interview, March 15, 2012.
Greaves, Jerry. Telephone interview, May 19, 2013.
Griffing, Brenda. E-mail, January 1 and 2, and March 12, 2013.
Gustafson, Bob. Telephone calls, July 8, 2001, and October 2, 2011.
Hannig, Bill. Telephone interview, January 21, 2013.
Hayer, Roland. Telephone interviews, April 14, 2008, and November 10, 2007.
Hazle, Chuck. E-mail, August 5, 2012, and April 2, 2013; personal interview, June 28, 2012; telephone interview, July 16, 2012.
Henn, Betty. Letter, December 10, 1995; personal interview, May 18, 1986.
Henn, Dick, Jr. Letters, February 1, 1997, November 21 and 25, 2001, and February 4, 2002.
Holder, Lorrain. Personal interview, May 20, 1986.
Holder, Nancy. Personal interview, May 20, 1986.
Holth, Jack. E-mail, September 21, 2012, and March 29, 2003; letter, March 4, 2005; telephone interviews, April 6 and 7, 2005, September 22, 2011, and October 31, 2012.
Honsperger, Ellen. E-mail, June 5 and 8, 2013; letter, June 10, 2013.
Householder, Tom. E-mail, February 19, 2006, November 12, 2012, January 21 and 22, 2013, and February 21, 2013; telephone interview, January 20, 2013; telephone call, February 28, 2013.
Howlett, Vince. E-mail, March 16, 2012.
Hugus, Barbara. Letter, November 28, 2012.
Hugus, Ed. Letter, January 7, 2005; telephone call, January 3, 2004.
Irish, Dick. Letter, June 21, 2004; telephone interview, February 21, 2013, May 12, 13, and 24, 2013; telephone interview, November 1, 2012.
James, Herb. E-mail, June 9, 2001.
Jarmain, Walt. Telephone interview, January 14, 2013.
Johnson, Roger E. E-mail, May 18, 2013; telephone interview, May 19, 2013.
Karol, Bob. E-mail, June 16, 2009, February 14, 20, and 21, 2013; letter, November 9, 2001; personal interview, August 17, 2006; telephone interviews, January 14, 2001, and February 13, 2013.
Karol, Robert. Letter, May 26, 2013.
Kerr, Stu. E-mail, December 25, 2012, May 30, 2013, and June 4, 2013; letters, March 30, 2010, and June 9, 2013; telephone interview, May 29, 2013.
Kintner, Chris. E-mail, June 15 and July 18, 2001; telephone interviews, September 30 and November 4, 2012.
Kintner, Christopher. E-mail, November 2, 2009, April 10 and 14, 2013, May 27, 2013; letter, May 24, 2011.
Kreager, Keith. E-mail, June 21, 2012.
La France, Rollin. E-mail, November 14, 2001, January 17 and 23, 2002, December 3, 2004, June 18, 2009, March 30, 2013, April 2, 4, 6, and 7, 2013; letter, May 26, 2013; telephone interview, February 13, 2013.
Lamport, Dick. E-mail, June 30, 2012; personal interview, June 29, 2012.
Lance, Clark. E-mail, March 8, 2012.
Lance, Harold. Letter, July 27, 2001.
Linick, Chuck. E-mail, June 28, 2009, February 21, 2012.
Lynch, Michael. Letter, November 27, 1992; telephone interview, January 13, 2013.
Maltby, Gordon. Telephone call, February 28, 2013.
Massey, Jason. E-mail, April 21, 2013.
McLaird, Lee N. Letter, May 3, 2012.
Mishne, Mickey. E-mail, January 12 and 14, 2002; letters, February 19 and October 13, 1996; telephone interview, January 11, 2001.
Morrison, Bob. E-mail, June 23 and 24, 2003; telephone interview, March 15, 2012.
Murphy, Nina. Telephone interview, February 28, 2013.
Parsons, Bob. Telephone interviews, October 25, 2012, March 24, 2013.
Perry, Bruce. Letter, October 15, 2012.
Primack, Marv. E-mail, March 21, 2013.
Reder, Dick. Telephone interview, September 22, 2011.
Reder, Richard. E-mail, February 17, 2012.
Riggs, D. Randy. E-mail, February 25, 2003, and July 20, 2009.
Rochford, Susan. Letter, January 28, 1997.
Rubini, Gunnar. Telephone interviews, March 19 and 25, 2013, and May 23, 2013.
Satava, Bob. Letters, April 29, 2001, and July 2, 2003; personal interviews, May 21, 1986, and October 29, 1995; telephone interviews, March 15, 2012, January 27, 2013, and September 30, 2012.
Schmidt, Bob. Telephone interview, January 13, 2013.
Seyler, Art. Telephone interviews, September 12 and 15, 2012.
Sitz, Jim. Telephone call, May 22, 2012.
Skirmants, Vic. E-mail, September 21, 2011, September 21, 2012; telephone call, September 22, 2011; telephone interviews, August 28, 2001, and September 22, 2011.
Smith, Russ. Telephone interviews, January 4 and October 28, 2012.
Snider, Bob. E-mail, February 25 and March 4, 2013.

Steger, Fred. Personal interview, June 17, 1986.
Steger, Jane. E-mail, October 8, 2012.
Stein, Robert. E-mail, April 8, 2005.
Stoddard, Chuck. E-mail, November 14, 2009, January 20, 2013, and March 21, 2013; telephone interviews, May 22, 1986, and August 28, 2001.
Tame, John. Personal interview, June 17, 1986; telephone interviews, May 13 and 14, 2001, June 13, 2003, and August 5, 2008.
Troyan, Fred. E-mail, March 21, 2013; telephone calls, March 20 and April 11, 2013; telephone interviews, August 29, 2001, March 20, 2013, and April 11, 2013.
Truax, Michael. E-mail, March 13 and October 17, 2012.
Vack, Pete. E-mail, January 1 and 13, 2013.
Wearn, Doug. Telephone interview, July 1, 2009.
Weber, Joe. E-mail, February 7, 2012; letters, March 26 and May 7, 2012; telephone interviews, December 11, 2011, and March 29, 2013.
Woehrle, Jack. E-mail, August 27, 2009.
Wonder, Bill. Telephone interview, May 13, 2013.

Books and Periodicals

Anselmi, Angelo Tito. "Corrozzeria Italiana Advancing the Art and Science of Automobile Design," *Automobilia Societa per la storie e l'immagine dell-automobile*, 1980, pp. 37, 76, 80, 108.
Armstrong, Douglas. *The World's Racing Cars and Sports Cars*. New York: Hanover House, 1959.
Bly, Sheila. "Racing the Octagon at Put-in-Bay," The Checkpoint, June 1990, pp. 37–40.
Borgeson, Griffith. "Siata: The Never-Told Tale of a Very Great Little Marque." *Automobile Quarterly* 23, no. 2 (1985): 142–163.
Brown, J.A. "A Little Watkins Glen at Put-in-Bay." *Road and Track*, October 1955, p. 26.
De Boer, John. *Registry of Italian Oddities* (The Etceterini Register). Pittsburgh, PA: Riopress, May 1990.
Dodge, Robert J. *Isolated Splendor: Put-in-Bay and South Bass Island*. Hicksville, NY: Exposition, 1975.
Garrett, Amanda, and Lynn Ischay. "No Man Is an Island." *The Cleveland Plain Dealer*, October 17, 2004, pp. 6–16.
Glover, Ray. *NE Ohio Region of the SCCA, November 16, 2002*." 50th Anniversary Book. Cleveland, OH: SCCA, 2002.
Goodwin, Carl. "The Last American Road Race." *Vintage Motorsport*, March–April 2003, pp. 48–64.
_____. "MGs Return to Put-in-Bay. *Vintage Motorsport*, September–October 1990, pp. 68–69.
_____. "MGs at the Put-in-Bay Road Races." *Classic MG Magazine*, Summer 2001, pp. 8–11.
_____. "The Put-in-Bay Road Races." *Automobile Magazine*, October 1986, pp. 108–113.
_____. "Racing on Real Roads." *British Car*, February–March 2003, pp. 56–59.
_____. *They Started in MGs*. Jefferson, NC: McFarland, 2011.
Griffing, Len. "Put-in-Bay." *Sports Cars Illustrated*, October 1958, pp. 22–46.
Hitchcock, Meach. "Funny Face Auto Racing Team." *NE Ohio Blower*. Sports Car Club of America newsletter. May 10, 1959, p. 4.
Johnson, Brett. *The 356 Porsche: A Restorer's Guide to Authenticity*. Indianapolis: Beeman Jorgensen, October 1997.
Karol, Robert. "Put-in-Bay 1959." *Road and Track*, October 1959, pp. 58–59.
Kintner, Christopher. "MG Madness." February 29, 2004, pp. 1–9.
Lavery, John. "Put-in-Bay." *Road and Track*, October 1958, p. 54.
McComb, F. Wilson. *The Story of the MG Sports Car*. New York: St. Martin's, 1972.
Mishne, Mickey. The *Scrutineer* Yearbook, Cleveland Sport Car Club, 1951–1965.
The People History. "The Year 1957 from the People History." http://www.thepeoplehistory.com/1957.html.
Pollack, Bill. *Red Wheels and White Sidewalls*. Carpinteria, CA: Brown Fox, 2004.
Pollack, Susan R. "Bay Dreaming." *Detroit News*, June 12, 1988, pp. 1N–4N.
Satava, Bob. "Put-in-Bay Documentary Films." Lake Erie Islands Historical Society, June 1990.
Stanford, Don. *The Red Car*. New York: Grosset and Dunlap, 1954.
Vitrikas, Robert P. *MGA: A History and Restoration Guide*. Pawtucket, RI: Scarborough Faire, 1980.
"Waterford 25th Anniversary Brochure." Waterford Hills Road Racing, August 1983.
Wikipedia.com. "The People's History: The Year 1957." 2013.

Index

Abarth 21
Abbott, Tom 211
AC Ace 28, 31, 93, 150, 151, 168, 174
AC Bristol 31, 108, 188
Ahr, Kenneth 162, 181
Airport Motel 137
Airport Straight 19
Airport Turn 31, 198
AJS-7R motorcycle 250
Akron Airport sports car race 39, 89, 245, 246, 247, 252
Akron Cars 181
Alfa Romeo 12, 25, 100, 125, 127, 143, 144, 146, 174, 246; Giulietta 163, 165, 183, 185, 201, 240
Alfa Touring 2000 201
Allen, Charles 26, 126
American Le Mans series 252
American Sports Car Racing in the 1950s 85
America's Cup 176
Anderson, Leonard 224
Andrews, Barbara 129
Andrews, Reed 2, 14, 31, 34, 129, 169, 171, 189, 190, 199, 204, 241
Anidyne rotary engine 251
Argetsinger, Cameron 1, 12
Arnolt Bristol 17, 31, 32, 128, 130, 168, 188, 204, 214
Askew, Ken 99, 123, 125, 127, 128
Aston Martin DB2 59, 81
Austin-Healey 28, 29, 193, 203, 244, 245
Automobile magazine 2, 3
Av-Gas 130

B-17 airplane 251
B-24 airplane 163
B-29 airplane 243
Bailey, Dick 211, 214
Bailey, F. Lee 82
Baker, Chet 136
Baldwin Wallace College 43
Bandini 18, 25, 27, 76, 120, 122, 141, 142, 191

Barber, Lou 47
Barber, Quay 31
Barron, Jim 220, 223, 228
Barsantee, Bob, Jr. 100
Bass 7
Bassett, Terry 236
Battle of the Bulge 64, 65
Baughman, Sidney 168, 169, 174
Bayview Inn 137
Beasley, Al 25, 141, 142, 163, 191, 201, 241
Beasley, Ma 162
Becker, Hank 19, 45, 68, 101, 102, 151
Benham, Bill 96, 252
Berkeley car 187, 201
Berkley, Jack 215
Beverly, Bob 100
Binder, Eugene 70
Birchfield, Helen 36
Birchfield, John 4, 13, 17, 28, 36, 38, 42, 43, 53, 89, 93, 138, 166, 243, 244
Black, Don 104, 123, 125, 126, 127, 128
Black, Jim 9
Black, Pat 240
Black River Sports Car Club 43
Blackhawk Farms 130
Blaser, Joe 120
Blauschild, David 48
Blumberg, Al 32, 211
Bly, Dave 2, 20, 21, 232, 239, 241
Bly, Sheila 2, 20, 21, 232, 239, 241
Boardman, Malcolm 76, 79, 87
Bobsy sports racer 185
Bojalad, Joe 93, 107, 108, 110
Bojalad, Joey 110
Bolster, John 30
Book of Sports Cars 190
Bosley, Dick 10, 13, 40
Bosley Mk. 1 10
Bowling Green State University 3, 56
Boyce, Larry 32

Bradley, Bill 128, 149, 153, 160, 161, 163, 164, 190
Bradley, Norm 4, 13, 17, 18, 28, 36, 47, 192, 243
Bradley, Sophia 149, 160
Brainerd, Minnesota 130
Bridgehampton 1, 12, 15, 17, 130, 154, 183, 243
Bristol engine 168
British Car 3
Bronze Star 248
Brooks, Bill 69
Brooks, Bob 108
Brooks, Jim 108
Brow, Art 2, 20, 27, 28, 31, 65, 73, 83, 165, 166, 185, 193, 236, 239, 241
Brow, Dutch 64, 73, 236, 241
Brown, Clifford 4
Brown, Georgia 245, 246
Brown, Gordon 220, 224
Brown, Joe 3, 10, 40, 56, 101, 104
Brown, Richard 141, 162
Brubeck, Dave 4
Brynfan Tyddyn 17, 66
Bugatti 22, 33, 41, 150
Bugatti Type 35 45, 86
Bugatti Type 55 19, 63, 95
Bugatti Type 57 86
Burnett, Barnie 148, 165, 167
Burry, Don 215

Cadwallader, Ralph 4, 23, 29, 36, 41, 56, 171, 232, 239, 240, 241, 243, 249
Cal Sales, Inc. 106
Calgary, Alberta Olympics 245
Callicoon, New York 71
Caparon, Michael 20, 125
Carrera PanAmerica 251
Carrera Speedster 167, 187
Carroll, Jim 39, 46, 52, 151, 244, 246
Carroll, Sally 3, 36, 46, 246
Carrozzeria Motto 76
Case Western Reserve University 246

Index

Castrol-R 130
Catawba 16, 20, 21
Catawba Avenue 19, 38
Cavan, Ed 199
Cemetery Corner Curve 2, 25, 84, 199
Center for Archival Collections 3, 56
Central Ohio and Put-in-Bay Racing Enterprises 213
Chagrin River Road 16
Chanute AFB 142
Chapman, Colin 77, 79
Charter, Stephen 3, 56
Chicago Region SCCA 1
Chinetti, Luigi 79
Chris Craft 16
Chrysler Allard 127
Cincinnati Gang 89
Cipelle, Frank 32, 214, 219, 224
Cisitalia 10, 40, 65
Citroen 4CV 28
Clark, George 50, 102
Clark, Jim 96
Clark, Norm 172
Classic MG 3
Clemens, Carol 3
Cleveland Art Museum 168
Cleveland Plain Dealer 3, 25, 30, 45, 57
Cleveland Skating Club 89
Cleveland Sport Car Club 2, 3, 4, 10, 11, 12, 13, 17, 21, 25, 36, 39, 50, 81, 88, 89, 93, 119, 132, 165, 244, 246, 249, 253
Cleveland Yacht Club 11
Clift, Bob 219
Clifton, Jon 142, 191
Colaizzi, Bob 241
Cole, Phillip 77
Colonial Ballroom 23, 126, 173
Colonial Inn 192
Columbia (yacht) 176
Columbia University 255
Comey, John 18, 17, 20, 28, 31, 41, 63, 89, 95, 96, 101, 150, 241
Comey, Joy 89
Conrero Alfa 166, 182
Constant, Harry 23, 25, 98, 99, 115, 163, 181
Cook, Richard 169, 170, 173, 188, 189
Cooper Climax 30, 126, 141, 142, 144, 145, 146
Cooper Straight 25, 143, 199
Corvette 22, 167, 173, 244, 245
course record (89.90 mph) 31, 169
Cowan, Bob 40
Cowell & Hubbard 246
Coyne, Mike 70
Cranage, Elvadore Jr. 160
Crescent Bar 140
Cricket 4, 10, 13, 40

Crosley engine 26, 28
Crown Hill 38
Cumberland 188, 252
Cunningham, Briggs 1, 89, 176
Curran, Doc (John) 23, 187, 203

Dachshund (dog) 13
Dahl, Henry 77, 80, 83
Dasey, Homer 167
Davis, David E., Jr. 2, 3, 128
Davis, Ernest 16
Dayton Sports Car Club 253
Dean Van Lines Special 253
Deen, Dorothy 94, 106
Delaware Street 38
Detroit Region SCCA 25
Dever, Jim 88, 233, 239
Dever, Neil 201, 203
Diemel, Dudley 203
Dietrich, Chuck 1, 25, 27, 29, 31, 45, 68, 88, 92, 93, 128, 140, 142, 145, 146, 153, 160, 161, 164, 187, 188, 203, 252, 240
Dietrich, Suzy 30, 36, 40, 45, 184, 188, 201, 233, 239, 241
DKW 28
Dodge, Robert, J. 3, 42, 49, 56, 58
Donald Duck camera 254
Donley, Bill 211
Doretti 94, 105, 106, 161
Douglas Skyraider 97
Downey, Jack 100, 123, 125, 127
Drivers' meeting 43
Dubel, Andre 217, 228
Ducati 198, 250, 255
Dunlop 95
DuPont, Marcel 148
Durbin, Ralph 25, 28, 32, 41, 87, 88, 99, 101, 127, 128, 146, 214, 223

Economaki, Chris 3
Edgar, William 85
Egloff, Fred 1
Eichenlaub, Edward 148, 167, 168, 174
Eichenlaub, Jim 148, 161
8th Air Force 251
Eisenhower, Dwight 4
Elder, Dave 182, 201
Elkhart Lake 1, 12, 15, 17, 46, 71
Ellington, Duke 3, 136
Ellmers, Charlie 2, 9, 22, 23, 29, 31, 40, 42, 45, 52, 87, 89, 97, 122, 140, 142, 153, 170, 190, 197, 204, 232, 239, 241
Ellmers, Ruth 2, 22, 46, 89, 122, 125, 204, 239
Elva 1, 30, 139, 141, 145; Mk II 186, 187; Mk III 160, 162, 163, 164, 174, 190, 203; Mk IV 195, 203, 223, 225
Emerald Necklace MG Club 3, 36

Emerson, Ollie 240
Etzkorn, Jim 44, 159, 163
European Automotive 120

Fageol, Lou 27, 31
Fairthorpe 162
Fergus, Bob 41, 65, 198
Ferrante, John 31
Ferrari 22, 30, 50; America 175; Mexico 118; Mondial 1; Monza 1; 166 31; Testa Rossa 1; 250 LWB 33
FIA motorcycle GP 251
Fiat: Balilla 41, 45, 52; Bianchina 201; Nardi 600 17, 191, 197, 255, 250; 600 28; 600 Multipla 17
Fiat-Abarth Zagato 18, 24, 28, 192, 201, 217
Findlay, Ohio 252
Fine Cars Inc. 14, 102
Finn Class 8
Fischer, Ed 223
Fitch, John 1
501st Parachute Infantry Regiment 248
Flickinger, Paul 7, 86
Floyd, Frank 170
Ford, Manley 3, 56, 160, 241
Ford Tri-Motor airplane 15, 21, 45, 50, 137, 191, 200
Forlenza, Bob 3
Formula Atlantic 29
Fort Industry Auto Sports Club of Ohio 211
Foss, Charlie 3, 56
Fox Motel 137
Frazer Nash 20, 31, 168, 188, 190, 198
Friendly Inn 59
Frosty's Pizza 7
Funny Face Auto Racing Team 22, 59, 89, 103, 122, 138, 142, 153, 159, 187

Garlinghouse, Jack 223
Gates, Dick 64
General Competition Rules (GCR) 181
Gent, Dick 10, 13, 27, 40, 45, 65, 142, 250
Gent, Richard, Jr. 67
German Grand Prix 136
Giant's Despair Hill Climb 71, 174
Gibraltar Island 7, 8
Gifford, Curt 188, 204
Gingerman Raceway 252
Gleason, Cal 114, 118
Goggomobil 28, 201
Golden Gate Bridge 251
Goodwin, C. Ray 69
Goodwin, Carl 3
Goodwin, Nancy 3, 236

Index

Goodyear Tire and Rubber 165
Gorris, Bill 18, 37, 42, 96, 103
Grant, Will 28, 162, 201
Grassow, Karl 27
Green, Bill 1
Greenacres, Ont. 99
Gregory, Masten 1
Greyhound Bus 117
Griffing, Brenda 247, 248
Griffing, Len 171, 247, 248
Guerrieri, Reno 217, 224, 228
Gustafson, Bob 223

Haas, Carl 31
Hall, Ben 28, 31, 108, 129, 150, 168, 170, 174
Hallock, Tom 30, 126, 141, 144, 145, 146
Hamilton, Chico 17
Hancock, Ed 101, 127
Hannig, Bill 104
Hannig, Jack 104
Harewood Acres 99, 245
Harrison, Gordon 169, 188, 228
Harvard Business School 248
Hassan, Chuck 89
Hazle, Charlie 69, 70
Heckman, Dick 22
Heineman, Louis 95, 215, 216, 223
Heineman's Winery 95, 215, 216
Henn, Betty 2, 13, 18, 22, 27, 28, 32, 33, 36, 38, 40, 42, 54, 55, 93, 96, 109, 115, 136, 190, 201, 215, 232, 234, 239, 241, 248, 249, 252, 254
Henn, Dick 13, 18, 27, 30, 33, 36, 38, 40, 54, 60, 89, 93, 95, 96, 109, 137, 138, 173, 190, 213, 215, 243, 248–250, 252, 254
Henn, Dick, Jr. 5
Henning, Carol 210, 216, 219, 228
Henry, Chuck 23, 118, 140, 162, 240
Hier, Al 184, 185
Hier, Kaye 184, 185
Hill, Graham 96
Hill, Phil 1
Hitchcock, Ben 54, 98, 153, 170
Hitchcock, Meacham 29, 89, 98, 153, 170, 181, 193, 203
Hitchcock, Spook 54, 153
Hoffman, Max 27
Holder, Barbara 175
Holder, Lorrain 2, 33, 169
Holder, Manny 2, 16, 142, 168, 169, 172, 174, 175, 188, 200, 204
Holder, Nancy 2
Holder brothers 25, 31, 169, 170, 194, 195
Holth, Carol 3, 32, 211, 214, 223, 224, 226

Holth, Jack 3, 32, 211, 214, 223, 224, 226
Honsberger, Ellen 230, 236
Honsperger, Skip 230, 236
Houlehan, Ed 32, 211, 218, 223
Householder, Tom 106, 144, 147, 161
Howell, Elmo 77, 85
HRG 77, 86
Hugus, Ed 83, 88, 126, 128, 141, 198
Hutchinson, William 168

Indianapolis Motor Speedway 253
Indy 500 246, 253
International Automotive Media Competition 247
Irish, Chuck 4, 13, 41, 45
Irish, Dick 4, 10, 11, 13, 40, 41, 50
Island Airlines 200
Isle of Man TT 251
Isolated Splendor 42
Ivanyi, George 2, 185
Ivanyi, Steve 137, 185
Iwo Jima 97

Jaguar 22, 33, 50; C-Type 1; D-Type 1; E-Type 249; XK-120 36, 47, 98, 103, 243; XK-140 17, 33, 115, 141, 249; XK-150 253
Jaguar-Cleveland 84, 166
James, Herb 137
Jarmain, Walt 158
Jayne, Penny 89
Jayne, Ted 52, 87, 89, 152, 168, 170, 172, 187
Jeffords, Jim 89
Joe Parker Garage 19, 20, 38, 61, 62, 93, 158, 194, 198, 243
Joe's Bar 194, 202
Johnson, Earl 10, 40
Johnson, Roger 230, 236
Johnston, Sherwood 89
Juan Manuel Fangio 136, 197

Karol, Bob 17, 28, 251
Keller, Bernie 31, 149, 153, 168
Kerr, Stu 145, 146, 251
Kersey, Tom 203
Keystone Garage 77
Kieft MG 77, 85
Kimberly, Jim 1, 89, 245
Kintner, Bettsy 55, 89, 252, 253
Kintner, Bob 40, 42, 89, 96, 252, 253
Kintner, Cheryl 253, 254
Kintner, Chris 36, 55, 241, 253, 254
Kintner, Christopher Henn 252, 253
Korean War 45

Kovach, Joe 19, 20
Kuhn, Bob 27, 76, 84, 88, 198

LaFrance, Rollin 3, 23, 191, 184, 188, 250, 255
Laguna Seca 154
Lake Erie 21, 25, 88, 136
Lake Erie Communications 96, 165, 251, 252
Lake Placid Olympics 245
Lakewood High School 85
Lamport, Dick 69
Lamport, Dick, Jr. 69, 70, 168
Lancia B20 GT 250
Lang, Jim 191
Langham Road 38
Latimer, Jerry 219
Lawrence, Joan 211
Lawrenceville, Illinois 243
Leica IIIf 246
LeMay, General Curtis 72, 85, 89
Lester MG 17, 29, 31, 93, 103, 125, 168, 172, 188, 204, 252
Lewis, Sam 76
Lightning Class 11
Lime Rock 130, 154
Linsay's Tavern 16
Linton, Otto 241
Linton, Roger 3, 56, 229, 241
Liscowski, Mary 60
Liscowski, Walter 60
Lisicki, Bert 103
Lisicki, Jim 103
Lister-Jaguar 176
local dog 60
Lockbourne AFB 46, 73, 85, 99, 142
Lola 30
Lonz Winery 197, 203
Lossman, Bob 13, 31, 40, 67, 158, 216, 244
Lossman Motors 65, 158
Lotus 28, 30, 33, 77, 79, 188, 190, 192, 201, 204, 248; Mk VI 199
Lownsdale, Gary 33, 236
Lownsdale, Paulette 236
Lunken, Ebby 89, 245
Lyman boat 7, 16
Lynch, Michael 85

Malion, Bill 165, 189
Maltby, Gordon 167
Manakiki Country Club 3
Mansfield Hill Climb 189
Manting, Jack 31, 99, 102, 110, 127, 188, 198, 204
Marblehead 20
Marcel Riveau 18
Markman, Charles 190
Marsh, Don 29, 65, 103
Martin, Burdette 160, 161
Martini Super Vee 29
Maserati 1
May, Lt. Leo 188, 189

McBryde, Ed 168, 174
McCarter, John 217, 228
McCluggage, Denise 176
McConnell, Ron 101
McLaird, Lee 3, 56
Mentor Harbor Yachting Club 11, 88
Merdeka (yacht) 9
Metropolitan Sports Car Club 10
MG 12, 21, 22; MGA 203, 253; MGB 254; MG-TA 29, 244; MG-TC 12, 22, 23, 27, 33, 54, 65, 84, 88, 140, 174, 189, 201, 246; MG-TD 13, 17, 19, 23, 25, 25, 32, 33, 45, 46, 58, 68, 75, 140, 165, 174, 201, 244, 248, 249, 252; MG-TF 23, 26, 88, 140, 65, 174, 201
MG Car Club 2, 39, 254
MG Motors 159, 166
MG Vintage Racers 254
Michelin 95
Mid-Ohio Sports Car Course 1, 254, 252
Middle Bass Island 5, 6, 197, 203
Milan Hill Climb 140
Miles, Ken 191, 197, 250
Mille Miglia 15, 196
Miller, Al 162
Miller, Ron 186
Miller's Ferry 16, 17, 21, 42, 43, 58, 136
Mishne, Mickey 3, 20, 21, 30, 31, 182
Miske, Bo 20, 31, 165, 189, 198
Mitchell/Giurgola and Thorp 255
Mollman, Bob 167
Momo, Alfred 79, 176
Monaco 147
Moncur, John 62, 102
Mong, Gerry 185
Monk, Thelonius 17
Monkey Stable 85, 103, 125
Moretti 76
Morgan 31, 71, 173, 188, 189, 198
Morris Minor 28, 29, 101, 166
Morrisett, Len 163
Morrison, Bob 18, 42, 96, 119, 188, 190
Mulligan, Gerry 136
Munz brothers 86
Murray, Leon 224, 228

Nardi 76
National Guard 200
National Speed Sport News 3, 245
Navarro, Joe 220, 228
NE Ohio Region SCCA 4, 16, 188, 199, 249, 252
Nelson Ledges 252
New England MG T Register 254

New Parliament House of Australia 255
New York Central RR 50
Nichols, Frank 30, 141, 160
North Bass Island 5, 6
North Hollywood Motors 191
Northwest Ohio SCCA 17, 33
Norton, Dick 211
Norton Manx 250
Novak, Art 211
Nurburgring 251

Oakland County Sportsman's Club
Offenhauser engine 31, 149, 253
Ohio National Guard 18, 96
Olivetti typewriter 197, 250
101st Airborne Division 248
Orr, Roy 16

P-38 airplane 243
Palm Springs 1
Park Hotel 137
Parker, Charlie 3
Parravano, Ron 85
Parsons, Bob 149, 191
Patterson, Alan 62, 66, 226, 227
Payne, Tom 23, 31, 151, 181, 203, 224
Pebble Beach 1
Pell, Bud 167, 174, 188, 199, 204, 216, 219, 228
Pell, Craig 218
Pennsylvania Railroad Army Reserves 255
Penske, Roger 23, 189, 219
Pepper, Art 4
Perch 7
Perry, Oliver Hazard 5, 16, 23, 198
Pervo, Chuck 4
Pickrel, Bill 201
Pikes Peak 252
Pirelli 95
Pittsburgh Grand Prix 226
PM Magazine 249
Porsche 1, 12, 77, 149, 153; Carrera 23, 203, 204; 550 30, 104, 188; 550 RS 31, 168, 196; RS60 30; Speedster 99, 100, 148, 171, 174; Spyder 2, 16, 25, 127, 128, 131, 142, 198, 203, 204; 1300 77, 214, 219, 224; 356 Registry 167
Porsche Club of America 78
Port Clinton 7, 21, 45, 50
Preston, Howard 128
Put-in-Bay Reunion 3, 56
Put-in-Bay Wine Festival 39
Put-in-Bay Yacht Club 11

Quartullo, Fred 148, 149

Race Communications Association 249, 252

race trophy 132, 152, 153
Raceway Equipment 245
Rand Corporation 54
Randle, Bill 62, 68, 70, 85
Rattlesnake Island 6
Reder, Dick 32, 211, 223, 224
Reinhart, Johnny 23
Renault Dauphine 28, 101, 201
Reynolds, Fred 167
Rippel, Bob 159, 166
Riverside, California 130, 154
Roach, Max 4
Road America 1, 142, 154
Road & Track 190, 191, 197, 255, 250
Road Atlanta 252
Rolliflex 246
rolling start 93
Roncarelli, Robi 220, 223, 228
Round House Bar 195
Rubin, Dan 76
Rubini, Gunnard 77, 79, 88
Rumrunners nightspot 2

Saab GT 28, 162, 201
Sachs, Eddie 253
Sachs, Mel 25, 27, 141, 142
Samm, Robert 28, 192, 201
Sandusky, Ohio 17
Sandusky Register 215, 227, 228
Sandusky Yacht Club 101
Sargent, Jack 220, 228
Satava, Bob 2, 22, 32, 33, 60, 130, 232, 234, 239, 241
Sceptre (yacht) 176
Scheid, Cornelius 10, 13, 40
Schmidt, Bill 18, 96
Schmidt, Bob 42
Schmidt, Nancy 18, 96
Schwedler, Bill 228
Schwendler, William 188
Scott, Ed 217, 227
Sebring 30, 41, 49, 243, 252
Seyler, Art 57, 83, 84
Seyler, Lucile 84
Shaker Heights 16
Shaker High School 51
Sharrigan, John 220, 228
Shea, Bob 22, 63, 65, 125, 142, 151, 185
Shelby, Carroll 1
Sheppard, Dr. Sam 20, 62, 79, 80, 82, 88
Shoemaker, Ben 28
Siata 19, 21, 25, 27, 31, 142; Gran Sport 26, 41, 50, 77, 80, 83, 126, 127; Spyder 41, 46, 51, 64, 127, 132, 144, 145, 184, 201; 208S 31, 75, 76, 82, 84, 88
Simca 64, 101, 166
Sinbad (yacht) 9
Singer 77
Skirmants, Vic 3, 32, 213, 214, 217, 223, 224

Smith, Russ 163, 165, 181, 182, 185, 189
Snell Foundation 131
Snider, Bob 144, 147, 161
South Bass Island 4, 5, 6, 188, 203
Spear, Bill 26
Speed Graphic Camera 193
Sports Car Club of America 10, 40, 81, 93, 96, 132, 181, 188, 249, 252
Sports Cars Illustrated 248
Sports Cars Ltd. 40, 48, 50
standing start 93
Stanguellini 76
Staufer, Bill 2, 25, 117, 165, 171, 184, 186, 201
Staufer, Pat 117
Steel Cities Region, SCCA 104, 128, 167
Steger, Fred 2, 9, 23, 97
Steger, Gerry 9, 97
Steger, Jane 9
Steigerwald, Jerry 86
Stein, Bob 24, 28, 201
Stephenson, Bruce 1
Stica, Tony 29
Stoddard, Chuck 19, 21, 22, 31, 76, 96, 120, 122, 132, 141, 145, 163, 168, 174, 183, 185, 201, 252
Stoddard Import Motors 187
Stone, Dave 28, 201
Stout Field 142
Strategic Air Command 72
Studebaker 23, 59
Swan, Herb 31, 149

Tame, John 2, 23, 26, 143, 153, 181, 183, 201, 240, 241
Tanner, Martin 160
Targa Florio 15
Thistle Class 8, 11, 16
Thompson, Connecticut 26
Thompson boat 7

Thompson Raceway 76
Thompson Road 38
Tipton, Charles 203
Tobin, Jerry 219
Toledo Avenue 38
Tony Pompeo 76, 83, 120
Tony's Place 143, 190
Torrey Pines 1
Treible, John 3, 36
Triumph 12, 21, 31, 33, 189; TR2 16, 82, 87, 94, 172; TR3 191
Trofimov, Ivan 163, 168, 174, 201
Troyan, Fred 18, 64, 82, 137
Truman, Harry 4
TRW 1, 22
Turner, Clark 162
Turner sports car 28, 165, 193, 203
Tweety Bird 26, 122, 145
Tyrone, Whitey 137, 186

Uhr, Jack 81, 108, 185, 186
Ulmer, Ron 203
Underwood, Lake 1
United States Air Force 253, 254
U.S. Army Reserves 249
U.S. Grand Prix, Austin, Texas 252
University of Pennsylvania 254

Vaughn, Sally 39
vehicle dynamics 251
Vero Beach 49
Victory Park 137
Vintage Motorsport 3
Vintage Sports Car Club of America 226
Virginia International Raceway 130, 154
Volkswagen 28, 101, 252
Vollmar, Paul 187

Walleye 7
Walters, Phil 1

Ward, Mike 129
Warren, Pennsylvania 77, 80, 83
Waterford Hills 32, 130, 210
Watkins Glen 1, 12, 15, 17, 46, 71, 130, 154, 252
Watson, A.J. 253
Wearn, Doug 30, 186, 187, 203
Weaver, Al 140
Webb C. Ball 246
Weber, Joe 75, 87
Wehrheim, Jeanne 240
Wehrheim, Joe 240
Weisenbach, Paul 245
Weisenburger, Dave 139, 167, 169
Western Reserve Academy 191, 193, 197, 254
Wherry, Jack 86
Whistler, Willard 182
White, Frank 10, 40
Whiting, Herb 78
Wilder, Stephen 167, 168, 171, 173
Williams, Bob 241
Williams, Linda 241
Wilmot Hills 130
wine festival tents 42
Winograd, Harvey 30
Wintermude, Norman 129
Woerhle, Jack 241
Wolf, Don 139, 167, 168, 171, 172
World War II 1, 45, 163, 247, 248, 249
World's Fastest Bus Driver 117
Wright-Patterson Airforce Base 26, 76, 253
Wyllie, Doc 30

Yares, Dick 64, 120

Ziegler, Hap 106
Ziegler, Phyliss 107
Ziegler, Ralph 94, 105
Zimmerman, Andy 10, 13, 36, 40, 243

Milton Keynes UK
Ingram Content Group UK Ltd.
UKHW051953241124
451466UK00015B/279